Investigativ

David Leigh

Investigative Journalism

A Survival Guide

palgrave
macmillan

David Leigh
City, University of London
London, UK

ISBN 978-3-030-16751-6   ISBN 978-3-030-16752-3   (eBook)
https://doi.org/10.1007/978-3-030-16752-3

Cover illustration: eStudioCalamar

This Palgrave Macmillan imprint is published by the registered company Springer Nature Switzerland AG
The registered company address is: Gewerbestrasse 11, 6330 Cham, Switzerland

PREFACE

Few—if any—textbooks like this are available. The author combines an academic background with a prominent track record in investigative journalism. This is therefore intended to be a candid practical guide for journalism students interested in investigative reporting in print, online, or video. It will be useful to media professionals who themselves want to do more work in this demanding field and also to anyone in the wider public with a concern for keeping democracy alive.

The book is based on long insider experience of adversarial writing. It sets out to describe the key enemies and dangers that investigative journalists face, with the intention of better equipping those reporters for professional survival. The idea is to provide guidelines for people who want to develop the discipline and flair they will need to succeed as public interest reporters in an often hostile environment.

This is not, however, a training manual of the kind which explains how to do basic journalistic interviews, make freedom of information requests, manipulate spreadsheets, or scrape data. There are many such technical handbooks already accessible, some of which are indicated in the appendix. Nor does this guide include more than a minimum of media theory and history.

Instead, the book takes a broad and essentially practical approach, with autobiographical aspects. It offers an analysis of institutions, laws, techniques, problems, and case-histories from the field. The first chapter reviews the existential challenges faced by modern investigative journalism. Chapter 2 is an introductory account of the historical tension between commercial greed and liberal ideals of public service which culminated in the Watergate generation of investigative reporters. The rest of the book gives specific examples of investigative stories alongside a systematic analysis of the obstacles which the would-be investigative reporter faces in such work.

Chapter 3 dissects two key case-histories. These were the journalistic exposures of UK minister Jonathan Aitken and the UK's giant arms manufacturer BAe. Chapter 4 discloses the perils and pitfalls of carrying out investigations while working for a media boss. Chapter 5 focuses on the obstacles the law places in the way of the probing reporter and provides methods to defeat legal bullies. Chapter 6 unearths the ways intelligence agencies threaten the work of journalists. Chapter 7 shows why conspiracy theories can lead excitable investigative reporters astray. Chapter 8 documents how over-enthusiasm and personal vulnerabilities can also derail reporters (and sometimes get them killed). Chapter 9 explains that the new need for collaborative international work on a large scale has reduced the scope for the lone mavericks of yesteryears. Chapter 10 considers "fake news" from a fresh angle, chronicling the menace of bogus "investigations" published by the mainstream media. Chapter 11 rounds off the case histories with a single detailed study of the Trafigura toxic waste scandal, showing how modern investigative reporters can combine across borders to defeat their many enemies. Chapter 12 looks to the future with a certain amount of optimism. An appendix lists some basic public sources of key types of information.

Investigative journalism, by its nature, is highly culture specific. A lot of investigative work is about "feel"—a sense of where to go in a particular society, at a particular moment, to find things out and get them successfully published. Techniques that succeed in one legal or administrative environment frequently do not cross over into another. The context of this book is therefore inevitably primarily British, but many of its more general ideas and attitudes will also be relevant to investigative journalists worldwide. So will the realisation, particularly outlined in Chap. 9, that journalists from the northern hemisphere and from the developing south can nowadays work fruitfully together. The right kind of mindset is what matters.

My postgraduate students at City, University of London, debated many of these topics with me for 12 years. I am also grateful to Jeannie Mackie above all, and to Rob Evans, Paul Lashmar, Adrian Gatton, Elena Egawhary, James Ball, James Oliver, and Sara Beremenyi for entertainment and encouragement; and, for particular pieces of help, to Meirion

Jones, Lindsay Mackie, and Fred Laurin. I owe a sizeable debt to Godfrey Hodgson, Sally Sampson, and the Gatsby Foundation for launching the Anthony Sampson chair at City University in honour of one of Britain's finest journalists. The Monty Python script extract is quoted in Chap. 3 by permission of Methuen. I should also like to thank those editors who over the years gave me a job: Eric Mackay at the *Scotsman*; Ben Bradlee at the *Washington Post*; Robin Lustig at the *Observer*; Roger Bolton at *This Week*; Charles Tremayne at World in Action; and Alan Rusbridger at the *Guardian*. They helped me learn the trade and pay my rent, which are things for which an investigative reporter should always be grateful.

London, UK   David Leigh

Contents

About the Author

David Leigh Anthony Sampson Professor of Reporting at City University of London 2006–18 is one of Britain's best-known investigative journalists. He was head of investigations at the *Guardian* 2000–15 and at the *Observer* 1980–89. He was a TV producer at *This Week* and *World in Action* 1989–97 and the first Laurence Stern Fellow at the *Washington Post* 1979–80. He is one of the founder members of the International Consortium of Investigative Journalists based in Washington DC; was a trustee of the Centre for Investigative Journalism in London 2008–14; and is a director of the independent press regulator IMPRESS. He has won numerous UK and international journalism awards in a 40-year career. His books include biographies of Michael Foot and Howard Marks; an account of Prime Minister Harold Wilson's relations with the intelligence services; and a study of secrecy in British life.

CHAPTER 1

Introduction

Investigative journalism in the public interest—the daily supply of truths about the world that would otherwise be hidden—only has a short history. The phenomenon originated largely in the nineteenth century. Thanks to the work of a later generation of writers, editors, and moviemakers—the Watergate generation—it went on to achieve an iconic status in the West and became seen as the lifeblood of democracy itself.

I believe that investigative journalists are vital to a decent society. But we need to acquire the right tools to survive in the job. For in the present century, this concept of truth-telling investigative journalism is under considerable threat. Government propagandists, repressive judges, corrupt officials, criminals, commercial bullies, and cynical tabloid proprietors—these people have always been the enemies of honest reporters, and their powers remain strong. But another hostile force is also growing. The idea of truth itself is under plausible attack.

Many Western journalists, myself included, were brought up with ideals that now feel almost naïve. Believing that we help to make democratic societies work better, we were professionally occupied with attempts to distinguish fact from fiction. Our quest was to establish what actually was, or was not, the case. So we found it very jolting in the twenty-first century, when *truth* itself became a despised notion.

"Speak Truth to Power: A Quaker Search for an Alternative to Violence" was the title of a US pamphlet, published in the 1950s at the height of the Cold War with the Soviet Union. This group of pacifist authors wanted to tell the US military that a looming Third World War could be avoided.

© The Author(s) 2019
D. Leigh, *Investigative Journalism*,
https://doi.org/10.1007/978-3-030-16752-3_1

1

They wrote: "Our truth is an ancient one: that love endures and over-comes; that hatred destroys" [1]. This tough religious message about one kind of truth was subsequently adopted by US journalists, and its meaning morphed into a more glib job description. "Speak truth to power" became a largely unexamined slogan ministering to the professional self-importance of Western news reporters (see [2, 3]).

For what happens the other way round, when power speaks bullyingly to truth? US President Donald Trump's uninhibited Twitter account appears to provide an unwelcome answer. Politicians and other powerful people who simply don't believe in the usefulness of truth have learned to manipulate new online forms of mass media, conveying visceral messages that energise their supporters, even though those messages often consist of downright lies. At the same time, the professionals of the so-called mainstream media (MSM) are targeted for volleys of abuse that delegit-imise them.

Ironically, this "post-truth" campaign to destroy factual journalism has friends on the left. Counter-cultural analysts and anarchists such as Julian Assange of Wikileaks seek to demonstrate that just as history is only writ-ten by the victors, so the "MSM" newspapers are all only written to peddle a capitalist narrative [4].

They are joined on the far right by a network of well-funded bloggers who denounce the mainstream media as merely a liberal conspiracy. On Breitbart or Infowars, activists paint a weird picture of themselves as the insurgent underdogs, victims of political correctness imposed upon them by the BBC or the *Washington Post* or CNN or the *Guardian* [5, 6]. "Reality" seemed to become a contestable thing. Have the post-modern claims that truth is only relative seeped out of the campus to culminate in the likely wreck of serious journalism?

When I started out as a reporter in the 1970s, life for my colleagues was a series of battles to publish what we were confident were simple and necessary truths. We were inspired by the heroic myth of Watergate. We took on powerful newspaper bosses like "Tiny" Rowland at the *Observer* and William Rees-Mogg at the *Times*, and led resistance from their staffs. We challenged Britain's judges: and we halted trials with our revelations. We published supposedly confidential documents, broke the rules by interviewing jurors, and faced down accusations of libel and contempt of court. We defied the knee-jerk secrecy of the military and the intelli-gence agencies to reveal spies, to defend whistleblowers; and to expose blacklisting, bugging, nuclear scandals, propaganda, and assassinations. We shot down false conspiracy theories and attacked corrupt or lying politicians. One of the pivotal moments of my own career came when one such—cornered British cabinet minister Jonathan Aitken—publicly vowed in revenge to destroy me as "the cancer of bent and twisted journalism" [7]. (Luckily for me, he didn't succeed.)

My colleagues and I, particularly on the *Guardian* and the *Observer* in London, two papers where I was head of investigations, saw ourselves in this way as foot-soldiers in a War on Lies. We won awards over 40 years of exposure journalism and felt our activities were self-evidently useful. We did not see ourselves as peddling either a leftist Marxist "truth" or a capitalist "truth". The current fundamental assault on our professional values was something we were slow to see coming.

For now the "legacy media" are almost too weak to resist ideological attacks. The giant Internet tech firms have sucked the money out of them. No single organisation can nowadays easily produce massive, unanswerable investigations which dominate the culture, as the once-famous *London Sunday Times* Insight team used to do. Instead, much news is consumed in a fragmentary landscape where what money there is comes with clicks—websites essentially trolling their own readers to elicit almost unconscious, twitch reactions. The 24-hour news cycle feeds on stories printed with little oversight—replaceable, correctable, deletable, forgettable. Truth becomes almost irrelevant, when interesting fakes and lies get more clicks [8].

A toxic swirl of hyper-partisanship, media fragmentation, and "fake news" is polluting the information water supply. This makes life harder for credible journalism. The often-brilliant tradition of Western exposure reporting that we have all inherited may yet be eventually overwhelmed by its many opponents. But if such journalism were ever to disappear, ordinary citizens would be condemned to a bleak political future. For it will be a future in which no-one will bother any longer to ask the question: "Is it true?" Instead, people will merely demand "Whose side are you on?"

That wouldn't be good news. But there are ways to resist these dangerous developments. I hope that from handbooks like this, journalists of all kinds can learn how to practise and defend genuine investigative reporting. In the uncertain world we inhabit, it is needed more than ever.

References

1. American Friends Service Committee. 2 March 1955. Speak Truth to Power A Quaker Search for an Alternative to Violence. Accessed October 28, 2018. http://www.quaker.org/sttp.html.
2. Edelstein, David. Journalists Speak Truth to Power in 'Spotlight', 8 November, 2015. Accessed October 28, 2018. https://www.cbsnews.com/videos/review-journalists-speak-truth-to-power-in-spotlight/.
3. Stverak, Jason. Franklin Center for Government and Public Integrity. Accessed October 28, 2018. http://americasfuture.org/investigative-journalism-speak-truth-to-power/.
4. Leigh, David, and Luke Harding. 2011. *Wikileaks: Inside Julian Assange's War on Secrecy*. London: Guardian Books.
5. Mulhall, Joe. 2017. It's Just Not Politically Correct to Talk Openly About Islam's Rape Culture. *Guardian*, March 7. Accessed October 28, 2018. https://www.theguardian.com/commentisfree/2017/mar/07/breitbart-threat-to-europe-postwar-liberal-consensus.
6. Snyder, Michael. 14 August 2013. 19 Shocking Examples of How Political Correctness is Destroying America. *Infowars*. Accessed October 28, 2018. https://www.infowars.com/19-shocking-examples-of-how-political-correctness-is-destroying-america/.
7. Harding, Luke, David Leigh, and David Pallister. 1999. *The Liar*. London: Guardian Books.
8. Vosoughi, Soroush, Deb Roy, and Sinan Aral. 2018. The Spread of True and False News Online. *Science*. Accessed October 28, 2018. http://science.sciencemag.org/content/359/6380/1146.

CHAPTER 2

A Short History of Investigative Journalism

LIVING THE WATERGATE DREAM

There is a children's playground game called Blind Man's Buff. One child is blindfolded and feels around, trying to catch hold of the others and identify them. Naturally, all the other targets do their best to dodge out of the way. The exuberant journalist Bruce Page, when he headed Britain's *Sunday Times* Insight Team during its heydays in the 1960s, used to say, with his touch of a blunt Australian accent, that investigative journalism was "Just like Blind Man's Buff .... played with open razors" [1]. His gruesome mental image of a set of old-fashioned cut-throat razors has long stuck in my mind. It catches just how difficult decent investigative journalism is to do well, and just how brutal and blundering the power of the media can be when it's done badly. You're attacking other people, and frequently drawing blood.

Yet when such journalism is carried out effectively, it is regarded in the west as a glamorous activity—so glamorous that the people (men, mostly) who do it get to be played by movie stars. Robert Redford, Dustin Hoffman [2], Al Pacino [3], Benedict Cumberbatch [4], Mark Ruffalo [5]—just to name a few. In these movies, the investigative reporter is a dogged—sometimes cantankerous—character, who exposes the truth virtually single-handedly, driving the popular narrative storyline of David and Goliath. The actor playing the probing journalist is one of Hollywood's iconic caped crusaders—up there in the pantheon along with Humphrey

© The Author(s) 2019
D. Leigh, *Investigative Journalism*,
https://doi.org/10.1007/978-3-030-16752-3_2

Bogart, the cynical yet incorruptible private eye, and Clint Eastwood, the grim cowboy avenger who leaves all the black hats dead on the ground.

Where does this romanticised and highly male picture of journalism originate? In a word, Watergate. It was in the early 1970s—more than 40 years ago—that two young men brought down the then president of the US, Richard Nixon. They exposed the fact that he had been running a crooked re-election campaign, using the full armoury of the US administration to bribe, bug, and burgle his opponents—in short, to steal the election. That story went down in history as Watergate, after the name of a mundane Washington DC office building. A bungled break-in at the opposition Democrat campaign headquarters took place there, igniting the saga [6].

It's a sign of the mythic power of that name, Watergate, that—more than a full generation and a new century later—media people are still trying to christen scandals after it. When there was an uproar about a property transaction by the wife of the then Labour prime minister, Cherie Blair, British tabloid newspapers started referring to "Cheriegate" [7–9]. Julian Assange of hacking-site Wikileaks dumped out a hoard of classified US embassy cables and sought to suggest that wickedness was being revealed, by calling it "Cablegate" [10]. Later, the then UK Labour Party leader Jeremy Corbyn had himself videoed sitting on the floor of a train carriage to campaign against overcrowding. When it transpired the carriage may not in fact have been full, his political opponents sought to label the saga "Traingate" [11, 12].

Even in the Internet age, the zombie term lives on. The Trump presidential election campaign saw so-called Pizzagate [13]. This slogan encouraged a gunman inflamed by fake claims about Clintonite sex abuse to fire off shots at the door of a pizza parlour. Some obscure anti-feminist and conspiratorialist allegations among the US video gaming community also circulated online in 2015 under the tag "*#gamergate*" [14]. Many such hashtags might have been posted by teenage boys in their back bedrooms—whose own parents were not even born themselves at the time of the original Watergate burglary. The "Gate" suffix was once a historical fact, and now it's turned into a potentially misleading meme.

Watergate did certainly inspire me and my contemporaries to want to become journalists. Nowadays, looking a bit ruefully in the mirror, I suppose that I was then at an impressionable age. I too was a young reporter when Watergate broke, serving out my own apprenticeship 400 miles away from Fleet Street, on the Scotsman newspaper in Edinburgh. And I'd not been long out of university, where in the 1960s, we'd been confident in our belief that everything was changing in western society—and we could make it change faster. We wanted to sweep away the lies, the wars, the secrecy, and the corruption that we were convinced lay all around us. Watergate was our icon. A few years later, when I won a US journalist fellowship, I bounced into the old L St. office block of the *Washington Post* to work with its national desk reporters. It felt like entering Olympus, home of the gods.

The 1960s were a transitional moment in European and American societies. The post-war baby-boomer generation were just reaching their dissident maturity. Yet it is not simply middle-aged nostalgia for those exciting times that prompts these reflections. Watergate influenced a whole generation because in many ways it was—and remains to this day—a true classic of investigative journalism.

There are, of course, questions we should ask about the way it has been romanticised.

WATERGATE: THE MYTH

The narrative of Watergate was that two nobodies from the paper took on the most powerful man in the world and using straightforward professional skills, they won. Notice that I say "won". I could have said "and democracy prevailed" or "so the truth finally came out". But that's only part of the picture—the most respectable part, perhaps. Successful journalists do what they do because—as well as all the noble reasons they like to boast about—they also have a more primitive instinct. It's the instinct of the hunter: the young men of the tribe pulling down a big beast. Adversarial journalists, much like adversarial trial lawyers perhaps, are people who like to fight. And who like to win. That testosterone part is sometimes glossed over in the romantic versions.

The story of Watergate became distorted in other ways too, in the process of becoming the legend. First of all, it was turned into a best-selling book. It was written up by the two young reporters themselves, Bob Woodward and Carl Bernstein, and was called *All the President's Men*. With that volume, the process of mythologising, or even of novelisation, began. One of the book's myths was of a crucial, shadowy source who the duo met in an underground garage, and who came to be known as Deep

Throat [6, p. 71]. But according to the pair's literary agent David Obst, the early outline for the book did not in fact contain any character called Deep Throat. It was a sober, drier, third-person history of political events, offered as a narrative in a relatively conventional way.

The publishers were disappointed.

So the story was re-drafted to depict a heroic David-and-Goliath struggle by 28-year-old Bernstein and 29-year-old Woodward. Deep Throat was exhumed with his office nickname (taken from the title of a pornographic film) and written up with a highly dramatic role. This version was more replete with human interest and the book sold very well [15, pp. 243–6, 16]. The actual Deep Throat—Mark Felt, as it transpired, then No 3 at the FBI—detested the way his leaking was fictionalised. According to Woodward and Bernstein biographer Alicia Shepard, he particularly hated being called "Deep Throat" and is said to have slammed down the phone on Woodward after the book came out [15, 16]. Critics also argue that Deep Throat's judicious leaks to the "Post" were not uniquely telling, and neither were they in fact the vital information that overthrew the president. Nixon successfully got himself re-elected in 1974 despite the scandal. It was congressional investigations thereafter, which actually brought the President down.

Following the publication of *All the President's Men*, a further distortion took place. The film rights were sold. Woodward was transformed into the handsome actor Robert Redford, and Bernstein into the equally photogenic Dustin Hoffman. Their boss at the Post, the patrician Ben Bradlee, was played memorably by the gravel-voiced Jason Robards [2]. The 1976 film was reasonably accurate, but only within the necessary limits of Hollywood melodrama. Thus, the two scared reporters are made to bang on Bradlee's door late at night and tell him, as he stands in his bathrobe out on the lawn, "Deep Throat says our lives are in danger". This never actually happened in just that way.

It is still inspirational, of course, to watch such a fine old movie. In the narrative, Woodward and Bernstein overreach themselves, and they find themselves floundering whilst trying to incriminate the White House (journalism is blind man's buff!). As a result, there are humiliating official denials of one of their stories and an angry showdown with Deep Throat in a moodily lit underground car-park. The Oscar-winning climax comes in that re-imagined night-time scene in front of Bradlee's house where the *Washington Post*'s editor is made gruffly to tell the youthful pair of reporters:

Nothing's riding on this except the, uh, First Amendment to the Constitution, freedom of the press and maybe the future of the country.

Not that any of that matters. But if you guys fuck up again, I'm going to get mad. [2]

The film's finale is also unforgettable. The artillery salutes marking Nixon's 1974 presidential inauguration boom away against the drumbeat of Woodward and Bernstein's typewriters. Then a rattle of teleprinters crescendo to a thunder as front-page headlines spell out that Nixon is finally resigning. The forces of darkness are defeated! Manual typewriters as working tools have of course since become completely obsolete. So have teleprinters. So indeed have the roaring newsprint presses as an emotive image: comparable iconic images nowadays tend to revolve around smartphone screens, online chat snippets, and underground bunkers full of computer servers. Woodward and Bernstein's reporting technologies have been almost entirely swept into the dustbin of last century's history, along with hot metal, flongs, compositors, and linotype machines.

But the many investigative lessons embodied in the Watergate movie are still timeless good ones. We shall explore them in the course of this handbook. Here are seven to start with—bosses need careful handling; successful investigators don't work alone; much depends on human sources; you don't need fancy equipment; patience is necessary; being hated comes with the territory; and above all, that it's always hard to get it right. The echo of Nixon-style misdeeds in the 2016 Trump presidential election campaign, remind us also of another journalistic lesson that is timeless—that the forces of darkness can always regroup.

THE SEVEN LESSONS OF WATERGATE
GOOD TO WORK IN PAIRS
YOU NEED HUMAN SOURCES
YOU DON'T NEED FANCY EQUIPMENT
YOU HAVE TO BE PATIENT
PEOPLE WILL HATE YOU
IT'S HARD TO GET IT RIGHT
YOU'RE GOING TO HAVE A BOSS

THE IDEOLOGY OF TRUTH-TELLING

Watergate, then, is still rightly the icon, the creation myth that sustains the morale of intrepid journalists everywhere. But its ideology of truth-telling did not come out of the blue.

Historically, I would suggest there can be considered to be two types of Anglophone exposure journalist: illiberal and liberal. These opposites make more sense in a media context than traditional political divisions between left and right. The illiberal types are people who, broadly speaking, use the opportunities offered by the mass media to exercise power and make money. Often highly effective, the illiberals tend to be violently partisan, inflaming their already like-minded audiences against selected targets. The *London Daily Mail* and Fox News in the US are notable examples of media who thrive using these techniques.

Liberal journalists, on the other hand, have come over time to see themselves more idealistically as agents of democratic reform—as countervailing powers, revealing faults in society and in society's official picture of itself. They believe there is a demand for "the truth" as a form of public service. In a totalitarian country, dictators and their cronies will shamelessly tell lies until—with luck—such a disconnect from the real world eventually overwhelms them. Democracies, on the other hand, are thought to have a self-correcting mechanism thanks to a free press. Independent reporters can turn over stones, bear witness, and give a voice to the otherwise voiceless. This is claimed to be useful, even essential, to the community.

There are thus two clashing visions of investigative journalism. One tends to punch down: the other more often punches up. This clash of visions has caused plenty of confusion over the last century and a half. It is one of the reasons for the paradox that journalists are simultaneously despised and revered in western popular culture. In all opinion polls, the slimeball with the reporter's notebook comes out as one of the least trusted individuals ever. Yet people flock to see movies with a fearless investigator as hero, and they support journalists who get locked up or murdered by authoritarian regimes. The persistent reporter in the raincoat is simultaneously seen as noble, and as utterly ignoble.

The confusion is deepened by two things. Liberal journalists, particularly in the US, made a big mistake when they attempted to shake off the depravity of the yellow press by preaching a gospel of pseudo-scientific "objectivity" (rather than simply one of honest reporting). It has been difficult to straighten out the intellectual tangles caused by this false notion of journalistic objectivity, which does not and cannot exist. Journalism is always selective.

The second cause of confusion is that brutally commercial or partisan journalists of the illiberal kind often drape themselves in the rhetoric of liberalism. They too claim to be exposing social evils, rather than merely whipping up the mob for their own ends.

WT Stead's "New Journalism"

The early and colourful career of William Stead bears out some of these paradoxes. Stead, a full-bearded Victorian Englishman, was a fine and brave editor. He was a role model for his most legendary successor at his provincial newspaper—Harry Evans, who went on to launch the famous *Sunday Times* Insight Team in 1967. Evans wrote of his own time as editor of the *Northern Echo* in the engineering town of Darlington:

> Sitting in the chair of the great 19th-century editor-campaigner … I could see Stead's letter accepting his appointment, still standing, framed on a bookcase: 'What a marvellous opportunity for attacking the devil!' [17, p. 15]

The published text of Stead's letter actually reads: "What a **glorious** opportunity of attacking the devil isn't it?" [18]. It is typical of the slipperiness of facts, that Evans may have in fact slightly misquoted the great man. Nonetheless, "Attacking the devil" sounds a public-spirited ambition, not to say an evangelical one.

Unfortunately, the devil in his turn made some inroads into Stead's own behaviour. The most lurid investigative stunt that Stead pulled off was intended to dramatise the scandal of child prostitution. It did make him notorious; it did sell a great many copies of the Pall Mall Gazette, the editorship of which he had taken over in London. He did contribute to legal reform, raising the age of sexual consent from 13 to 16. But the story also landed Stead in jail.

And when one examines the details of the exploitative way in which he behaved towards 13-year-old Lizzie Armstrong, it is no wonder he was locked up. Even Rupert Murdoch's brazen twentieth-century editors, in the most prurient heyday of the UK's now-shuttered *News of the World*, might have blanched at going so far to stand up a story.

Stead claimed, in what may have been one of the earliest uses of the word in this context: "I am an investigator". He wrote, his stance quite recognisable to liberal journalists today: "We are … compelled, in the public interest, to publish". But this pious remark came in the course of a thoroughly hucksterish teaser for his upcoming "long, detailed report dealing with... sexual criminality":

> Notice to our Readers: A Frank Warning
> ....We have no desire to inflict upon unwilling eyes the ghastly story of the criminal developments of modern vice. Therefore we say quite frankly to-day that all those who are squeamish, and all those who are prudish, and all those who prefer to live in a fool's paradise of imaginary innocence and purity, selfishly oblivious to the horrible realities which torment those whose lives are passed in the London Inferno, will do well not to read the Pall Mall Gazette of Monday and the three following days. [19]

Those readers, subsequently queuing day after day to part with their pennies, had their expectations fully met. Headlines included: "The Violation of Virgins", "Virgins Willing and Unwilling", "Confessions of a Brothel Keeper", and "Strapping Girls Down". The first day culminated with "A Girl of 13 bought for £5". Dangerously perhaps, Stead claimed cabinet ministers were involved in sex abuse, and that a high figure in the police force was said to have raped his own daughter. Soon afterwards on 7 November, Mr Justice Henry Lopes told an Old Bailey jury (not very dispassionately) that Stead was "a disgrace to journalism" [20, p. 9]. These were, he said:

> disgusting and filthy articles—articles so filthy and so disgusting that one cannot help fearing that they may have suggested to innocent women and children the existence of vice and wickedness which had never occurred to their minds before. [21, p. 123]

Stead had faced a problem common to many investigative journalists. He had certainly heard lots of anecdotes, from Salvation Army campaigners and police officers, but had no hard facts to stand up his story. If teenage girls in London were being trafficked and raped, there were unlikely to be eyewitnesses willing to go on the record about it. So he staged an event of his own.

He hired a former brothel-keeper to obtain a girl. And so little Lizzie Armstrong, from the slum district of Lisson Grove in London, daughter of a drunken mother and a violent father, was duly produced. Her mother, it was claimed, had knowingly sold her into prostitution. Later, however, when it all backfired, her mother said she had believed Lizzie was being offered a respectable job as a servant. Lizzie, herself, with no idea of what was going on, was towed round to the house of an elderly woman midwife/abortionist, who subjected her to a virginity test. She was then taken to a "hotel" (actually a brothel), given chloroform to sniff, and put to bed—only to wake up in fear.

> The purchaser entered the bedroom. He closed and locked the door. There was a brief silence. And then there rose a wild and piteous cry–not a loud shriek, but a helpless, startled scream like the bleat of a frightened lamb. And the child's voice was heard crying, in accents of terror, "There's a man in the room! Take me home; oh, take me home!"And then all once more was still. [19]

This intruder was Stead himself, demonstrating to his own satisfaction that what he headlined as "The Maiden Tribute of Modern Babylon" was actually taking place. He wrote, mysteriously: "I can personally vouch for the absolute accuracy of every fact in the narrative".

The story was a mixture of crusading zeal and what a later century might have called "fake news". In 1885, Stead was to get 3 months in jail for masterminding this abduction and indecent assault of little Lizzie. The rival Times commented sanctimoniously:

> It is matter for rejoicing that a test case has shown that one of the gravest of the charges against the English populace—the charge of selling their children for infamous purposes—cannot be substantiated. [20, p. 9]

Stead was proudly unrepentant about what he called his "New Journalism". Prominent on the front pages to the very end, in 1912 he was one of the most famous of the passengers who went down with the Titanic.

NELLIE BLY: "BEHIND ASYLUM BARS"

At the turn of the twentieth century, basic literacy and steam technology were of course transforming the reach of print newspapers and building a whole industry out of what came to be known as tabloid journalism. The ambiguities of this new and powerful mass medium were on show on both sides of the Atlantic. Whilst Stead was causing uproar in London, Nellie Bly transfixed New York with her 1887 stunt, headlined "Behind Asylum Bars".

She was trying to get a job on the *New York World*. The gutsy 23-year-old reporter agreed to go undercover and, by acting penniless and crazed, to get herself sent to the notorious asylum on Blackwell's Island, off Manhattan. The rationale was the sober "public interest" of liberal journalism. Nellie recorded piously that her editor instructed her:

> We do not ask you to go there for the purpose of making sensational revelations. Write up things as you find them, good or bad; give praise or blame as you think best, and the truth all the time. [22]

But the presentation in the paper was, of course, precisely one of sensational revelations, complete with true-crime style woodcuts:

> Inside the Madhouse....Nellie Bly's Experience in the Blackwell's Island Asylum; ... the Story of Ten Days with Lunatics; How the City's Unfortunate Wards Are Fed and Treated; The Terrors of Cold Baths and Cruel, Unsympathetic Nurses; Attendants Who Harass and Abuse Patients and Laugh at Their Miseries. [22]

How else could such investigation be made to pay except as a piece of sensational theatre? Even her by-line, "Nellie Bly", was a stage name, adopted from a popular song. (Her real name was Elizabeth Cochrane.) *Ten Days in a Madhouse* certainly set the template for all subsequent undercover exposures of prisons, orphanages, and institutions that abused the vulnerable. More than a century later, the undercover reporter for a memorable BBC exposure who videoed abuse in an old people's care home, owed a debt to Nellie Bly [23]. But the fearless Bly herself went on to perform numerous other more pointless stunts, including a circumnavigation designed to beat Jules Verne's fictional *Around the World in 80 Days*. When she died, her obituary concluded: "The feat that made her famous was her trip around the world" [24, p. 13]. That, predictably, was the one that did not have any social value at all.

MUCKRAKING AND THE RISE OF THE "INVESTIGATIVE REPORTER"

Such an early miasma of sensationalism did not make investigative journalism very respected. US President Teddy Roosevelt launched an attack on it in terms close to the heart of every beleaguered politician and chief executive ever since. He sought to quote John Bunyan in Pilgrim's progress, on:

The man with the Muckrake, the man who could look no way but down-ward with the muckrake in his hands; who was offered a celestial crown for his muckrake, but who could neither look up nor regard the crown he was offered, but continued to rake to himself the filth of the floor. [25, pp. 415–24]

Roosevelt, who was a blustering optimist, denounced "muckrakers" for their negative attitude to important people who were often only trying to do their best:

The men with the muckrakes are often indispensable to the well being of society; but only if they know when to stop raking the muck… There are beautiful things above and round about them; and if they gradually grow to feel that the whole world is nothing but muck, their power of useful-ness is gone.

Roosevelt was accusing such journalists of being not truth-seekers, but perpetrators of a false picture of the world. The accusation stung. Reporters who wanted to become socially acceptable subsequently found it easier to present themselves as "objective" social scientists and stenographers of the powerful, rather than as attack dogs. It was not until decades later in America that the pendulum swung.

When it did, at the height of the Cold War with Russia, the change was thanks to McCarthyism. The PhD researcher Elena Egawhary has traced what appears to be the first use of a key phrase to this era, nearly a quarter of a century before the excitements of Watergate. It came about as a reac-tion to the US media's passivity, which was being exploited by Senator Joe McCarthy and his repulsive aide, the late Roy Cohn. (It is perhaps no accident that President Donald Trump in 2016 turned out to have learned some of his media techniques at the feet of Cohn himself. Trump once employed him as his lawyer).

McCarthy used his legally fireproof Congressional platform for anti-communist witch-hunting. He read out lists of purported "communists", knowing that the media would mindlessly re-publish them. It was, in essence, another successful "fake news" operation.

In response, some journalists began to re-think the technique of "dead-pan reporting"—what *Hartford Courant* editor Herbert Brucker called "the publication of a suspected or unknown lie without qualification, just because a noise-making Senator issued it from behind Congressional immunity" [26, p. 8]. Another US editor, Basil Walters, made a speech on the same topic, saying optimistically:

> Deadpan reporting is for Pravda, not for free American newspapers....to counter this trend, newspapers must turn more and more to great reporters ... *They will be known as investigative reporters*. Their function will be to audit government. [27] (author's emphasis)

HARRY EVANS AND THE *LONDON SUNDAY TIMES*

Yet it was not until the large generational disruptions of the 1960s that Walter's vision of "investigative reporters" materialised to any degree. It did so on both sides of the Atlantic. In the UK, in 1967, the irreverent provincial northerner, Harry Evans, became editor of the staid *Sunday Times*. He brought design flair and meticulous craftsmanship to the job. But he also shook it up with a series of massive investigations that were respecters neither of the political "Establishment" nor of Big Business. Instead of fawning, he attacked. This appealed to members of a youthful generation who were marching against their governments, and occupying universities.

For Evans, the great enemy of journalistic truth was the law. The spectre of Britain's oppressive Official Secrets Act hampered his team's research to expose the Philby scandal. Kim Philby had been given high rank in Britain's intelligence agency, MI6, whilst all the time secretly working for the Russians—an embarrassing fact which had been assiduously covered up by the secret agency and the politicians. Britain's "arcane" and "bizarre" [17, p. 24] civil law of confidentiality was also used to try and ban publication of the 10-year-old political diaries of government minister Richard Crossman, which revealed disagreements around the cabinet table. But most famous of all, the archaic rules of contempt of court were used to try and block his revelations about the thalidomide case.

Thalidomide was an inadequately tested drug given to pregnant women suffering from morning sickness. It caused the birth of hundreds of cruelly deformed babies. Invented by a German firm, Chemie Grunenthal, as a "wonder drug", it was marketed in Britain by Distillers (Biochemical), an offshoot of a giant drinks firm. The parents were receiving puny amounts of compensation in litigation that dragged on for a decade against Distillers' fleet of lawyers. Under what was then British law, it was considered punishable contempt of court to write about civil proceedings that were under way, even if, as in the case of thalidomide, the litigation had gone on interminably, and none of the reasons for the private settlements would ever see the light of day in a courtroom. Evans eventually obtained some of the legal documents (by covertly paying £10,500 for them) but was unable to publish their revelations. The case went all the way to the European Court of Human Rights in Strasbourg, and Distillers were eventually shamed into paying up.

The old contempt of court rules were reformed. It is now no longer possible to suppress discussion of wrongdoing in Britain merely by issuing a writ. Furthermore, journalists are now allowed to inspect the "pleadings" in civil cases, as they wind their way through the slow-motion joustings which may lead to an out-of-court settlement. Looking back to the 1970s, one marvels at the number of British judges and lawyers who were prepared at the time to find abstract reasons to prevent the truth coming out about a horrible scandal.

But once again, the thalidomide triumph has been romanticised with the passage of time. Philip Knightley, one of the key members of the Insight Team of reporters who broke the story, subsequently confessed:

In journalism schools and media courses they use the thalidomide scandal as an example of campaigning journalism at its finest: fearless journalists take on a huge corporation which is behaving badly towards child victims of the corporation's horror drug and, after a long, bitter battle, win for them decent compensation. But, in truth, that is too simple and the reality is much more ambiguous … the full story is as much about the failures of journalism as about its triumphs. [28, p. 155ff]

He went on:

All the scientific material to rebut Distillers' defence was available to anyone who had the inclination and time to find it… Bruce Page warned that we had no right to feel triumphant … half in jest, he said any book we wrote on the campaign should be called, 'How The Sunday Times Gradually Recovered From Its Own Mistakes And Did Something About The Thalidomide Scandal—Just In Time'.

And Knightley said this, too: "I suppose that at the back of all our minds also was the inconvenient fact that we had come to the thalidomide scandal via what critics of the press call chequebook journalism: the buying of information".

Ray Fitzwalter and the Poulson Case

Harry Evans was not alone in his crusades that changed the journalistic weather. Another provincial northerner to galvanise British investigative journalism at the same time was the campaigning "World in Action" TV series boss Ray Fitzwalter, seen by his colleagues as "Doughty, puritan, [and] plain-speaking" [29, p. 116]. Fitzwalter was the son of a Lancashire factory worker. He brought down a senior Conservative statesman, Reginald Maudling, the most prominent of many politicians who were shown to be taking money from a corrupt property developer and architect, John Poulson.

Fitzwalter too had to fight his way through the thorns and brambles of British law to expose unwelcome truths. Maudling, who was Home Secretary and a candidate for leadership of the governing party, deployed many libel writs against his journalistic opponents. Fitzwalter's worst struggle over the story, however, was with a body which at that time had legal powers over British commercial broadcasters—the Independent Broadcasting Authority, or IBA.

In 1973, they used those powers to try and ban outright the transmission of Fitzwalter's programme exposing Poulson. And they succeeded for a while. The IBA's members appeared to be less interested in exposing the truth than in protecting their political colleagues from "trial by television" [30, p. 198–9]. Fitzwalter was gloomy in later years about his failure to have Maudling arrested. But Poulson himself did go to jail, and Maudling, the crooked politician, remained free only to drink himself to death.

Vietnam, My Lai and the Pentagon Papers

In mid-century Britain, the biggest enemy of truth may thus have been the law. But in the US, it was the war. Specifically, the war in Vietnam. Faced with conscription, and the prospect of dying in a pointless slaughterhouse, the reaction of many young men was to burn their draft cards or hold up placards as they did in 1967, saying "Hell, no—We won't go!" Shortly afterwards, in 1969, the investigative reporter Seymour Hersh began to expose the My Lai massacre, in which some 347 villagers had been murdered, many by a platoon led by 26-year-old Lt William Calley. Hersh was to spend the next 3 years writing about the atrocity and its cover-up by the US Army, winning a Pulitzer prize and a stellar reputation [31].

My Lai's journalistic fame was only surpassed by the saga of the Pentagon Papers. In 1971, the *New York Times* started to publish extracts from a voluminous classified history of the US in Vietnam, handed to them by leaker Daniel Ellsberg, who had worked on the defence department's secret study, and was opposed to the war. The "Pentagon Papers", as they came to be known, showed how the war's origins merely lay in a scheme to contain China, and its bloody continuation was due to little more than a US wish to avoid humiliation. The study, as Ellsberg put it, "revealed a lot of high-level lying" [32]. The *New York Times* was hauled into court by President Nixon's Attorney-General John Mitchell, who sought an unprecedented gagging injunction.

That failed 6 to 3 in the Supreme Court, Justice Hugo Black ruling memorably:

> Only a free and unrestrained press can effectively expose deception in government. And paramount among the responsibilities of a free press is the duty to prevent any part of the government from deceiving the people and sending them off to distant lands to die of foreign fevers and foreign shot and shell. [33]

Ellsberg himself was put on criminal trial for theft and espionage. But the case against him also collapsed in 1973 amid the dramas of Watergate. It transpired that President Nixon's gang of "plumbers" had, among other Watergate-related crimes, broken into the office of Ellsberg's psychiatrist in the hope of getting some dirt on the leaker. A mistrial was declared due to extreme government misconduct. For his entire generation, Ellsberg's name became one to conjure with as a totemic whistleblower.

The iconic saga of Watergate itself, with its two bold young reporters, thus grew at the time out of an existing soil of widespread political dissent. It was also the culmination of a longstanding tradition of florid journalistic stunts going all the way back to Nellie Bly. By the early 1970s, this combination had fixed some bold notions into liberal Anglophone culture. These were that there can be such a thing as "the truth" about society; that it is regularly concealed by the powerful; and that heroic investigative journalists are the people to reveal it. These ideals have proved to be inspirational, and they have brought about some major journalistic successes.

But to succeed at the practice of investigative journalism requires, of course, much more than the mere possession of ideals. Would-be investigative reporters will only survive if they can also identify and overcome the whole range of potential particular obstacles that face them.

REFERENCES

1. Leigh, David. 2005. The Cliché is Right—The Lying Bastards Lie to Us. *Guardian*, January 10. Accessed October 31, 2018. https://www.theguardian.com/media/2005/jan/10/mondaymediasection.politicsandthemedia.
2. Redford, Robert, and Dustin Hoffman. 1976. *All the Presidents Men*. Warner Bros.
3. Pacino, Al. 1999. *The Insider*. Touchstone Pictures.
4. Cumberbatch, Benedict. 2013. *The Fifth Estate*. Dreamworks.
5. Ruffalo, Mark. 2015. *Spotlight*. Participant Media.
6. Bernstein, Carl, and Bob Woodward. 1974. *All the President's Men*. New York: Simon & Schuster.
7. Glover, Stephen. 2002. A Litany of Lies. *Daily Mail*, December 10.
8. Routledge, Paul. 2002. Not Many Conmen and their Lovers Can Rely on the PM's Wife. *Mirror*, December 10.
9. Pascoe-Watson, George. 2002. Cheriegate Scandal Deepens. *Sun*, December 10.
10. Assange, Julian. 2010. Cablegate: 250,000 US Embassy Diplomatic Cables. Accessed November 1, 2018. https://www.wikileaks.org/Cablegate-250-000-US-Embassy.html.
11. Tapsfield, James. 2016. Raging Jeremy Corbyn Stokes Feud. *Mail Online*, August 24. Accessed November 1, 2018. http://www.dailymail.co.uk/news/article-3756207/Raging-Jeremy-Corbyn-stokes-feud-tax-exile-Virgin-boss-Richard-Branson-admits-seats-free-ram-packed-train.html.
12. McTernan, John. 2016. Jeremy Corbyn Will Regret Picking a Fight. *Daily Telegraph*, August 24.
13. Associated Press. 2016. Pizzagate Shooting Suspect Ordered Held by Judge. *Albuquerque Journal*, December 5. Accessed November 1, 2018. https://www.abqjournal.com/902461/the-latest-son-of-trump-adviser-has-sent-posts-on-pizzagate.html.
14. Quinn, Zoe. 2014. All Gamergate Has Done is Ruin People's Lives. *Observer*, December 3.
15. Obst, David. 1998. *Too Good to be Forgotten*. New York: John Wiley & Sons.
16. Bernstein, Carl. 1998. He Wasn't in the Proposal. *New York Post*, September 23.
    Shepard, Alicia. 2008. Deep Throat's Legacy to Journalism. NPR online. http://www.npr.org/templates/story/story.php?storyId=98532461. Accessed 1 Nov 2018.
    Smith, David. 2017. The story of the man who brought down Nixon. Guardian, September 29. https://www.theguardian.com/us-news/2017/sep/29/mark-felt-the-man-who-brought-down-nixon-peter-landesman. Accessed 1 Nov 2018.

17. Evans, Harold. 1983. *Good Times, Bad Times*. London: Weidenfeld & Nicolson.
18. Stead, William. 1871. WT Stead to Rev. Henry Kendall. WT Stead Resource Site. Accessed November 1, 2018. http://www.attackingthedevil.co.uk/letters/kendall.php.
19. ———. 1885. Notice to Our Readers: A Frank Warning. *Pall Mall Gazette*, July 4, 6.
20. Unsigned. 1885. The Second Trial of the Defendants in the Notorious Armstrong Case. *Times*, November 11.
21. Plowden, Alison. 1974. *The Case of Eliza Armstrong: A Child of 13 Bought for £5*. London: BBC Books.
22. Bly, Nellie. 1887. Ten Days in A Madhouse. *New York World*, October 9. In *The Collected Works of Nellie Bly*, 2015. Golgotha Press.
23. BBC TV. 2016. Nursing Homes Undercover. *Panorama*, November 21.
24. Unsigned. 1922. Obituary of Nellie Bly. *New York Times*, January 28.
25. Roosevelt, Theodore. 1906. In *The Works of Theodore Roosevelt*, 1926. New York: Charles Scribner's Sons.
26. Brucker, Herbert. 1960. What's News. *Nieman Reports*. Accessed November 1, 2018. http://1e9svy22oh333mryr83l4s02.wpengine.netdna-cdn.com/wp-content/uploads/2014/03/Spring-1960_150.pdf.
27. Walters, Basil. 1951. Deadpan Reporting Is Passing. *Editor & Publisher*, December 8.
28. Knightley, Philip. 1997. *A Hack's Progress*. London: Jonathan Cape.
29. Birt, John. 2001. *The Harder Path*. London: Little, Brown.
30. Goddard, Peter, John Corner, and Kay Richardson. 2007. *Public Issue Television: World in Action 1963–98*. Manchester University Press.
31. Hersh, Seymour M. 1972. Cover-up. *New Yorker*, January 22.
32. Ellsberg, Daniel. 2008. Remembering Anthony Russo. *Anti-War Blog*. Accessed November 1, 2018. https://www.antiwar.com/blog/2008/08/07/ellsberg-remembering-anthony-russo/.
33. New York Times Co. v. United States, 403 U.S. 713 (1971).

CHAPTER 3

Two Case Histories: Jonathan Aitken and BAe

This chapter might well be subtitled "How to put a minister in jail". Jonathan Aitken was a glamorous and well-connected politician from an influential family. He was related to Lord Beaverbrook, the newspaper tycoon, and became a Conservative MP like his father. By the 1990s, he was in the government as the minister responsible for arms sales. His improper dealings with members of the Saudi Arabian ruling clan were eventually—thanks in part to my own activities as an investigative journalist—to see him sent to prison for perjury.

But the whole saga took years to play out. And I was not at all sure it was going to culminate the way it did. In fact, I thought I was the one who was going to be ruined. In the middle of a melodramatic libel trial, I remember shaking my wife awake at three in the morning—I couldn't sleep—and saying "Look, you need to know that we're going to lose this case. So I'll never work again". Aitken had denounced me in savage terms as "the cancer of bent and twisted journalism". And before my unexpected legal rescue, I felt resigned to going down in journalistic legend as the TV producer who told so many outrageous lies about a cabinet minister that he had cost his own employers millions.

These two linked case studies are about a form of journalistic warfare. They are not simply a veteran's war stories, however. They have general application. Many investigative journalists want to expose wrongdoing by the most powerful social actors. They see their role as "punching up" rather than punching down. In the societies we live in, their central targets

© The Author(s) 2019
D. Leigh, *Investigative Journalism*,
https://doi.org/10.1007/978-3-030-16752-3_3

are therefore often going to be chief executives and government ministers. But precisely because such people are powerful, they can often frustrate a reporter's efforts to get at the facts.

The case studies demonstrate a number of journalistic methods of attack. We will analyse two linked exposures of the relations between Saudi Arabia and the UK—the first revealed Aitken's dealings with the Saudi ruling family, and the second unearthed the way Britain's biggest arms firm, BAe, persuaded the Saudis to buy weapons from them. These are both sagas in which I was personally involved and where I can draw on insider experience.

The Investigation into Aitken

The Aitken saga embroiled a number of other reporters and editors in the pursuit of this slippery politician. The fight with him was psychologically demanding. It also threw up many professional problems. Some of those methods we used were controversial, and some instructive mistakes were made by the journalists (including myself).

Indeed, the whole affair began with a journalistic failure.

In the autumn of 1993, a rich Egyptian businessman, Mohammed Fayed, summoned the paper's then editor, Peter Preston, to a meeting at Harrods, the famous London department store. Fayed owned Harrods, along with Fulham football club and the Ritz hotel in Paris. He privately told the editor that Aitken, Britain's arms sales minister under the Conservative government of John Major, had been staying at Fayed's own Paris hotel at the expense of the Saudi ruling family and was having secret meetings with them about arms deals. Serving British ministers are not allowed to take money from foreigners in this way. If true, it was a resigning matter.

On the face of it, the *Guardian* had been presented with the story on a plate. But of course, journalistic life is never so easy.

Like so many scandals, the story was launched by allegations from a human source. When a source gives a newspaper unsolicited information, there are many questions to ask about his credibility. Was Fayed in a position to know these facts? Well, yes, he clearly was; he himself actually owned the Ritz hotel and controlled all its staff.

But was he a disinterested party, or did he have a personal axe to grind? He did indeed have an existing series of grievances against the British government—he was alleging at the time that government MPs had dishonestly extorted cash from him in return for asking parliamentary questions on his behalf. So he had a motive for painting a government minister in a black light, in ways that might or might not be correct.

Was he willing to stand up and go on the record with his evidence? No, he wasn't. He insisted that his role in the affair should be kept hidden and furthermore that he would only deal with one person—the editor himself.

Clearly, Fayed was not an ideal source. But journalists, like police officers, can't confine themselves only to taking information from vicars and boy scouts. The people who know about murky doings may have murky motives themselves. So Preston decided, correctly, that his source's allegations were well worth investigating. He also concluded, again correctly, that Fayed's off-the-record say-so was not worth much unless the paper could lay hands on corroborating documents—particularly Aitken's hotel bill.

However, Preston did make one key error. His mistake was in agreeing to Fayed's condition that he would alone deal with the Egyptian businessman. An editor is very foolish to try and become his own investigative journalist: it is like keeping a dog and barking yourself. An editor does not have an editor above him—so there is no-one to restrain him from making mistakes.

As a result of his mistaken decision, Preston ended up being controlled by his source. This proved fatal. He asked Fayed for a copy of the Ritz bill, which would confirm that Aitken had not paid for his own luxury stay. Fayed said he could not be seen to hand it over, because that would be bad for his hotel business. Instead, he persuaded the *Guardian*'s editor to agree to a scheme which became known as the "Cod Fax". Preston was to fax the manager of the Ritz, pretending to be Jonathan Aitken himself, and asking to be sent a duplicate of his bill. But the return fax number would really be that of the *Guardian*. The hotel manager in Paris would be in on the plot and would oblige.

This was all done, and it all went wrong. It became known that Preston had obtained the bill via what his political opponents called forgery. Aitken brushed aside the evidence of the piece of paper: he lied that it was the result of a clerical error. He said that his wife had actually paid the bill on his behalf.

The smooth-talking politician got away with this somewhat unlikely story because Aitken's political supporters were busy publicly denouncing

Preston and summoning him before parliamentary committees. One of them abused him as the "hound of hell". The government's top official, the then cabinet secretary Robin Butler, wrote a personal letter to Preston accusing him of crossing "the margins of criminality" [1, p. 80]. As a result, it was the *Guardian*'s controversial methods that became the story. The furore no doubt contributed to an exhausted Preston's decision to step down as editor of the *Guardian* shortly afterwards, in 1995.

THE *GUARDIAN* AND WORLD IN ACTION JOIN FORCES

Meanwhile, I was sitting across the river in an unaccustomedly glamorous 17th-floor office overlooking the Thames, with a fine view of St Paul's cathedral. I had moved over to work as a producer with Granada TV's investigative slot, "World in Action". Television journalism is not quite as idealistic a milieu as outsiders might imagine. The programme's canny top executive, Charles Tremayne, came in and said: "David, we need to kick off the next series. Do you think you can make a minister resign?"

Even by the bold standards of World in Action, this was an audacious request. I started to rack my brains. There were only two senior politicians in the John Major government that I personally knew had skeletons in their cupboards—one was secretly gay, and the other was Aitken, who had been pretty obviously lying to the *Guardian* about his Paris hotel bill. I had no wish to out homosexuals, so my team set to work on Aitken instead.

What were the steps we took in an effort to crack open Aitken's falsehoods? The first was obvious—it was to try and gain the co-operation of the *Guardian* itself. Their reporter on their stalled story, David Pallister, had been a former colleague I already knew as clever and trustworthy. I went to see the editor, Peter Preston. He agreed we could share the *Guardian*'s existing research material, and we would both publish the eventual findings simultaneously.

This was one of the first ventures into collaborative journalism for me. Over the succeeding years, it has flowered into a crucial tool for investigative reporters, particularly on cross-border projects. Old-school journalists are trained up to compete with each other for "scoops", hiding their discoveries from each other and trying to do down all rivals. But it actually often makes a lot more sense for investigative journalists to collaborate. It can give them more research resources, and better political cover. The synergy of simultaneous publication in different media can greatly add to the impact of the story, not dilute it. All it needs is a change of the journalists' conventional mindset. And perhaps a change of inner priorities, so that what matters most is loyalty to the story itself—a feeling that the truth ought to get out, come what may.

Making a Chronology

The next step was to conduct a massive task of research. At Granada, we set out to unearth every fact we could about Aitken's life and career. We fed it into a single large chronology. Making a chronology is a simple idea and one that of course has become a lot simpler thanks to word-processing: data can be easily interpolated, shifted about, and searched with key words. Despite the simplicity of the technique, it is the absolute bedrock of any investigative endeavour that is at all complex. A timeline imposes order on a mass of material. It provides a database for everyone's reference purposes. And, most useful of all, it can reveal previously unsuspected patterns of connections, and of cause and effect.

In Aitken's case, the chronology started to speak volumes as soon as it began to be compiled. It rapidly revealed a key fact to us—that Aitken's meeting with the Saudis had not been a one-off event, but part of a long-standing subservient relationship with one particular wealthy Saudi prince, Mohammed bin Fahd, who had an entourage of fixers and cronies. A striking pattern emerged of Aitken getting secret Saudi backing for his business ventures over many years, and of his links with a world of "commission" payments and bribery.

Finding Human Sources

This discovery in turn led us on a difficult search for human beings, who could confirm or explode the truth of our scenario and—just as vital—be persuaded to appear on television. Newspaper journalism can sometimes get away with vague reference to "sources". But investigative work on radio, by contrast, needs speaking voices; and television must have pictures as well, which are often extremely hard to get.

Some sources were easy enough to persuade on to camera: it just took travel and hard work. An affable aircraft salesman in Florida told us how Aitken had bought a private jet, acting on behalf of the Saudi prince. This US interviewee came from a media-savvy culture where appearing on TV was seen as normal. A health farm matron who had retired to the Canary Islands vividly described how Aitken had posed as the owner of her business, fronting for the Saudis. She had fallen out with Aitken and left under a cloud: so her words would need corroboration.

Other sources were harder to persuade. The limousine-drivers who were hired to ferry Aitken and his prince about on his visits to Britain had all benefitted from showers of Saudi largesse: not just big tips, but even family medical bills. They weren't going to kill the goose that laid golden eggs. But one marked our card: thanks to him, we traced Aitken's former secretary, Valerie Scott. Secretaries can be key sources: they tend to know a lot but also tend to have been undervalued by their bosses. She was willing to tell the truth, but refused adamantly to appear on-screen.

We solved that problem in a controversial way. We hired an actor to appear before the camera, speaking Scott's words. It was true that we put the legend "actor" up on the screen. And it was true that the words were an actual transcript of Scott's own interview. But what we did was, in retrospect, at the absolute edge of acceptability. The audience saw an attractive woman speaking with a winning manner. They would have seen a similar sight with the real Valerie Scott, but there is no getting away from the fact that they were not looking at her, but at a different person.

In our search to get the truth out on camera, we also used what might be seen by some to be even more questionable methods. Sir Frank Williams came on: whilst filmed, he confirmed under sympathetic interviewing that it was Aitken who had arranged Saudi sponsorship of the famous Williams motor-racing team. I don't think we mentioned to him beforehand that our intention was to mount an attack on his benefactor.

And we certainly did not mention that such an attack was our intention when we invited Irene Maggs, Aitken's local party chair from his Thanet constituency, to appear and contribute to what we told her was our planned TV profile of a rising political star. We edited both their interviews with scrupulous fairness, and neither of them had any complaint afterwards. Nevertheless, we were deceptive. I felt it was all in a good cause and we had no alternative. But others might disagree.

TV Reconstructions

Another technique that can arouse controversy is the use of reconstruction and theatrical techniques. Our eventual half-hour documentary was extravagant in doing this. We decided that the most engaging way to tell the story was to turn it into a parody of the 1962 hit movie, *Lawrence of Arabia*, starring Peter O'Toole. We played the film's stirring theme music throughout, but called our production *Jonathan of Arabia*. We used actors kitted out in burnous and Arab robes to stage mock encounters in desert tents. Most fanciful of all, we hired a camel called Topsy from a circus, and towed her up and down on Blackpool beach, to stand in for the sands of Arabia.

These antics were frowned upon by our more staid colleagues working on current affairs programmes such as BBC Panorama. But they raise a genuine technical issue. How do you turn dry investigations with complex political or financial material into something a mass audience will want to watch? The World in Action mission was essentially democratic, in that it sought to find visual methods which would encourage ordinary people to stay with significant stories to the end. Theatrics, irreverence, comedy, sauciness—these were not only marks of subversive states of mind, but also deliberate tools to carry an investigative narrative forward.

The alternative is to abandon the ambition to run serious video investigations in any quantity in the mass media. Such programmes will be confined instead to print, or to a handful of prestige productions aimed only at elites and opinion-formers. That's what happens nowadays, since World in Action's demise. But even the most sober-suited investigative journalist will always need to carry on asking themselves the big question that World in Action posed: "How can I get people to pay attention to my work?"

"Hatchet Jobs" Versus "Fairness"

One of the most interesting attacks on us was made by Aitken after the transmission of Jonathan of Arabia. He protested that it was a "hatchet job". It was certainly true that the programme constituted an unrelenting assault on his character and contained no testimonials of any kind to his love of animals, say, or his Christian faith. We did not give both sides of the story. This raises an important ethical question which every would-be investigative journalist needs to clarify in their mind. Do they need to be fair?

On the face of it, the answer is obvious. Of course, one needs to be fair. But what does fairness mean? Here is an imaginary news item:

Yesterday a plane crashed on landing in Bolivia killing all 37 passengers on board. But 3,740 other planes around the world landed safely.

Is that fair, or is it absurd?
Here is another invented statement:

Hitler exterminated 6 million Jews. But he said they deserved it.

That statement too, is something we would not call fair. We can all recognise this kind of false "balance" and misleading "impartiality".

For the purposes of investigative journalism, I have always been rather attracted by the definition of fairness provided in a sketch by Monty Python, the by-now rather whiskery British TV comedy series. In a parody of the solemn interviewing style of investigative programmes, they purported to profile Britain's notorious gangsters, the Kray Twins, by probing their associates:

> *Interviewer*
> *I understand he also nailed your wife's head to a coffee table. Isn't that right Mrs O' Tracey?*
> **Camera pans to show woman with coffee table nailed to head.**
> *Stig*
> *Yeah, well, he did do that. Yeah, yeah. He was a cruel man, but fair* [1]

"Cruel but fair" strikes me as a useful definition of the correct approach that an investigative journalist should aim for.

This kind of journalism should try fearlessly to expose wrongdoing. It is not there to provide a balanced portrait or to win friends. Where "fairness" comes in is that in the course of an exposure, no matter how harsh, one must never distort, mislead the audience, or falsify the facts.

THE LIBEL TRIAL

Aitken's reaction to the preview of our film in that morning's *Guardian*, was to try to stop the programme going out, first by issuing a writ against the paper, and then by calling a dramatic press conference in which he termed the allegations "wicked lies". He said, memorably and brazenly, that he would defeat us with "the simple sword of truth and the trusty shield of British fair play". This was a masterclass in the art of doubling down. It did not work, because Granada's bosses were made of sterner stuff and went ahead with transmission [2, p. 98ff].

We had hoped to provoke Aitken and gain greater impact for our programme by the deal for simultaneous publication with the *Guardian*. But we had miscalculated how violently the politician would react. And he had miscalculated how hard we would be to intimidate. As a result, the wheels began to turn and rumble for an unstoppable major libel trial, somewhat like the railway mobilisation plans which launched the First World War. The stakes for both sides became frighteningly high.

Our lives were consumed by litigation for the next couple of years. I would not recommend it. We won because the new *Guardian* editor, Alan Rusbridger, did not give in, despite being told by his counsel, George Carman, that Carman was losing the trial. As we fought on, we managed to identify a loophole in Aitken's lies. Our research showed that his wife—whom he claimed had paid his hotel bill for him in Paris—might have actually been in Switzerland at the time.

An extraordinarily fine reporter, Owen Bowcott of the *Guardian*, went and somehow obtained confirmatory documents from the basement of a bankrupt hotel outside Geneva. We served legal "third-party disclosure orders" on British Airways and a car hire company, who turned up the relevant—and conclusive—dockets in their files. It was a novel kind of investigative journalism, conducted by a (highly expensive) legal process. Aitken's case collapsed midway through the trial. The *Guardian* ran a front-page splash story headlined "He Lied and Lied and Lied". Aitken declared himself bankrupt [2, p. 199], and eventually went to jail. After his release, he found religion and has since taken holy orders [3].

LESSONS FROM THE AITKEN CASE
DO:
MAKE A CHRONOLOGY
GET DOCUMENTS
FIND HUMAN SOURCES
COLLABORATE
BUILD A NARRATIVE
DON'T:
LET YOUR METHODS BECOME THE STORY
BE CONTROLLED BY YOUR SOURCE

**BORE THE AUDIENCE
BE TOO "FAIR"
PROVOKE A LIBEL SUIT**

The BAe Investigation

The Aitken investigation was a melodrama: but BAe was a slog. It took almost seven years. It also posed a very different suite of investigative problems. With Aitken, we journalists knew from the start what we were trying to prove: but with BAe, we had very little idea of what was really going on. It was blind man's buff. The investigation eventually succeeded—to an extent at least—thanks to the novel use of documents, other people's lawsuits, human sources, cross-border collaboration, and cautious relationships with the police. Along the way, it demonstrated the accuracy of the saying "It's always the cover-up": for it was only when the British Prime Minister Tony Blair stepped in to try and block exposure of the truth that the story really caught fire.

It was then, at last, that we were able to publish the allegation which all parties had been desperate to conceal and which enabled the *Guardian* to write another striking front-page splash headline: "BAE ACCUSED OF SECRETLY PAYING £1BN TO SAUDI PRINCE" [4]. Prince Bandar, son of the Saudi defence minister, had even also been presented with a free gift of his own jumbo jet. This was all to help persuade the Saudis to make the biggest arms purchase in British history. Saudi Arabia had bought from the UK what was in effect an entire air force, at very high prices. Bandar had his free Boeing 747 specially painted in the silver and blue colours of his favourite American football team, the Dallas Cowboys.

There are two useful lessons we gained from the BAe experience. The first is that Rome wasn't built in a day. We accumulated knowledge only bit by bit. Obviously my colleagues and I did not spend those seven years doing nothing but write about the company. Other stories intervened and we returned to the subject from time to time only when there were developments. But we needed to learn patience and to keep plugging away at the case.

The second lesson is that business corporations are much harder to investigate than governments and politicians. Public officials recognise, at least nominally, that they have civic duties to explain themselves to parliament, to council meetings, to committees and inquiries and even, via Freedom of Information requests, to the ordinary citizen. They may well be lying their heads off, but at least they feel constitutionally obliged to provide some responses.

Private companies are different. They provide some basic statutory information in their published accounts, but otherwise they don't have to engage with political opponents, and they certainly don't have to engage with journalists. Annual reports and shareholders' meetings are normally little more than tailored showcases for the image a company wishes to project. Trying to prise facts out of big business can frequently consist of little more than flinging yourself against a wall of silence built by public relations officers. In their playbook, this is the best tactic because it starves any controversial issue of the oxygen of publicity.

Finding Documents in the National Archives

The 9/11 atrocities of 2001, in which Islamist terrorists flew planes into the twin towers of the New York World Trade Center, had an almost accidental result. They managed explicitly to outlaw overseas bribery by British companies for the first time. This was because British legislation followed the US in the wake of 9/11. They criminalised the kind of international money-laundering which it was believed had helped the terrorists.

Until then, British government officials had taken the cynical attitude that bribery of UK public officials was a wicked crime, but bribery of foreigners was a very good way of doing business. My colleague Rob Evans and I were at the time running investigations back at the *Guardian*. We thought it would be a good idea to highlight British hypocrisy in view of the new laws. In particular we hoped to expose the activities of Britain's official arms sales department, then going under the bland name of DESO, the "Defence Exports Services Organisation".

Curious about DESO's origin in the 1960s under a Labour government, we went to the National Archives. There in bunkers at Kew, on the outskirts of London, are stored official papers open to the public after 30 years. We unearthed secret reports from the time, which were lying largely forgotten in old files. They openly advised Harold Wilson's administration that one must pay bribes to sell arms. In particular, a later 1971 dispatch from our ambassador in Jeddah calmly explained that Saudi sales always required bribery of the defence minister, Prince Sultan: "Sultan has, of course, a corrupt interest in all contracts" [5]. It dawned on us that because Saudi Arabia is a family business, Sultan was, more than 30 years later, *still* the defence minister, and BAe was still selling him arms. We had a story, even if it was about events in the past.

LAWSUITS IN JERSEY

Crucial documents emerge from all sorts of places. Another excellent source of documentation about companies can be found in law courts, especially where there have been unsavoury goings-on. People fall out, especially about money. A smart local journalist on an offshore paper in the small Channel island of Jersey gave us our next break. He spotted some litigation there which the parties were attempting to keep secret. They had gained orders preventing local publication. It involved the foreign minister of Qatar, another oil-rich oligarchy in the Middle East. Qatar too had purchased arms from Britain. Because of the new British anti-bribery laws, a local bank became uneasy about millions of pounds that was mysteriously deposited in the name of anonymous trusts, and they froze these offshore assets. The Qatari minister was trying to get his money back.

It began to look as though this was another BAe-linked suspicious transaction. We also learned that the Serious Fraud Office on the British mainland, tasked with enforcing the new law, was taking an interest. In later years, lawsuits brought by agents or middlemen claiming to be deprived of their "commissions" on transactions like this were to be a fruitful source of information. But for now, our stories went nowhere: in a pattern that was later to become familiar, the Qataris effectively bought their way out of trouble. They paid over a fee of £6m to the Jersey authorities for "any damage perceived to have been sustained" [6] and the case was dropped.

HOW TO STIMULATE SOURCES

At this stage, we learned another important lesson: the more you keep on publishing prominent stories, the more you stimulate fresh sources to come forward. This is something that can make investigative work on print or online outlets much more productive than doing exposure stories in the more laborious field of television. There, you tend to only get the opportunity of a single programme, with one shot at the target.

The first source who approached us was an unlikely character called Eddie Cunningham, who lived in Runcorn, on Merseyside in the north of

England. His message? "You've got no idea what's really been going on. But I can tell you". Cunningham said that he had been working informally for a travel company, which acted as a "front" for BAe. Since a recent gigantic Saudi-BAe arms deal known as Al Yamamah had been proposed, senior members of the Saudi air force had been coming over to London, ostensibly for training. Eddie's job had been to use a secret BAe budget to "entertain" them. The entertainments provided had ranged from prostitutes to more bizarre items such as canteens of gold and silver cutlery. His motive for talking to us? He had been laid off, because BAe were getting jumpy, and they wouldn't pay him his due.

Cunningham presented us with a characteristic source problem. How could we possibly stand his story up? We could not proceed unless we got confirmation that he did have the secretive relationship with BAe that he claimed. But he had certainly not been provided with monthly pay slips. We could not make freedom of information requests to a private company.

What we could do, however, was use the then provisions of the Data Protection Act to have Eddie make on our behalf what is called a "Subject Access Request". If you pay £10, any organisation, not just a public body, is legally obliged to give you copies of personal data they hold about you. (As BAe's lawyer no doubt advised them when they received Eddie's request.) The company responded by sending over copies of his complaining correspondence and their replies. The file was no doubt shorn of any embarrassing internal memos, but that did not trouble us: we had gained the confirmation of Eddie's *bona fide* connection with the company. That enabled us to print more stories.

As a result, our phone rang again. This time it was a businessman called Peter Gardiner who actually owned one of the travel companies BAe had been using. His message to us: "You've still got no idea what's really been going on". Gardiner's motives were again straightforward: a jittery BAe had pulled out, driving his company into collapse. He explained that BAe had operated a "slush fund" on a much greater scale than our previous source realised. They had been paying out millions to Saudi officials right up to the head of the Saudi air force. In a bizarre but apparently typical operation, Gardiner might be required to fly an entourage of up to 30 wives and children over to Los Angeles to do some shopping—and then charter an entire jumbo jet to fly them home with their cargo of classic cars, furs, and other expensive loot. Furthermore, Gardiner possessed boxes and boxes of documents with copies of detailed invoices that he had sent on for payment to BAe.

CHEQUEBOOK JOURNALISM?

Peter Gardiner's treasure-trove of documents presented us with a common dilemma. Were we going to practise what is known as "chequebook journalism"? This is a question that journalism students often ask about. At the bottom end of the market, it is not much of an ethical problem. Tabloid journalists pay for stories and advertise openly that they do. "Kiss and tell" revelations can fetch fair sums, although it is a common experience for members of the public to find their stories have been already tickled out of them while they have come away with much smaller amounts than those of which they had dreamed.

Prison officers, police constables, defence ministry clerks—these kinds of relatively lowly sources will sell names, addresses, and other titbits to the tabloids. A series of trials arising out of investigative reporter Nick Davies' phone-hacking revelations, demonstrated a strangely equivocal attitude among British jurors. They proved willing to convict public officials who took such bribes, but also happy to acquit the reporters who offered them the money [7].

At the serious investigative end of the business, there is also an equivocal attitude. As *Sunday Times* journalist Philip Knightley recalled over his paper's thalidomide exposure, the journalists were uneasy because they paid several thousand pounds for an expert's court files, tainting the purity of their legal battle (see Chap. 2). In the case of Jeremy Thorpe, the Liberal party leader acquitted of conspiracy to murder, we discovered at the time by interviewing a juror what a damaging effect chequebook journalism could have. Their deliberations had been tainted when it was revealed in court that the Crown's star prosecution witness stood to get £50,000 from the *Telegraph* papers for his recollections, but only half as much if the defendant was acquitted (see Chap. 5).

Yet more recently, the *Telegraph* was seen to triumph when they paid £150,000 to an intermediary able to lay his hands on a disc of every British MPs' expenses claims [8]. After a good deal of further investigation, the paper was able to reveal—to great acclaim—that many of the expense claims were bogus or outrageous. It led to a string of exposures, sanctions, and even the criminal convictions of politicians. Yet other papers such as the *Sun* and the *Times* were not willing to engage in this piece of chequebook journalism. They were reported to have previously refused to buy the files [9].

I have faced this problem myself: I once in 2003 self-righteously refused to pay £20,000 to a private security source who was willing—for cash—to reveal that he had infiltrated an anti-arms trade group of campaigners on behalf of a weapons firm. My reasons were a mixture of principle and practicality—I recoiled at rewarding such a bad person. But also, my paper didn't have that kind of money. And furthermore the story didn't seem big enough to be worth it. I was then wryly amused to see the exposure subsequently appear in the *Sunday Times*. Not only had its journalists been more morally flexible (and better resourced) than me—they had also unearthed a better story. It turned out that the security firm involved had significant political connections. The *Sunday Times* had made the right call [10].

So this is not a question to which there are absolute answers. One of the good reasons for not paying large sums is that it can tempt people to make things up. In Britain and the US, most serious newspapers and broadcasters will therefore tell you that they don't pay for investigative stories. What they tend to mean is that they don't *normally* pay for stories. In my experience, there is often a certain amount of wiggle-room. You don't pay for stories, but you might pay travel and hotel "expenses". TV companies will very reasonably pay "disturbance fees" for one's trouble in turning up to be interviewed. You might not pay for a story, but you might buy the supporting documents for legal use.

My own view is that modest payments can sometimes be useful, but are best avoided if possible. In Peter Gardiner's case, his boxes of Saudi documents were clearly vital. But we didn't want to be accused of paying large bribes whilst claiming to expose the paying of bribes by other people. Our compromise to get the story off the ground was to point out to him that, in future, book publishers, TV, and movie companies would be bound to be interested in his revelations. We would help with introductions. Gardiner was not driven primarily by greed, and he agreed to co-operate.

Off we went. We wrote many more stories. This time, when the phone rang, it was a highly confidential source who was adamant that he did not want his identity to be disclosed. He feared retaliation, and he feared the tax authorities. His message was the same again: "You've got no idea what's really been going on".

I cannot give too many details about this informant, even a decade later, for obvious source protection reasons. But I had to board a plane, and arrange a cloak-and-dagger meeting by a remote seashore. What he told me there was stunning. He explained that BAe's Saudi "slush fund" was itself just a small part of the story. The arms giant had been operating a worldwide system of secret payments on weapons deals to all sorts of countries, funnelled through a network of agents or middlemen. The money was sluiced through a BAe front company, kept off the books, and incorporated offshore in the British Virgin Islands. Its name was Red Diamond Trading, and my source handed me copies of offshore bank statements that gave proof and enabled us to publish [11].

Collaborating with the Authorities

BAe maintained a stoical silence throughout all our disclosures. But they successfully managed to dissuade any other newspapers or broadcasters from picking up our stories. We were now at an impasse. This led us to try and think laterally, and to turn outside for help. We started to collaborate in two different directions. Our first collaboration was controversial in some eyes. We went to the authorities—in this case, Robert Wardle, then head of the UK's Serious Fraud Office, which took the lead in bribery cases. We offered to co-operate, and handed over to him all our evidence of British government complicity, as well as our key source, Peter Gardiner (with his consent, naturally).

Wardle was willing—rather to our surprise—and he set up a heavy-weight investigation aided by a team from the Ministry of Defence police. In our ignorance, we did not grasp at the time that in fact he and his staff had been quietly fuming ever since their attempts to probe the Qatar connection had been blocked. (Investigative journalism is like blind man's buff.)

Why was this move of ours controversial? I have met quite a few journalist colleagues who think it is just wrong to work with the police. They say journalists must be independent and never be seen to act as informers or agents of the state. These principles are perfectly correct. But I don't think they rule out certain forms of co-operation, on a case-by-case basis.

My own analysis is that my primary task as an investigative journalist is to obtain information. Was talking to the Serious Fraud Office (SFO) going to help me obtain more information about BAe's behaviour? I believed it was, for the simple reason that the police had powers which journalists do not possess. The SFO were able to serve orders on the company, for example, forcing them to disclose the identities of their confidential agents around the world, and the nature of their banking arrangements. They were able to arrest people and interrogate them. They were also able to approach foreign authorities and ask them to investigate people and bank accounts in those countries.

Naturally, the authorities are not supposed to pass sensitive investigative information back to journalists. But there were legitimate ways some of this material could seep back to us. The police might talk to sources who were also in touch with us, for example. Or, as happened in one such case, the police would send a detailed request for assistance to their counterparts in South Africa, explaining what they had already discovered. The local police leaked such interesting material to their own South African journalist contacts, with whom we were collaborating.

That gave us stories we could publish in the UK perfectly legitimately, along such lines as this:

> More than £100m was secretly paid by the arms company BAe to sell warplanes to South Africa according to allegations in a detailed police dossier seen by the Guardian. A lengthy affidavit from the SFO in London, leaked to the Mail & Guardian newspaper in South Africa accuses BAe of 'covert' behaviour and of withholding information. SFO principal investigator Gary Murphy says in the affidavit... "I believe that BAe have sought to conceal from the SFO the involvement of [defence minister aide] Fana Hlongwane..." [12]

And when a bullying Saudi Arabia and a compliant British government started leaning on lawyers and police to suppress their inquiries, anger and frustration also grew among the honest officials. Our phones once more started to ring.

COLLABORATIVE JOURNALISM

As the links with South Africa's *Mail & Guardian* demonstrate, our other move to break the journalistic impasse was to reach out to different media organisations. These collaborations work best as a two-way street, in which both sides get something they need. We linked up with a TV team in Sweden who were already investigating BAe transactions in the Czech Republic. They were looking for a Briton who could play an undercover role. Soon my colleague Rob Evans, disguised as "Dr Miller", a British PR man, was being secretly filmed in Prague as he explained to Czech politicians that he was engaged in a damage-limitation exercise on London's behalf, and what did they know of corrupt payments?

This grainy footage was to star in a Swedish documentary exposing massive corruption in Eastern Europe. Fred Laurin, their reporter, had his own sources in Stockholm, with information which he shared with us.

Similarly, we joined forces with a Romanian investigative journalist, Paul Radu, to work on the transactions around the sale of some elderly frigates to Bucharest; and we worked with local journalists in Tanzania to investigate the particularly disgraceful sale of an overpriced military radar which the poverty-stricken country did not even need.

This last was a striking demonstration of one particular value of cross-border collaboration. We were trying to identify the confidential middleman in the Tanzanian sale. When I flew to Dar-es-Salaam, the local journalists said everyone knew his name, which they told me. But they said, of course they could not print it inside the country for fear of repercussions. However, if I went back to London and published the name in the *Guardian*, the local journalists said they felt they would be safe enough to reproduce it. And so we did. In a situation like that, all the journalists win [13].

Collaboration got a little bit more tricky for us in the final stages of the BAe saga, when Prime Minister Tony Blair was prevailed upon by the Saudis to order the SFO investigations to be shut down. This turned what had until then been a lonely campaign by one newspaper into a noisy national scandal. We joined forces with BBC Panorama, and its formidable reporter Jane Corbin—for both of us had separate sources revealing the biggest scandal of all: the monster secret payments to the Saudi defence minister's son, Prince Bandar.

I suspect we were each grateful politically for the other's support, in this dangerous territory. We were supposed to publish simultaneously. Unfortunately, the story got the better of me. We ended up in an unseemly scramble to see who would publish first, and the BBC claimed they had won by getting out an initial version on their website. Jane wrote, to my annoyance,

> *Until Panorama broke the story* of secret payments into accounts controlled by Prince Bandar, the former Saudi ambassador to the United States, no journalists had got to the heart of the matter. [author's emphasis] [14]

This does, I will admit, show that my claim is optimistic that reporters find it easy to put aside their rivalries.

The BAe saga did end with a result, but it was a long time coming. The US department of justice picked up the investigation the British SFO had been forced to put down. And on 6 February 2010, Rob Evans and I were at last able to write:

The arms giant BAe yesterday agreed to pay out almost £300m in penalties as it finally admitted guilt over its worldwide conduct in the face of long-running corruption allegations. [15]

The BAe investigation did show that it was possible, using some straightforward techniques and some innovative ones, to crack the wall of secrecy round the behaviour of a big corporation. Our long crusade did also lead eventually to a strengthened Bribery Act, and to a series of further exposures of corrupt misdeeds by other companies. But it was never going to be the kind of quick reveal that gets industry awards for scoop of the year. Sometimes investigative journalists just have to live with that.

LESSONS FROM BAE

CORPORATIONS ARE HARD TARGETS

ROME WASN'T BUILT IN A DAY

YOU NEED DOCUMENTS

YOU NEED LAWSUITS.

YOU NEED HUMAN SOURCES

DON'T PAY BIG MONEY

COVER-UPS CAN BECOME THE STORY

THINK LATERALLY

THE AUTHORITIES MAY CO-OPERATE

COLLABORATE WITH OTHER MEDIA

ALWAYS KEEP ON WRITING!

REFERENCES

1. Wilmut, Roger, ed. 1989. *The Complete Monty Python's Flying Circus: Just the Words*. London: Eyre Methuen.
2. Luke, Harding, David Leigh, and David Pallister. 1999. *The Liar: The fall of Jonathan Aitken*. London: Guardian Books.
3. BBC. 2018. Jonathan Aitken Becomes Prison Chaplain. *BBC News*. Accessed November 8, 2018. https://www.bbc.co.uk/news/uk-44668185.
4. Leigh, David, and Rob Evans. 2007. Bae Accused of Secretly Paying £1bn to Saudi Prince. *Guardian*, June 7.

5. Morris, Willie. 1971. Arms Procurement in Saudi Arabia. *National Archives*. Accessed November 8, 2018. https://www.theguardian.com/baefiles/page/0,,2095803,00.html.
6. Barnett, Antony, and Conal Walsh. 2002. Riddle of Sheikh's £100m Secret Fund. *Observer*, June 2.
7. O'Carroll, Lisa. 2015. Four Senior Sun Journalists Acquitted Over Payments to Officials. *Guardian*, March 20.
8. Lewis, William. 2012. Witness Statement. Evidence to the Leveson Inquiry into the Culture, Practices and Ethics of the Press. Accessed November 8, 2018. http://webarchive.nationalarchives.gov.uk/20140122145147/http://www.levesoninquiry.org.uk/wp-content/uploads/2012/01/Witness-Statement-of-William-Lewis.pdf.
9. Brook, Stephen and Audrey Gillan. 2009. MPs' Expenses: How Scoop Came to Light. *Guardian*, May 18.
10. Campaign Against the Arms Trade. 2005. 2005 CAAT Steering Committee Statement on Spying. Accessed November 8, 2018. https://www.caat.org.uk/about/spying.
11. Leigh, David, and Rob Evans. 2007. BAe's Secret Money Machine. *The BAe Files*. Accessed November 8, 2018. https://www.theguardian.com/baefiles/page/0,,2095840,00.html.
12. ———. 2008. BAE Paid £100m to Secure South African Arms Deal, Police Files Allege. *Guardian*, December 5.
13. Leigh, David. 2007. The Arms Deal, the Agent and the Swiss Bank Account. *Guardian*, January 15.
14. Corbin, Jane. 2007. Princes, Planes and Payoffs. *BBC Panorama*. Accessed November 8, 2018. http://news.bbc.co.uk/1/hi/programmes/panorama/6718831.stm.
15. Leigh, David, and Rob Evans. 2010. BAe Admits Guilt. *Guardian*, February 5.

CHAPTER 4

Investigative Journalists and Their Bosses

A Mutiny at the *Times*

It's two in the morning. I'm alone on the newsdesk on the deserted floor of the Times in New Printing House Square, at the far end of Fleet St. Who is in charge of the clattering train? I am. I'm 29 years old and I'm the juniormost night reporter, doing the graveyard shift. I slide open the news editor's desk drawer, where I know there's kept a spare key to an adjoining glass-walled office. It belongs to my immediate boss, Charlie Douglas-Home—Old Etonian, Guards officer, Home Editor, and Top Toff. For days, the newsroom has been swirling with rumours that Charlie is compiling secret blacklists of individual reporters, with a view to victimising the malcontents.

I mean to find out

In the course of this collision with the late Charles Douglas-Home in 1977, I did indeed succeed in breaking into his office, and I did confirm that he was compiling secret dossiers on the staff. Among the surveillance files on the "Other Ranks", I was mortified to find my own name. He wrote: "Leigh is frequently depressed, which he attributes to his conditions of work, but which I am more inclined to blame on his chaotic love life". (I was recently divorced.) It was made painfully clear that oiks like me and some others had little future on the "Top People's Paper"—as it used boastfully to style itself.

There followed on from this discovery a smallish staff mutiny among the reporters and their trade union "chapel". It was rapidly suppressed.

© The Author(s) 2019
D. Leigh, *Investigative Journalism*,
https://doi.org/10.1007/978-3-030-16752-3_4

The *Times* was then under the editorship of former Conservative candidate William Rees-Mogg, father of an infant who was later to flower into the parodiable right-wing MP Jacob Rees-Mogg. I decided this oppressive regime wasn't for me, and quit the paper.

Does my little personal anecdote confirm that investigative journalists are temperamentally unsuited to working for any sort of boss at all? Or does it show, on the other hand, that corporate bosses are bad people, who are nearly always going to be the enemies of free-spirited investigative journalists?

It is true that as a typically brash young reporter, I didn't much like being ordered about by anyone. That might support the view that investigative journalists are merely irresponsible egotists. But a piece of evidence to support the opposite interpretation can be found in the story of Harry Evans, one of the greatest British editors. Even at Evans' own exalted level, he himself had bosses who made his life impossible. Douglas-Home re-appears in Evans' story, again as something of a villain, but this time playing the role of henchman to tycoon Rupert Murdoch.

Evans made his reputation as the crusading editor of the *Sunday Times* and founder of its famous Insight team. But Murdoch bought the paper. He did not find Evans' liberalism to be congenial: he persuaded him out of his *Sunday Times* stronghold in 1981 to take over the daily *Times*. The following year, Evans, who says he was resisting Murdoch's schemes to turn the paper into "an organ of Thatcherism", was undermined and eventually ousted. Douglas-Home got Harry Evans' editorship for himself.

A striking contemporary cover of the satirical magazine *Private Eye* reproduces a news photo of Evans looking over the proprietor's shoulder as he holds up an outstretched copy of the venerable *Times*. Rupert Murdoch's gloating fantasy speech bubble reads: "It says here you've been fired" [1]. Evans wrote gloomily in his memoirs:

> Douglas-Home …was the figleaf behind which Murdoch began the rape of the Times as an independent newspaper of unimpeachable integrity. [2, p. xxvii]

A Mutiny at the *Observer*

Such questions of journalistic integrity were thrown into sharp relief for me by my own next personal confrontation with a boss. I was by now at the *Observer*, where I found myself working for the late "Tiny" Rowland. This extremely tall businessman with icy pale-blue eyes was as unsavoury a proprietor as Murdoch. In some respects, he was worse. Murdoch does not personally commit criminal offences, but Rowland made much of his money via his Lonrho company by paying bribes to African politicians in return for trading concessions. Conservative prime minister Edward Heath famously called him "the unpleasant and unacceptable face of capitalism".

Rowland purchased the loss-making *Observer*, a British Sunday paper which had a distinguished anti-colonialist reputation in Africa, because for him, it was simply one more means of exercising commercial influence.

My personal situation posed some ethical problems. I was in charge of investigations for the paper, many of them controversial, throughout the heyday of the radical Thatcher government in Britain. Was it possible for me and my colleagues to be honest journalists whilst working for a crook? Surprisingly perhaps, for a number of years, the answer turned out to be "Yes". We were given free rein to write story after story, no matter how embarrassing or infuriating for the government. On 12 successive weeks, to Mrs Thatcher's growing rage, we published unflattering front-page articles about the money-making schemes of the prime minister's own son, Mark.

Our run of journalistic freedom was not, of course, because of Tiny Rowland's commitment to the principles of independent investigative journalism. It was a temporary convergence of interests. Rowland had fallen out with the Thatcher regime for a rather bizarre reason: he longed to buy Harrods, the iconic London department store, and he believed the British government had unfairly helped it fall into the hands of his rival, an Egyptian businessman called Mohammed Fayed. The more enraged Mrs Thatcher became, the more delighted was the proprietor.

Naturally, this delightful space within which we could work freely as journalists did not remain available for ever. Rowland could not resist abusing his power over us in the end. He obtained (no doubt through more bribery), a copy of a secret government report which revealed that his arch-enemy Fayed had not been using his own funds to purchase Harrods, contrary to his claims. Rowland then prevailed on the *Observer*'s editor, Donald Trelford, to publish a special midweek edition of the paper containing the leaked report, merely so Rowland could wave it at a Lonrho shareholders' meeting.

Nor did his prostitution of Britain's oldest Sunday paper stop there. One morning shortly afterwards, I parked my company Passat as usual at our office building next to Battersea power station (Tiny had acquired among other things the UK import franchise for Volkswagen, and so we

were all issued with fine, large vehicles, presumably obtained at a dis-
count). When I reached my desk, there was an unwelcome surprise. An
executive thrust a bundle of papers at me. They were from a supposedly
secret source, accusing the arms company BAe of bribery in warplane sales
to Saudi Arabia and Jordan. The "dossier" was colourful, but vague.

I was suspicious. "Is it a Lonrho story?" I asked. As I was later to testify
to an inquiry by the *Observer* directors, I then said "I won't do it". Nor
was I alone. Eventually, nearly every other single senior journalist refused
to write it, including the business editor Melvyn Marckus and the distinguished outside author and arms sales specialist Anthony Sampson. By the
time I went off on an Easter ski-ing holiday in France with my family, I was
happy that we had scotched Tiny's nefarious schemes.

I returned to find the newsroom in an uproar. A senior editor had published the dossier story in the *Observer* after all, in my absence. News of the
internal rows had promptly been leaked to a Labour MP, who had publicly
denounced the *Observer* in parliament for corrupt journalism. I myself was
being fingered as the leaker and Trelford was getting calls for my sacking. I
asked my deputy, Paul Lashmar, "What's been going on?" He said: "I leaked
it" "Oh", I said "why did you do that?" "Well, David" he replied "I just
asked myself what you would have done and then I did the same".

Nor did the mayhem end there. It is a red line with reporters on self-
respecting papers that a proprietor should not write the news. Yet it transpired that Tiny really had been personally responsible for the story's
appearance. Trelford, his editor, had been whisked off on Lonrho's private
jet to Iran to help promote Tiny's interests there. On the plane, the editor
had been introduced to a crony, the late arms dealer Wolfgang Michel,
who had pressed the BAe "dossier" into his hands. Lonrho were at the
time in business with Dassault, British Aerospace's great rival.

The journalists' union branch demanded the so-called independent
directors of the *Observer* intervene and protect us from this sort of corrupt
proprietorial pressure. But the directors conspicuously failed to help. They
said their only role was to protect the editor. Trelford informed them he
himself had felt no pressure and therefore needed no protection. He had
merely promoted the story to his staff and put it on the front page, he said,
because "My curiosity as a newspaper man was naturally aroused" [3].

I resigned from the paper in despair [4, pp. 548–57]. Paul Lashmar
followed me out the door at the *Observer*, going to the TV series World in
Action. Robin Lustig, the gifted executive who had originally hired me
and who subsequently became the voice of the BBC's World Tonight, wrote:

I knew that I would soon have to leave as well. I had been profoundly uncomfortable as the rows intensified...As my sympathy was entirely with the mutineers, I was in an impossible position and in September 1989 I handed in my notice. I was not alone: the paper's chief foreign affairs correspondent Neal Ascherson and the literary editor and poet Blake Morrison both left at the same time. [5, p. 211]

What remained of the *Observer* was finally purchased by the *Guardian*, in something of a fire sale. As Lustig records, Trelford retired to the island of Majorca and in 2014, at the age of 76, fathered his sixth child, Poppy.

This saga, which severely dented a once-fine paper, was a striking demonstration of what happens when investigative journalists try to stand up to their bosses. Mostly, they lose out.

There were also two significant ironies. The first was that Tiny Rowland's allegations of bribery were actually not wrong: years later, we found evidence of an astonishing global pattern of apparently corrupt behaviour by British Aerospace. Trelford was to claim this vindicated his earlier stance. But, of course, it does not solve the ethical issue we had faced. Investigative journalists owe it to their readers to be free to look at evidence dispassionately, and only publish if satisfied of its reliability. They can't let their hands be tied by the agenda of a proprietor without betraying those readers. There was a classic conflict of interests.

The second irony was one that I only discovered many years later. When I resigned, I thought that at last I would be free to defend myself and tell the truth about what had been going on behind the curtain at one of Britain's most distinguished journalistic institutions. I wrote a lengthy article detailing the corrupt practices I had witnessed. I took it to the *Guardian* in London, owned by the Scott Trust (of "Comment is free, but facts are sacred" fame), and then edited by the late Peter Preston. The piece appeared, after a certain delay [6]. Much later, after Preston had retired, I learned that it had in fact very nearly been suppressed. "Peter didn't want your article to be published" my source explained "He thought it would antagonise Tiny Rowland, and he wanted Tiny to sell him the *Observer*".

This time it was journalists at the *Guardian* who mutinied against their boss and saved my bacon. The then media editor, Georgina Henry, with the support of the then features editor Alan Rusbridger, defied their own editor, and printed my words. So even at a supposedly high-minded organisation like the *Guardian*, the corporate boss can be just as much a threat to journalistic endeavours, as at a more rabidly capitalist firm. Bosses are bosses the world over.

Living with a Boss

These stories show how sometimes an investigative reporter simply has to part company with their employer. It may be out of a prudent instinct for self-preservation. It may even be that conscience requires them to resign on principle. (Perhaps best not to make a habit of that if you need to pay the rent.) However, there is also an underlying moral to these personal anecdotes. I want to illuminate the very first rule of survival as an investigative journalist. If you intend to get started in your career, you must absorb the fact that you're most probably, in one way or another, always going to have a boss.

It is a fundamental truth that investigative journalists can rarely succeed by working alone. You can certainly express yourself very freely online these days, and the barriers to self-publication are much lower than they used to be in the pre-electronic era. But the solitary blogger lacks resources, legal cover and, above all, impact. This makes worthwhile exposure journalism difficult. So if you want to practise serious investigative reporting, it is probably inevitable that you will end up having to have to work with some sort of media organisation.

It does not have to be a conventional newspaper. The organisation could be a non-profit, a book-publisher, a news agency, an activist NGO, a website, or a broadcaster. You could be employed, or could be a freelancer. But whatever the format, someone out there is going to decide whether to give the would-be exposé writer a job, or whether to publish any of their findings. The bigger the media organisation, of course, the more there will be a hierarchy of editors, editors-in-chief, managers, donors, proprietors, or shareholders with whom the individual exposure journalist must contend.

A Mutiny at Fox: Jane Akre and Steve Wilson

The problem is widespread. Take the experience of a couple of wannabe investigative reporters who went to work for a Fox News TV station in Florida, part of the stable controlled by Murdoch. Journalists Jane Akre and Steve Wilson eventually went on camera to recount—in painful if sometimes droll detail—the story of what happened to them. In a Canadian documentary and accompanying book called "The Corporation" [7], they recalled how their first task was to shoot a boastful trailer for Fox. It touted their new role as "The Investigators", complete with smoke machine effects and melodramatic shots in silhouette.

The duo went on to produce a story about the fact that much of the cows' milk in the US was laced with bovine growth hormone—a chemical produced at the time by giant manufacturer Monsanto, whose use was banned from Europe on animal welfare grounds. Although "Posilac" was touted to increase US dairy farmers' profits, there were also claims it might be carcinogenic.

Shortly before the pair's exposure story on local TV was due to air, letters from Monsanto lawyers arrived, addressed to Roger Ailes himself, the then chairman of Fox News in New York. They expressed "great concern" and threatened "dire consequences for Fox News" if the broadcast went out. Monsanto advertised extensively on Fox TV stations, including not just for the growth hormone, but for products such as Nutrasweet, the artificial sweetener, and Roundup, the pesticide. Akre and Wilson say they were asked to kill the story, or else to make misleading changes. They were also asked to keep Fox's behaviour vis-à-vis Monsanto secret, they say. They dug in their heels and, as a result, eventually lost their jobs. According to Wilson, he expostulated to his bosses that they were only being fired for one reason:

> We stood up to this big corporation, we stood up to your editors and we stood up to your lawyers, and we said, 'Look, there ought to be a principle higher than just making money!'

The couple went to court, claiming they had in effect been victimised for whistleblowing. They won $425,000 at their first court hearing some years later, but lost on appeal. The case turned in part on whether the Fox TV station was legally required by the state of Florida to broadcast accurate news. The answer turned out to be—apparently not.

So their bosses defeated them. And the law defeated them. And so did Big Business. The case is instructive, but the story's moral is not necessarily the obvious one.

Were this pair of upright journalists martyrs to a good cause? Or were they just idiots from the outset? Some people might say no-one in their right minds would go to work for Fox News in the expectation that they would be allowed to upset corporate apple-carts by practising that kind of adversarial journalism. The company's reputation is well known, not to say notorious. Is it possible that the duo allowed their vanity, having a great career opportunity as "The Investigators" dangled before them, to get the better of their judgement? It might be tempting to say to Akre and Wilson: "More fool you".

A Mutiny at CBS: Lowell Bergman and *The Insider*

That could, however, be an unfair conclusion. In the history of famous media confrontations, another similar, if better-known collision is recorded between a dogged journalist and his bosses at a major US TV channel. That also involved Big Business. It had other parallel features. But the key difference this time was the outcome: the story went out triumphantly in the end, and the producer concerned got to be lionised as a hero in the subsequent movie—played by Al Pacino, no less.

The investigative producer concerned—Lowell Bergman—certainly deserved his personal accolade for confronting not only the US tobacco industry, but also for challenging his own editorial and corporate hierarchy at CBS. The Michael Mann movie that resulted was called *The Insider* and was released in 1999. It had a very different flavour to the one previous landmark film about investigative journalism—the celebrated Watergate movie of 1976, with its homage to tough-minded *Washington Post* editor Ben Bradlee. As Bergman wryly observes

> In 'All the President's Men,' the editors and reporters are heroes. That's not the case here. [8]

The editors and anchors at the famous CBS news programme "60 Minutes" proved unwilling to transmit Bergman's ground-breaking interview with a tobacco industry whistleblower. The whistleblower possessed key scientific evidence about false industry claims that nicotine was not addictive. But he had broken a non-disclosure agreement: CBS bosses professed themselves too scared of a legal opinion that they might be sued.

As the film recounts, in what Bergman emphasises is a fictionalised "historical novel" rather than a pedantic documentary, this cowardice left Bergman himself absolutely furious, and his vulnerable source high and dry. CBS never aired the explosive interview until it was eventually published elsewhere. Bergman made himself unpopular with his colleagues by revealing to the *New York Times* just how much self-censorship had taken place. He then left CBS.

This outcome demonstrates once again how disruptive it is to the career of an investigative journalist if they pick a fight with their bosses. But it also shows that the forces of suppression can be defeated—not least by the power to make events public. Journalists who know other journalists and can leak to other media outlets possess a useful weapon. The power to leak can improve the odds in favour of the reporter during any internal battle with bosses—provided, of course, that they are prepared to be more loyal to their story than to their future prospects.

The foot-dragging behaviour in television as detailed in *The Insider* was not a one-off event. More than 17 years later, during the era of Trump, there was an intriguing echo of it at another major network. In October 2016, Trump's rancorous election campaign was to see him exposed for making the "grab them by the pussy" remarks about women. Afterwards, The *Washington Post*, which broke the story, quoted an NBC executive saying that NBC News had actually possessed details for nearly four days beforehand of the sensational footage of Trump making these lewd statements. But they did not broadcast it.

The network sat on the recording at the height of a frenzied political campaign whilst, it was said, the company's lawyers continued to review the material. As a result, NBC News was scooped by the *Washington Post*. Having received a tip from a source, the paper only took five hours to vet and post its story [9]. It doesn't take a genius to work out that somebody privy to the Trump material held by NBC may have decided to don the Al Pacino/Lowell Bergman white hat, and send the apparently suppressed story to the newspapers.

THAMES TV AND DEATH ON THE ROCK

It is optimistic to imagine that the truth will always out in these circumstances. Television can be more structurally vulnerable to self-censorship than are traditional newspapers. One reason for this is that TV channels are not, as a rule, primarily journalistic organisations. They are entertainment media, which bolt on some news bulletins and current affairs documentaries. Their primary culture is not journalistic, and their senior executives are accountants and entertainment industry moguls. Their linkages to government, to advertisers, and to their own commercial subsidiaries or affiliates, are often more elaborate or extensive than those of newspapers. Acts of journalism can therefore often seem a threatening irritant, rather than a central raison d'etre of the company.

If you work anywhere on commercial TV, you feel this atmosphere. At one point in the 1990s, I moved over from print to the world of British television, to join a long-running current affairs series called This Week. The programme's soaring signature tune from the Karelia Suite by Sibelius marked a major appointment-to-view for millions of people in the pre-Internet age. As an on-screen reporter who was ultimately funded by flowing streams of advertising revenue, I revelled in TV's generous budgets, freedom to travel, and willingness to tackle big stories.

But these opportunities came with new pressures. We made an investigative documentary about Britain's then equivocal attitude to Saddam Hussein's Iraq. Although Saddam was a monstrous tyrant, elements in Whitehall and Westminster were only too happy to see money being made by selling him weaponry under the counter. We wanted to expose this.

But for the TV company, it was a delicate moment. This Week was made by Thames TV, a commercial firm which held a licence from the government to broadcast in the London area. That licence was up for renewal, a process in which the then Thatcher government could decide to whom it would grant the franchise. We edited our film, and the finished version rapidly escalated upwards through the executive ranks.

Soon the team ended up closeted with the director of programmes, David Elstein, in a tiny office at Thames' Euston Road headquarters. Elstein mused: "At such a moment in the company's fortunes, do we want to tweak the government's tail?" I remember how naively thunderstruck I was, coming from the simple world of print journalism, to realise that this was how television worked. In fairness to Elstein, when there was an immediate hubbub of protest at Euston Road, he withdrew his concerns. The show went out.

Two things happened subsequently, both of them deeply ironic. The first was that our Saddam documentary had no effect on the government at all: they had no reaction either in public nor, as far as I know, in private either. We were wrong to think that they cared one way or the other what we broadcast about the Iraq issue—or possibly, they were relieved that we appeared to know as little as we did, when the real truth was much more sinister. One lesson that investigative journalists can usefully try to convey to their bosses is that premature self-censorship may turn out to be not only ethically wrong but also stupidly unnecessary.

The second irony was more grave. It transpired that we had all been worrying about the wrong programme. A long-running row with the Thatcher government had exploded, over another This Week film called "Death on the Rock". Under a courageous editor, Roger Bolton, this documentary exposed the way British special forces had, in effect, executed an IRA team planning to plant a bomb in the British base of Gibraltar. The IRA "soldiers" had been shot whilst unarmed and not carrying explosives, facts which the Thatcher administration seemed to feel were best left unexamined.

Along with others, George Thomson, the head of the then broadcasting regulator, the Independent Broadcasting Authority, concluded that Mrs Thatcher was so angry at the programme-makers' defiance that she determined that Thames would not have its franchise renewed [10, p. 104]. And so it came to pass in 1991. Despite the fact that "Death on the Rock" was proved to have been carefully and accurately made, the company was deprived of its licence, and we journalists were all thrown out of work.

Probably, self-righteous reporters should learn some countervailing lessons from this episode too. It teaches us that company bosses are not necessarily being foolish when they fear that acts of investigative journalism are going to be potentially dangerous to all concerned.

MUTINY AT THE BBC: JIMMY SAVILE

So commercial greed can cause some of the difficulties that investigative journalists have with their bosses. And powerful politicians will bring about other obstacles that get thrown into a reporter's way. But there are yet further problems with bosses, demonstrated starkly by events at the British Broadcasting Corporation.

The BBC, which is effectively a tax-funded state broadcaster, has certainly had to struggle with cohorts of would-be political censors over the near-century of its existence. The battles are well known. They included, for example, the hostility to Peter Watkins' blocked documentary *The War Game* in 1965, which showed the effects a nuclear strike would have on Britain. In 1971, former premier Harold Wilson tried to have another documentary, *Yesterday's Men*, stopped on the grounds it deceived and ridiculed Labour politicians. And *Maggie's Militant Tendency*, a "Panorama" documentary broadcast in 1984, attracted huge libel damages from vengeful Conservative politicians and helped cost the then director-general Alasdair Milne, his job.

But the bosses at a public service media organisation like the BBC, despite being supposedly devoted to non-commercial values, can themselves also be an enemy to investigative journalism. BBC bosses' behaviour may be skewed by just as many corporate or personal interests as if they were ruthless capitalists.

This was painfully demonstrated in the 2012 case of Jimmy Savile. The celebrity presenter of "Jim'll Fix It", a prominent figure at the BBC, was exposed after his death as a predatory paedophile who had exploited his position. But Liz McKean and Meirion Jones, the BBC's own two investigative reporters who uncovered this, found that their journalism was suppressed and their own positions were made impossible. Civil war broke out at Newsnight, the programme they worked for. A Christmas tribute programme to Savile was already in the works, made by another department. Their exposure story only finally got out when it was taken to a rival channel, igniting a fuse which led to top executives, up to the level of BBC director-general, George Entwhistle, losing their own positions in a firestorm of scandal.

Far from being thanked for their efforts, McKean and Jones ended up feeling they were being punished. Both had to leave. Furthermore, when a second internal team of investigative journalists from BBC Panorama set out to investigate their allegations of BBC suppression, Panorama's own top staff too ended up deciding it was best for them to leave the corporation.

McKean died of a stroke at 52, four years after quitting the BBC. She said at the time: "I think the decision to drop our story was a breach of our duty to the women who trusted us" [11]. Her obituarist David Grossman wrote: "The episode left Liz feeling let down and isolated by an organisation she had once regarded as a benevolent employer" [12].

Meirion Jones recalls: "We were told at the time that you won't be sacked, but over a year or two years you'll realise you are being treated as an outsider, that you will never be trusted because you blew the whistle, and you will find yourself leaving" [13]. He believes BBC executives regarded the pair as "traitors" for speaking up. "Everyone involved on the right side of the Savile argument has been forced out...There is still sadly a small group of people at the BBC who think that the only problem with Savile was that it was exposed and if it had stayed hushed up, everything would be fine".

It is true that it is always particularly tricky to investigate a tumour of corruption inside one's own organisation. But Jones' sizeable BBC track record also included conflict with outsiders. He handled the award-winning exposure of toxic dumping by an international oil company Trafigura, in the teeth of well-funded external litigation against the BBC and other journalists. He identifies one of the problems with BBC bosses as a general culture which is the enemy of pioneering reporting:

> They always talk about encouraging original journalism but people are not rewarded for that. Not getting into trouble is a way of getting promoted. If you break stories the chances are you are going to cause trouble. It's the civil service element of the BBC. Because it's such a large organisation. To some extent it works like the civil service in that you will inevitably rise if you don't blot your copybook. [14]

How to Make Your Boss Like You

This chapter may appear to characterise media bosses purely as the enemy. I have indeed known some journalists who go to work every day in order to glower at their editors and mutter about conspiracies against them. But this does not improve their output. I have also myself had bosses who were masterly, inspirational, supportive, and dedicated. I am enormously grateful to them, because without their help I could not have found things out and got them published.

So here is an important final point to be made: despite their role in restraining you and frustrating you, it is a good idea to try and look at the world through the eyes of your boss. A corrupt media environment does indeed often unfairly inhibit investigative reporting, but there are also genuine problems which investigative journalists will pose for an employer. Investigative journalists, to be frank, can be a real pain.

Their work can be expensive. To detach a whole reporter, or worse, an entire team of reporters, from their day-to-day duties in order to pursue a lengthy investigation, costs a lot of money, which has to come out of some editor's budget. Cars, plane tickets, hotels, hiring experts, or foreign fixers—the expenses claims can mount up shockingly fast. What might seem a reasonable budget for an hour-long TV documentary, can be insanely expensive for the *Auchtermuchty Gazette.*

Even worse than the expense can be the uncertainty. Editors have daily or weekly slots to fill. Newspapers have more flexibility than TV and magazines, and websites have fewer issues about length. Nevertheless, the kind of journalism they all like best is the sort that approximates a factory product—it is of a predictable standard size and will become available at regular intervals. Investigative journalism is not like that. Its results cannot be guaranteed. Sometimes it will simply fail to deliver. Often the timescale is unpredictable, and sometimes the length is enormous. For a commissioning editor, this is all something of a nightmare; and some of the methods of managing the nightmare, such as over-commissioning in order to have a steady supply of viable investigative stories, can just end up causing more confusion and ill-feeling.

Furthermore, an investigative story, even if it is delivered successfully, may be a very unattractive editorial product. Editors like broad-brush, brightly coloured, easy-to-understand allegations that a casual viewer can quickly take in. But in order to be legally safe, many of the wordings of an investigation may be vague, cautious, or excessively muted. It is vital to be meticulous and not all the facts may be known on first publication. This may make a story seem pedantic or even confusing. Exposures of crime, fraud, or other wrongdoing may involve the laborious picking apart of cover stories, false transactions, and efforts at concealment. Dry details of accountancy discrepancies may be required. The result can be, to be honest, very tedious.

The "detective" mindset can also produce an equally tiresome and sometimes obsessional approach in the reporters who put together investigative copy or cut together an investigative programme. After too long a period of trying to penetrate other people's secrets, the journalist can sometimes lose all perspective. I remember once exploding in rage at a hapless news editor in London because he failed to see the significance of an obscure discovery I had made involving a case of bribery in darkest Romania. I was right—the facts turned out to be significant. But he was right too—those facts were crushingly boring, and he didn't want to put them on his news list.

Allied to this are the personality problems that investigative journalists sometimes develop. Confronted day by day in the outside world with powerful people telling them lies or uttering threats, the successful investigative reporter needs to develop a thick skin; an inner self-confidence; and a willingness to go into battle. Unfortunately, these necessary attitudes can then also bleed over into belligerent internal dealings with colleagues and bosses. The charitable word for these traits is "cantankerous". The less charitable words are all unprintable.

And finally, the story which arrives on an executive's screen so late and lengthy—and seemingly dull—may nevertheless turn out to be explosively dangerous. If it is any good, it will attract the ire of those powerful people and their massed ranks of high-priced lawyers. At best, there will be complaints which will take hours of executive time to deal with. At worst, there will be frighteningly expensive lawsuits, hostile pressure from powerful connections at the very top of the organisation, and the prospect of the sack for a relatively dispensable editor if it all goes wrong. The old BBC witticism about internal scandals is potent: "Deputy heads will roll".

INVESTIGATIVE JOURNALISTS CAN BE:

EXPENSIVE

IRREGULAR

OBSESSIVE

CANTANKEROUS

UNCERTAIN

BORING

DANGEROUS.

Not having your story published is nevertheless one of the most frustrating and infuriating aspects of the investigative reporter's life. So is there any way of checking what's going on with your bosses? Is the "spiking" of your material their fault or actually your fault? Reporters need sensible advice, not paranoia, when organisations are reluctant to run their stories. So here is a very short checklist of what to do to minimise the aspects that could be your fault.

First, try and deliver copy that is reliable. That means don't offer unrealistic delivery dates. It means don't promise more than you can deliver. It means honesty. There is not an uncommon situation, particularly in the world of TV, where investigative reporters can get a commission and some development money before discovering that their original sales pitch was over-optimistic and there isn't actually a story. As they've already spent the money, there is then a dangerous incentive for exaggeration or even fakery. This is how investigative journalism makes itself disreputable and unpopular.

Secondly, don't get stuck in a groove. A measure of tenacity, or even obsessiveness, is valuable. But to spend every waking hour chasing a single story tends to put blinkers on a reporter after a while. They come to believe that every minor development in their quest is journalistically interesting. Often, it isn't. Take a long walk. Find something else to write about for a while.

Finally, don't forget that you are in the news business. An elaborate investigation into one of the many scandals that plague the world is more likely to find an outlet if it chimes with the current zeitgeist, and even more so if it relates to a live news story. Lengthy evidence of sexual misconduct by, say, Donald Trump is not really very interesting when Trump is merely an obscure New York property developer. It is more intriguing when he becomes TV celebrity host of "The Apprentice". The story is gripping when Trump becomes president of the US. And it is truly hot news if the week before he has strongly denied such allegations and controversy is raging.

On the other hand, if the president has already resigned because of similar evidence published last week by others, then your story has lost out in this game of snakes and ladders. It goes off the front page and slithers right down towards the bottom of a snake again.

Likewise, if a giant asteroid has just crashed into the White House, vaporising all within, you might as well forget your sex-scandal investigation. No-one will want it.

As a reporter, there is no point in becoming indignant that you are forced to be a player in this irrational game. The sensible thing to do is to accept that news timing and the news environment are fundamental factors, and set out to handle your bosses accordingly. Finding things out is only half your task. The other half is the job of actually getting them published.

HOW TO DEAL WITH BOSSES-

BE RELIABLE DON'T GET STUCK IN A GROOVE TRY TO FIND NEWS PEGS.

REFERENCES

1. Cover. 1982. It Says Here You've Been Fired. *Private Eye*, February 26.
2. Evans, Harold. 1994. *Good Times, Bad Times.* London: Weidenfeld & Nicolson.
3. Trelford, Donald. 1989. What the Editor Said. *Guardian*, July 3.
4. Bower, Tom. 1993. *Tiny Rowland: A Rebel Tycoon.* London: Heinemann.
5. Lustig, Robin. 2017. *Is Anything Happening? My Life as a Newsman.* London: Biteback.
6. Leigh, David. 1989. Why I Quit the Observer. *Guardian*, July 3.
7. Bakan, Joel. 2004. *The Corporation: The Pathological Pursuit of Profit and Power.* New York: Free Press. Documentary version. 2016. The Corporation: 10th Anniversary Cut. *Cinema Politica.* Accessed November 2, 2018. https://vimeo.com/ondemand/thecorporationcp.
8. Bergman, Lowell. 1999. A Talk with Lowell Bergman. *PBS Online.* Accessed November 3, 2018. https://www.pbs.org/wgbh/pages/frontline/smoke/bergman.html.
9. Farhi, Paul. 2016. NBC Waited for Green Light from Lawyers. *Washington Post*, October 8.
10. Potschka, Christian. 2012. *Towards a Market in Broadcasting: Communications Policy in the UK and Germany.* London: Palgrave Macmillan.
11. McKean, Liz. 2012. Reaction to Inquiries into BBC Newsnight Savile Reports. *BBC News.* Accessed November 3, 2018. https://www.bbc.co.uk/news/uk-20787592.
12. Grossman, David. 2017. Liz McKean Obituary. *Guardian*, August 20.
13. Jackson, Jasper. 2015. BBC forced out team behind Savile expose says ex-Newsnight journalist. *Guardian*, July 29.
14. Ponsford, Dominic. 2015. Meirion Jones: 'Everyone on Right Side of the Savile Argument Has Been Forced Out of the BBC'. *Press Gazette*, July 29.

CHAPTER 5

Journalists Versus the Law

News Is What Somebody Doesn't Want You to Print. All the Rest Is Advertising

Nobody really knows who coined this phrase. British turn-of-the-century newspaper tycoon Lord Northcliffe and US press tycoon William Randolph Hearst are rival apocryphal candidates. The provenance of the quote may therefore be shaky: but every practising reporter knows it is true.

It means that energetic reporters often can't help colliding with the law. Investigative journalists seek to uncover the wrongdoing that other people don't want known. Yet there are far too many information laws in western countries which serve to help people with things to hide. The situation is paradoxical: investigative reporters see themselves as being on the side of the angels, yet they are repeatedly accused of being lawbreakers as they try to publish the facts.

Part of the problem is the twofold nature of the media. Commercially minded publications purchase intrusive paparazzi pictures and send the children of celebrities crying home from school. Hunting in packs, their reporters "monster" innocent victims of crime trying to get through their own garden gates. They have hacked phone messages in order to read other people's intimate titbits that ought to be private. They incite mobbing and witch-hunts of their chosen targets—and generally act like heartless burglars of any information which they can exploit or distort to turn a profit, get clicks, or do down a rival.

© The Author(s) 2019
D. Leigh, *Investigative Journalism*,
https://doi.org/10.1007/978-3-030-16752-3_5

Many information laws have been crafted with an eye to stopping this sort of brutish behaviour. They are interpreted, particularly in Britain, by judges sniffily unsympathetic to the concepts of free speech. In the US, the press is protected by the First Amendment to the constitution, preventing any curtailment of media liberty. This certainly gives US journalism more freedom, particularly in regard to what they say about public figures—but it is still perfectly possible there to bring cynical lawsuits in the hope of strangling investigative journalists into bankruptcy.

I once published a small mention of a US fraudster inside a larger piece of research. The fraudster invested thousands of dollars (which it later turned out he had embezzled in the first place) into hiring a prestigious Washington DC law firm to launch a worthless suit against us for defamation in the state of Delaware. He simply wanted to keep us off his back while he pursued his scams. It cost us more than $300,000 to deal with him. A Russian oligarch used a similar expensive tactic on the International Consortium of Investigative Journalists. It is an aspect of what Ian Hislop, British editor of the satirical magazine *Private Eye*, memorably calls "censorship by judicial process" [1].

The past half-century has seen a long series of battles to improve the arthritic attitudes of judges and officials towards the exercise of free speech in the public interest. Some of the fights have been lost: some have been won to the point that the information environment, particularly in the UK, is now rather more sensible. By 2018, campaigners there had, for example, achieved a limited freedom of information regime, reduction in threats of contempt of court, and a more manageable libel law.

But the wars are far from over. As recently as 2018, the British high court so little understood the basic function of journalism that it attempted to create a privacy law that people raided or even questioned by the police should be prima facie entitled to anonymity [2]. The law, and its lackeys, represent some of the worst practical dangers that would-be investigative journalists face. Lawyers can earn their pay by suppressing your work and destroying your livelihood. To survive, you often need to learn to challenge the law, and you sometimes need to learn how to defy it.

Harry Evans, crusading editor of the *Sunday Times* in the 1970s, set the benchmark with his high-profile collisions with the courts. By insisting on publishing, he fought iconic battles against the then one-sided laws of confidentiality and contempt of court, and he got them reformed.

It is a mark of his success that the positions taken up by officials and judges at the time now seem not merely mistaken, but downright absurd.

Who nowadays would seriously advocate banning a book of ministerial diaries because it mentioned differences of opinion round a cabinet table that took place 10 years before? Who would argue with a straight face that no-one should be allowed to know of the evidence in a medical compensation case that had been pending, unresolved, for years? These were the arguments made at the time for censorship of the way the cruelly toxic drug thalidomide had been marketed and against publication of Richard Crossman's ministerial diaries. In the Crossman affair, the Attorney-General of the day, Sam Silkin, attempted to rely on the opinion of a judge whose words nowadays have a ludicrously feudal ring:

> Disclosures would create or fan ill-informed or captious public or political criticism. The business of government is difficult enough as it is. [3]

Defying the Law: Jury-Vetting, Harman, Thorpe, Ponting, *Spycatcher*

As a young reporter starting out in London the 1970s, I was surprised to discover the way real-life journalism worked in what was then Fleet Street. Lots of facts were well known, but couldn't be printed. It was relatively easy, it seemed, to find things out: but very hard to get them actually published. This made it possible for people like me to develop a career in investigative journalism by simply challenging everyone else's routine assumptions of secrecy.

It led to some turbulence. In 1978, we exposed in the *Guardian* the scandal of "jury-vetting" in an Old Bailey trial of anarchists alleged to be planning bombings. Police had been secretly checking out the political backgrounds of their jurors and excluding those they thought "undesirable". Our method was to disregard dire warnings of contempt of court, and simply to print a list we had obtained, detailing the jurors in the case and the supposed objections to them. Some apparently had relatives with convictions; one woman had once made a complaint against the police; another's address was "believed to be a squat".

The judge was furious at this act of journalism, halted the trial, and reported me to the Director of Public Prosecutions for "an outrageous intrusion into confidential matters". The general public were indignant, but on our behalf, however, not on the government's. Jury-vetting was curtailed, and instead of being arrested, I was given an industry award [4, p. 176]. The trial re-started with another vetted jury, and the defendants' counsel recalls:

> I can remember a sense of dawning wonderment as the foreman said 'not guilty' twenty-seven times. Even more amazing was the reaction of my solicitor, who leapt up and kissed me. [5]

This technique, of pushing back the boundaries of so-called contempt of court by sheer defiance, proved workable. We similarly published a sheaf of internal Home Office documents exposing prison conditions. They had been obtained during a civil court case brought on behalf of a prisoner by the legal process of compulsory "discovery". In fact, they had largely already been read out in open court, but, absurdly, we were not supposed to have copies of the files. The government tried to punish our source, Harriet Harman, the principled lawyer at the National Council for Civil Liberties who gave us the papers. Eventually, after dragging her through the courts, they lost at the European Court of Human Rights in Strasbourg. The case did Harman no harm: it boosted her profile and she was to become deputy leader of the Labour party [5].

With more mixed results, we used such techniques of legal defiance in the case of Jeremy Thorpe, the then Liberal Party leader accused of trying to murder his gay lover. My colleague Peter Chippindale and I wrote an innovative, but in our view perfectly legal, "instant book" containing a detailed account of all the prosecution evidence given in public preliminary hearings at a local court in Devon—in advance of the main trial. Our rationale was merely to give the world relevant information. But publishers, printers, distributors and bookshops were all so fearful that, although we eventually found a brave publisher in Hutchinson, our sales were hit.

Worse happened after Thorpe's trial, when a juror revealed to us their significant reasons for acquitting him. The *Guardian* refused to publish. A magazine editor, the *New Statesman's* Bruce Page, late of the *Sunday Times* Insight Team, was more courageous. He printed, but we were all hauled up before the then Lord Chief Justice, Lord Widgery, and accused of contempt of court. Our lawyer pointed out that there was actually no law against what we had done, and to our astonishment, Widgery agreed. (He was soon after forced to stand down from the bench, on grounds of dementia.) [5]

My then bosses and lawyers were willing to take a successful risk in another landmark case a few years later. In 1984, the jury at an Old Bailey official secrets trial were packed off out of the room, whilst the judge, the late Sir Anthony McCowan, confided behind their backs to the prosecutor that he wanted to order the jury to convict—whatever the jurors actually thought about the matter. On trial was defence ministry official Clive Ponting. He had leaked documents showing that parliament was misled about the circumstances in which the British had sunk (with the loss of more than 300 lives) the General Belgrano, an Argentinian naval cruiser. The Belgrano had been torpedoed by a nuclear-powered submarine during Britain's mini-war to take back the Falklands islands.

Ponting claimed that by revealing the truth to an MP, he had acted "in the interests of the state". It was one of the few legal defences written into the then version of the notoriously oppressive Official Secrets Act. The judge, a former would-be Conservative candidate—announced that in his view the "interests of the state" were the same as the policies of the government of the day—that is, the political interests of the then Conservative prime minister Mrs Thatcher.

Normally, everything said in the absence of the jury in the course of a trial is considered too dangerous to print, for fear of being accused of contempt of court. But again, there is no specific law against it. We decided at the *Observer* that the jury deserved to know what was intended to be done to them, and went ahead to publish the full courtroom report that Sunday morning, despite the dangers.

Ponting himself was grateful, writing: "This article was a real turning-point. Now the public would know exactly what had happened" [6, p. 194]. Opinion was again strongly on our side. We were not prosecuted, and the jury triumphantly acquitted the whistleblowing official in despite of the judge [7, p. 71].

This tactic—to publish first and fight about it later—has developed into a very successful journalistic tool over the years. For example, the Thatcher government was strikingly defeated in the *Spycatcher* affair in the 1980s. A bigoted MI5 officer, Peter Wright, wrote his memoirs. Or rather, they were ghost-written for him by the World in Action TV journalist Paul Greengrass. The British authorities got injunctions—legal gag orders—to suppress not only the book, but all the disclosures about its contents that myself and other journalists had already started to print in the *Observer* and the *Guardian*. The government quoted the Official Secrets Act, and the laws protecting confidentiality.

The manuscript was smuggled abroad and rogue editions were published in Ireland and Australia by publishers Heinemann. The saga culminated in a farcical trial in Sydney. The British cabinet secretary, Sir Robert Armstrong, who was out of his depth in a world of irreverent Australians, made himself notorious by admitting to cross-examining lawyer Malcolm Turnbull that he had been "economical with the truth". The British lost the case, and a good deal more light was shed on the antics of the UK's secret police. Turnbull subsequently became Australia's prime minister [8, p. 75].

Open challenge like this is a particularly powerful tactic when, as in the *Spycatcher* affair, it is combined with the ability to publish across borders in multiple legal jurisdictions. A lawsuit brought in England will not determine what happens in the US—or in Ireland or Australia. In more recent years, online publishing has arrived, often based on remote servers located somewhere else from the place of publication. From a censorship point of views, national borders are largely dissolving. The Wild West world of Wikileaks has become one of the outcomes, publishing virtually unstoppable leaks on a global scale. There are resultant ethical problems, of course.

But the key limitation on the technique of "publish and be damned" is that, once again, it is the sort of investigative journalism that cannot be practised alone. I had to persuade Peter Preston, the then editor of the *Guardian*, to take a risk in printing the jury-vetting list. I failed to persuade him to print the Thorpe juror interview: but fortunately, there was in those days another editor in town, willing to take my work. And he was only willing to do so because a bold young lawyer, Geoffrey Robertson, was prepared to stick his own professional neck out and advise him that it could be done [5, p. 282]. The *Spycatcher* success involved the newspapers and the publisher, Brian Perman of Heinemann, in spending astonishing amounts of time and hard cash on fighting international court cases. They had to be persuaded of the value of these stories, and they also had to possess the resources to fight in the first place. It is not a game that solitary bloggers can play.

Bringing Legal Test Cases: Felixstowe Justices; Alvis; Tisdall

There is a legal technique which might seem safer—not to go in for cheeky defiance, but to go to law with test cases. The tiny appearance of my own name as a British legal footnote is thanks to the case of *Regina v Felixstowe Justices ex parte Leigh*. We challenged the policy of magistrates in this provincial port town who were refusing to give their names when they tried cases. There was an easy High Court victory against these small-scale judges, with a ringing judgement declaring court reporters to be "the watchdogs of justice" [9].

In a similar way, Rob Evans of the *Guardian* fought and won a series of open justice rulings over the years. The High Court in 2004 ruled that he should be allowed access to court files containing witness statements about alleged bribery in Indonesia, against the wishes of Alvis, the arms firm involved [10]. He established rights to see barristers' written arguments in civil cases; and in 2012, he obtained a landmark judgement that journalists could also see court papers in criminal cases, the judge pronouncing: "Open justice lets in the light and allows the public to scrutinise the workings of the law" [11]. (These particular battles would, of course, appear bizarre to reporters working in the US, where the case-papers in lawsuits can generally be inspected instantly online, upon payment of a modest fee.)

Bringing test cases is a very respectable way to behave. It sometimes has the altruistic result of improving the journalistic environment for everyone in the long term. Freedom of information requests, for instance, are so often denied by cynical government departments that it can occasionally become a point of honour to litigate them to the tortuous end, no matter how long it takes. Cases in the highly secretive family courts have also been partially opened up by campaigning journalistic litigants [12]. Investigative journalists, and even everyday news reporters, in recent years have come to realise they don't have to lie down in the face of obscurantist judges and officials imposing gag orders—they can stand up in court and fight instead.

However, there are downsides to bringing test cases. One is that an appeal to the good sense and good nature of the British judicial class can prove dangerously optimistic. The consequences of such naivety can be graver than just the potential waste of time and money. The then editor of the *Guardian*, Peter Preston, learned it the hard way when his miscalculations led to the jailing of an idealistic young Foreign Ministry official, Sarah Tisdall. More than 35 years later, I listened from the pews as the case was still being brought up as an issue by speakers at Preston's memorial service in St Brides, the journalists' church. The stain on his journalistic reputation was ineradicable, even unto death.

Preston embarked on a series of court cases in which he vainly claimed he had a legal right not to hand over a leaked document about US cruise missile arrivals that Tisdall had sent anonymously to the paper. The editor then crumpled and did finally hand it over. This enabled the government to trace the paper's source. Preston subsequently sought to palm off some of the responsibility on to the paper's lawyer, the late Geoffrey Grimes of super-respectable City firm Lovells, for advising him that he had a legal defence and making him keep the document safe. Preston wrote: "Don't call for a solicitor—because due process will drag you down" [13].

He was right on that particular point. But it was not the true underlying moral of the affair at all. The truth was that Preston and his executives had been incompetent from the outset in not destroying or at least hiding the document well in advance. And Preston himself could still have saved the day at the very end, by tearing up the piece of paper and taking the consequences. Outright defiance can sometimes be a better way of retaining the moral high ground than playing other people's legal games.

The Tisdall case was an exceptional event, however. The usual drawback to launching principled legal challenges is the simple one that it is so expensive and slow. That relatively straightforward Alvis hearing, for example, involved paying our barrister for 3 full days arguing in the High Court against some dogged and high-priced opponents. When cases have to be appealed, the costs soon skyrocket into the tens or even hundreds of thousands of pounds. If the media outlet loses the gamble, they have to pay the other side's costs as well. Even if they win, they will only recoup a portion of their legal bills.

And yet the immediate return in terms of publishable sensational stories can be quite minimal—the news moment may have long passed by the time of the final legal outcome. The kind of potential journalistic revelations that would, on their own merits, justify heavyweight legal expense of this kind, are rare.

LIBEL

The most fearsome denizen of the legal jungle is the law of libel. Thankfully the days have now more or less gone when the law was so oppressive that London became known as the libel capital of the world. But nothing can alter the fact that investigative journalists, because of the nature of their work, are in danger of committing libel with virtually every story that they handle. They are making accusations of wrongdoing and—if they are doing their job properly—naming names. But because this kind of journalism is so often like Blind Man's Buff—feeling about in the dark—mistakes can be made. And your enemies are often the kind of people who will try to not merely punish you, but to utterly destroy you.

Other types of information law can occasionally threaten a journalist's survival—confidentiality, privacy, data protection, or official secrets. But the existential threat from libel is ever present and continuous.

Do not imagine, either, that only young and inexperienced journalists are in danger. Readers may have been taken aback a few years ago to see a bizarre apology appeared spread over many columns of their national paper:

> Tesco has accepted a formal offer of apology by the Guardian in relation to the reports 'Tesco's £1bn tax avoiding plan—move to the Cayman Islands' and 'Every little bit helps: tax free pot of gold at end of Tesco's rainbow' … and a related editorial and podcast. In these articles we reported that Tesco had created an elaborate off-shore corporate structure to avoid paying up to £1bn in UK corporation tax on profits from the sale of its UK properties.… We also suggested that this corporation tax avoidance was hypocritical, having regard to Tesco's public stance on social responsibility, and that Tesco's response to the charge had been evasive. We now accept that these damaging allegations were unfounded and should not have been published. All profits generated by this sale and leaseback arrangement were earned by UK tax-resident companies and have been or will be included in Tesco's UK tax returns. **The use of Cayman Island companies in the scheme was for legitimate stamp duty savings purposes.** [author emphasis]

After a total of 350 grovelling words, in daily newspaper terms equivalent to the length of War and Peace, the *Guardian*'s apology culminated:

> We have also agreed to pay a sum by way of damages to a charity of Tesco's choice and a payment by way of costs. [14]

The inside story of this affair shows two things—first, how even big papers are vulnerable to libel suits and, second how it is possible to push back against libel bullies. Far from being inexpert, the author of the original pieces was in fact a highly experienced *Guardian* business reporter (He was even a qualified accountant). His error was that in unravelling some highly complex offshore transactions, he mistook the nature of Tesco's tax-avoidance manoeuvre. He said they were dodging corporation tax on their profits.

The clue to how hard the *Guardian* fought back comes in the mysteriously opaque nature of that final sentence in the apology. It does not say just how much the damages and the legal costs actually were. This was undoubtedly at Tesco's request. It is believed that the damages were in fact no more than a relatively trivial £5000. All the extensive bluster of the agreed apology may have served to mask the extent of Tesco's legal retreat. For after the libel writ was received, the *Guardian*'s journalists had launched into intensive research; and so had others on the magazine *Private Eye*. From this it transpired that there was indeed a tax-avoidance manoeuvre carried out by Tesco, by creating Caymans offshore entities. But it was to avoid stamp duty, a routine tax on property sales, not corporation tax on their profits. The money involved was much less. Hence the vague sentence in the apology, referring to "legitimate stamp duty savings".

So even once a libel suit is under way, it is possible to use the legal process to stimulate more journalistic exposures, or even to use the compulsory process of legal "discovery" itself as a research tool. Libel threats and libel trials figure in many of the most significant exposure stories that investigative journalists have come up with—and their role will be further explored in some later chapters.

Reporters even managed to turn the brutality of the libel laws against the judiciary itself, in one piece of activist journalism. Lord Denning, a too-elderly judge by then whose famous Hampshire burr concealed a reactionary heart, published his own memoirs in 1982. In this book, he casually slurred black jurors in a recent riot trial, suggesting they would be biased in favour of others who were black. He had forgotten that, once out of the privileged arena of the courtroom, he was subject to the same law as any other citizen. On the *Observer*, we suggested to some of the indignant jurors that they could sue him for libel. We got a publishable story. And the 83-year-old Denning had to resign [15].

Similarly, the vagaries of the British libel law could not only be used to prevent publication, but actually exploited to enable it. I once wrote a book about the adventures of an Oxford-educated celebrity cannabis smuggler, the late Howard Marks. He privately admitted that he had bribed a bogus Mexican "secret service officer" to appear as a witness at his Old Bailey trial and bamboozle his jury by claiming Marks was secretly working as an informant.

The conundrum was that Marks refused to be quoted. It would have led to him being re-arrested for perjury. On the other hand, the publisher was not willing to put out a book in which I simply accused an acquitted person of being guilty after all. That would be an open invitation for Heinemann to be sued for libel under British law.

A study of the small print revealed, however, that the few available defences to libel included "consent". If a person consented to publication, he could not sue for libel afterwards. So we simply arranged for Marks to write a letter saying that he consented to the book being published (without of course, admitting that any of its allegations were true). This successfully squared the circle, and we were able to document the way in which the cannabis law had been made to look an ass [16].

It is also useful to know one of the oldest tricks in the British journalist's book—a stratagem more widely practised in the days when libel law was more fearsome and one-sided than it is today. This is simply to persuade someone to utter the defamatory accusation in a privileged setting, where the reporter will be free to re-publish it.

In practice, this means a statement either in open court or in Parliament. In the Jeremy Thorpe case, for example, his former gay lover Norman Scott blurted out to a Devon courtroom in 1976: "This is all because of my homosexual relationship with Jeremy Thorpe" [17, p. 229ff]. A biddable opposition MP, George Wigg, was encouraged by Harry Pincher of the Express in 1963 to use parliamentary privilege to unmask the Profumo affair, in which the Minister for War lied about having adulterous sex with Christine Keeler [18].

Obviously, getting MPs to assist in this way is not always easy to bring about in practice, and MPs who are willing do it run the risk of being regarded as unethical by their colleagues. The same tactic was, however, to be used successfully in 2009 to break a confidentiality injunction and expose toxic waste dumping by Trafigura (Trafigura, see Chap. 11). In 2018, an injunction to protect businessman Philip Green from allegations of sexual harassment, was likewise broken open in the House of Lords by Labour peer Peter Hain [19].

THE PUBLIC INTEREST AS A LIBEL SHIELD: CLINTON AND BLUNKETT

One key purpose of this chapter is to outline a basic approach which will enable you to write investigative stories without being paralysed by fear of libel suits. Its success does not rely on tricks or dodges, but on sound and ethical methods. This section deals with the current British situation as in 2018. US journalists need to go through a different set of routines to satisfy their lawyers and their insurers. But they do not have to contend with the same legal difficulties as their British counterparts. Some of the principles of fair reporting involved will nevertheless also be of ethical value to them.

The current legal environment in the UK is defined by the reformed Defamation Act of 2013. Its central plank is the concept of "the public interest". If a journalist is acting responsibly, they are allowed to make a mistake in the public interest. Even more significantly, they are generally allowed to publish material in the public interest which, right or wrong, they don't have to prove the truth to a courtroom standard. In a world of Blind Man's Buff and often reluctant witnesses, this can be crucial.

The basic rule permitting the publication of a defamatory allegation is that the editor concerned must have a reasonable belief, in all the circumstances of the case (making due allowance for editorial discretion), that publishing it is in the public interest. One of the fundamental requirements for achieving this status of "public interest" reporting is that the reporters and their outlet must have engaged in "responsible journalism".

What do these words "public interest" and "responsible journalism" actually mean? It is not completely simple. This is particularly so in the realms of sex. For example, US president Bill Clinton notoriously engaged in sexual activity, though short of intercourse, with a White House intern, Monica Lewinsky. This caused a scandal in 1998. But was it in the public interest to expose their doings? Clinton had committed no crime. Lewinsky by all accounts was a keen participant in their trysts. The relationship was outed not for public interest reasons, but by his unscrupulous political opponents. Their claims were ridiculous—that he should have been spending more of his time on his official work rather than abusing the White House tables and chairs for erotic purposes. People are surely entitled to a private, sexual life, even if they are public officials!

On the other hand, there was a disparity of power between the two individuals, which bears on the significant debates about sexual abuse in the US and elsewhere. It is possible that religious or conservative voters would be repelled and wish to alter their votes if they knew that Clinton, as a married man, was sexually incontinent. And should not the man who was the figurehead and role model for the entire American nation, be expected to behave better, even in his private life? It is hard to get unanimous agreement about the Lewinsky affair even from relatively sophisticated journalism students, when they come from different cultures in different countries. Some think writing about it at the time was obviously in the public interest; some think the complete opposite.

Let us take another case, this time from Britain—that of the then Labour home secretary, David Blunkett. In 2004, by hacking his voicemails (which was illegal) the *News of the World* got evidence that he had been having an affair with Kimberley Quinn, American publisher in London of the *Spectator*, a Conservative magazine. The Sunday tabloid went ahead and published, exposing the pair of them. It ignited a chain of events which led to Blunkett's humiliation and eventual resignation from office. Was the *News of the World*'s behaviour in the public interest? Blunkett certainly didn't think so: he pleaded with the newspaper's editor not to print, saying:

> Politics is one thing. Private life is another ... If you don't have a private life, you don't have anything. ... My private life is my own. I'm divorced ... I have always, always, kept my private relations private. I'm not a media star. I'm a politician trying to do a very difficult job.

The opposite argument was voiced to him by the then editor, Andy Coulson:

> But you are home secretary and I don't think you can use your right to privacy to bat back an accusation that you have had an affair with a married woman. [20]

Of course, many would find Coulson's hypocrisy revolting. At the time, he was not only committing information crimes for which he eventually went to jail but was also himself a married man having an affair with his boss, Rebekah Brooks [21]. This does not invalidate the point he made. There might well be a public interest in exposing the Labour Home Secretary's secret infatuation (although some might think the impropriety lay not so much in his secret *inamorata* being married to another person, as in her being a Tory).

I had a practical demonstration of the split views about Blunkett when I was working at the *Guardian*. The paper high-mindedly refused at first to publish the disclosure at all (unlike all the other papers), on the grounds that it was none of the public's business. Then it transpired that Blunkett's office might have helped fast-track a visa application for Kimberly Quinn's nanny. There was a screeching handbrake turn on the part of the *Guardian*, as it realised the public interest was in fact engaged and it had better start covering the unfolding big story along with everybody else.

If there are thus not always easy answers to the question of public interest, what is a conscientious investigative journalist to do? Fortunately, there are several formal definitions available which are helpful. Apart from the explicit ones in the standards codes of various newspapers and broadcasters, there is an official definition of when journalism is in the public interest which has been written as guidance for the Crown Prosecution Service. It was introduced during the regime of director of public prosecutions of Sir Keir Starmer QC, a human rights lawyer with sympathies for free speech, who went on to become a Labour shadow minister. I recommend it.

DPP GUIDELINES ON PUBLIC INTEREST

(A) DISCLOSING A CRIMINAL OFFENCE

(B) DISCLOSING A PERSON HAS FAILED TO COMPLY WITH A LEGAL OBLIGATION

(C) DISCLOSING A MISCARRIAGE OF JUSTICE

(D) RAISING OR CONTRIBUTING TO AN IMPORTANT MATTER OF PUBLIC DEBATE. NO EXHAUSTIVE DEFINITION...BUT EXAMPLES INCLUDE PUBLIC DEBATE ABOUT SERIOUS IMPROPRIETY, SIGNIFICANT UNETHICAL CONDUCT, AND SIGNIFICANT INCOMPETENCE, WHICH AFFECTS THE PUBLIC.

(E) DISCLOSING THAT THE ABOVE IS BEING, OR IS LIKELY TO BE, CONCEALED. [22]

These guidelines are given to the Crown Prosecution Service to help them decide whether to bring prosecutions against journalists. They encompass the relatively straightforward idea that there is a public interest in the exposure of concealed wrongdoing, whether that wrongdoing is a crime, a failure to meet legal standards, or a miscarriage of justice.

But the guidelines also go further in extending the protective blanket of public interest to reports which merely raise "an important matter of public debate". So the investigative reporter's editor could claim a reasonable belief, and hence a public interest defence, if they are ventilating allegations of "serious incompetence which affects the public", "significant unethical conduct", or even just "serious impropriety". These categories leave journalists a lot of scope.

It will be noted that the DPP guidelines do not unequivocally answer the Clinton or Blunkett questions that I posed earlier. Personally, I would say that one could reasonably believe that the Clinton allegation should indeed be published on grounds of "serious impropriety"; and the Blunkett allegation could also be published on grounds of debatable "significant unethical conduct". But these terms are vague and arguable. Others might still disagree.

An investigative journalist does not have an instruction manual that gives simple boxes to tick. What is necessary is to understand the importance of always thinking in terms of the public interest, and of therefore being able to formulate coherent public interest justifications that can be presented to an office lawyer, and perhaps even one day be defended from the witness-box.

It is also important to grasp that these assertions of "public interest" would only protect the UK journalist wanting to write about Blunkett's or Clinton's sex life from being sued for *libel*. Unfortunately, this would not nowadays protect the British reporter from being sued—or indeed injuncted in advance—for *breach of privacy*. As the grip of UK libel law has relaxed, so the reach of privacy law has tightened. To fight off a privacy suit, the journalist would have a harder task. They would have to convince a court that their own rights of free expression, buttressed by the fact that they were acting in the public interest, were strong enough to overturn their target's "reasonable expectation of privacy".

As we have seen, people can have quite different cultural notions about privacy. One might point again to the Blunkett story, to show just how the growth of these privacy rulings threatens investigative journalism. Of course, it is the case that the *News of the World* engaged in an indefensible breach of privacy in the first place by hacking the politician's phone. No public interest could justify their criminal behaviour. But, rather as the police might find a dead body by an inadmissible search without a warrant, so too the tabloid journalists stumbled on the Home Secretary's secret liaison.

The politician was eloquent when approached, in explaining why in his view he had a "reasonable expectation of privacy" for his love-affair. He might well have succeeded in persuading a judge to grant him a gagging injunction in advance on those grounds. Had he done so, the further fact of the fast-tracking of a visa application for the nanny might never, of course, have come to light. Yet the visa circumstances clearly change the balance between the two opposing human rights. The visa affair shows there was the possibility of a political abuse of power or, at the very least, a lack of political judgement.

Acts of censorship tend to err on the side of suppression and silence: but democratic values (and the cause of investigative journalism) are better served if we err on the side of transparency. This is where journalists will often clash with the courts.

Responsible Journalism

The public interest defence against libel suits will not work if the journalist has been reckless or irresponsible. There is one single key step reporters can take to protect themselves and demonstrate that they are responsible journalists. This is to give their target the opportunity to comment beforehand. We British journalists developed a system for doing this in an organised way, over the years during which libel rulings were slowly refined by judges and eventually completely reformed by the passage of the explicit new defamation law in 2013.

We built a standard template for a libel letter. It looks like this:

THE LIBEL LETTER

Dear

We have received information as follows

   1. XXXXXXXXXXX
   2. XXXXXXXXXXX
   3. XXXXXXXXXXX

This raises matters in the public interest, which we think we ought to publish. Before doing so, as responsible journalists, we wish to give you the opportunity to comment if you wish.

If we do not receive a substantive response to these specific numbered points by XXXXXXX we shall proceed on the basis that you do not wish to amend or correct any of them, but do not wish to comment.

For the avoidance of doubt, we will not regard as substantive any generalised statement referring to unspecified "inaccuracies" or the like. We hope that you will recognise that we have approached you in a straightforward way, and will wish to respond in the same manner.

Yours faithfully

The first thing to be said about this libel letter is that it works. I never received a libel writ once I started to send out these letters. One of the reasons is that the act of sending the letter alters the balance of advantage. The ball is put in your opponent's court. In the old days of the unreformed libel law, the balance of advantage lay the other way: the recipient of allegations merely had to lie low and keep mum, knowing that the journalist was the one facing the dilemma of whether or not to print. The reporter carried the burden of proof for what they published, and the smartest tactic for a wrongdoer was to keep quiet.

The legal situation has nowadays been upended. The journalist has demonstrated their responsible behaviour by sending the letter, and by offering a fulsome willingness to be put right on any inaccuracies, in advance of publication. If the recipient now ignores the letter, they have put themselves in the wrong, and have demonstrably passed up their chance to set the record straight.

Of course, the letter is not merely a charade. It is a genuine offer to hear the other side of the story. Sometimes, because investigative journalism is like Blind Man's Buff, your allegations are mistaken. Or there is some aspect of events of which you are unaware which actually puts a different complexion on them. Take an invented example: you suspect the Attorney-General is a drunk because someone has sent you a photo of him falling down the steps in the street as he emerged from the Garrick gentleman's club. When he gets your letter, the politician explains, enclosing a copy of his discharge note from the hospital, that he was in fact having a small heart attack. You drop the story. And you're grateful. So is he.

People sometimes call this tactic "Right to Reply". I think that phrase, drawn from broadcasting parlance coloured by impartiality regulations, is misleading. So too is the habit some journalists have of sending letters peppered with questions to which they demand answers. These approaches muddy the waters. What you are doing with the libel letter is providing your target with an opportunity in advance—an ample and fair opportunity—to comment. Your stance is one of fair-minded inquiry.

A key aspect of the libel letter is that it is just that—a letter. It can be posted, but it is better done by email, which provides an automatic time-stamped audit trail of the correspondence. You need to write to your target, and avoid speaking to them in person or on the phone at this point, because one of your purposes is to generate precisely this documentary trail, the contents of which are unarguable, and which can be later produced in court.

The content of phone or indeed live conversations can always be disputed: but documents can't, as a rule.

Journalists new to this tactic often complain that it is simply too difficult to trace the whereabouts or the contact details of people they intend to be rude about. The answer is that it may seem difficult, but usually it's not. If you can't trace an individual, you can trace their publisher, or their mother, or the company where they work or their fellow board-member, and send the letter to them, with a request to forward it. If you can't find an email address, get in a taxi and put the note through their letterbox. Send three or four copies of the letter in different directions to guarantee that at least one gets through. And follow up with secretaries or colleagues to make sure that letter has been passed on. Make a written record of the steps you have taken, for when the recipient claims he never got your note.

Every phrase in the libel letter has its function. You say at the outset "We have received information that…" rather than "We accuse you of…" because you are demonstrating that you are inquiring with an open mind, not with partisan prejudice.

Next, you break down the allegation into numbered segments, and request that each be considered separately. This is to prevent some generalised response along the line that "It's all lies". The numbered list must contain each allegation that might be considered defamatory, at the highest level at which it might be understood by the reasonable reader.

There is no need to submit the exact wording you are proposing to use, nor to go into any more detail than is necessary for the recipient to deal with the allegation. There is certainly no need to disclose the source of your information. In the invented example above, you might say, perhaps, "1. You are an alcoholic 2. You recently fell down the steps of the Garrick 3. This followed a bout of heavy drinking". It's not a good idea to say, for example "It happened at 8pm on Thursday 29th of June". The calm response might be "This is totally untrue" (because it actually happened at 6.45pm on Wednesday, the 28th of June).

The next paragraph ("as responsible journalists we wish to give you the opportunity…") spells out your position on the public interest, and your intention to behave responsibly. When the recipient rushes off to a media lawyer, crying "How do we stop this?", this expensive legal specialist will understand that you are deploying a defence of public interest under the 2013 Act, and that you know what you are talking about. This will give them pause.

There follows an essential section—setting the deadline. It is one of the most important, and frequently the trickiest, parts of the whole exercise. In order to keep the ball in your opponent's court, you must impose a deadline and make clear that they cannot improve their position by simply ignoring your letter. But how long do you give them? The answer is—"As short a time as possible".

Conventional journalists brought up on the old libel law are dismayed by the whole idea of notifying a subject in advance that you intend to publish something unpleasant about them. Their training was to keep their opponent in the dark, and if at all possible, ambush them out of the blue. It was not irrational—for as soon as your opponent is tipped off, they can take action against you. They can go to court and seek a gag order. They can try to "spoil" your story by releasing a version of it to a rival that is more favourable to them; or they can ring up your editor and try to make your life hell.

Of course, you can still go ahead nowadays and ambush your subject, if you are certain that you have rock-solid witnesses and documents that will stand up in a courtroom. No matter how obnoxiously and irresponsibly you behave, "Truth" remains a complete alternative defence to libel—so long as you can prove it. But if you want the protection of a public interest defence, you have to provide an opportunity for comment in a responsible way.

So how short is a short time? It depends on common sense about the circumstances. If you are putting a simple allegation to someone who plainly knows the answer already, then the time given for a response can be very short. "You murdered your husband" is a proposition that would not need as long as 10 minutes to come up with a comment. On the other hand, a detailed allegation about the way someone was complicit in a complex fraud in Australia 15 years ago might justify a subject's plea for a few days to do the necessary research. It is a matter of judgement.

Working on newspaper stories, I personally found that we tended to give a deadline of 48 hours or less. I would also, if possible, always give someone another 24 hours grace if they pleaded good reasons for needing a delay. It made us look very reasonable and responsible. But you have absolutely no obligation to give someone extra time so that they can consult a lawyer and come up with a carefully tailored form of words in order to wriggle off the hook.

Of course, the lawyers have been working hard on ways to circumvent these libel letters of ours. That is why we include a warning that we will only take note of a "substantive" response. There was a period when lawyers would merely reply on behalf of their clients that the allegations contained "many inaccuracies" or the like, thus avoiding an honest answer as to what they disputed and what they admitted.

Likewise, lawyers acting for big companies can sometimes try to respond by sending lengthy but off-the-point public relations messages about their clients' virtues. They believe that journalists can be bamboozled into believing they are obliged to print this material. The truth is that journalists are mostly obliged, in the interests of "responsible" behaviour, to print whatever response to the actual allegations arrives from the other party, without adding disparaging comment of their own. But they are not obliged to publish PR statements that are irrelevant.

LEGAL BULLYING

The reality of life for investigative journalists is that they mostly have to deal not with actual lawsuits, but with endless attempts at legal bullying. You only have to look at the marketing material put out by media law firms to see how much of their stock-in-trade consists of sending out threatening letters.

One prominent London firm's publicity has depicted them as: "The leading law firm protecting the reputations of high-profile individuals, corporates and brands... dedicated to safeguarding the reputations of international corporations, brands, celebrities and high-profile business people" [23, 24].

Cynics might note that there seems less emphasis there on protecting the human rights of little folk. Rationally enough, the lawyers go where the deep pockets are to be found: this is also, of course, where the targets of serious investigative journalism are also generally located. The firm have been frank about their methods in their publicity material: "Today most corporate clients prefer us to work with them under the radar and without publicity, using the law to protect reputations without drawing attention to the issue" [25].

Another well-known companion firm in the "reputation management" business similarly use their website to advertise their methods: "Every day, [the firm] helps clients who are threatened with unwanted media interest, both in the UK and worldwide. The firm has an unrivalled track record in using its legal and strategic expertise to prevent the publication of adverse or intrusive articles, broadcasts or images. Where it is not possible to stop publication completely, [our] reputation ... means that we are well placed to influence what is published or broadcast, often working closely with the client's PR advisers".

These solicitors go on to boast of their backstairs skills:

All television broadcasters and most national newspapers have staff lawyers. Our lawyers know most of them well and are experienced in dealing with them. We find them receptive to our approach. It is in their interests that stories should be accurate and potential disputes avoided where possible. We will advise the staff lawyer of your interest and, if appropriate, outline your concerns regarding the proposed story.....

The Results: This may lead to important changes to the story from your point of view and, sometimes, a decision not to publish the story at all. Often this is all that is required to nip the matter in the bud. [26]

What do such legal tactics mean in practice? Often, it is likely that the investigative reporter will find themselves confronted by an ashen-faced editor waving what appears to be a terrifying legal letter. This will frequently arrive after the story has been published, or late in the day after the reporter has very responsibly notified the subject that they are about to be written about and inviting their comments. Typically, from my thick sheaf of such letters received over the years, I see one from an oil company's lawyers:

The articles are on any view gravely defamatory of our clients....[we] require the Guardian within 7 days...that it will remove these article from its website.

Here is an aggressive extract from another one, addressed over my head to my editor from lawyers for a Swiss bank:

LEGAL NOTICE- NOT FOR PUBLICATION...
The bank requires the Guardian to provide the following undertakings:

1. That it will not disclose ... any information concerning the identity of the bank's customers...
2. To deliver up to this firm with 24 hours a copy of the information and by that time to destroy all hard copy documents and to delete all electronic documents

And here is a characteristic piece of legal menace:

Your journalist...raises a number of questions and allegations concerning our client's tax affairs...Our client will take a breach of his rights extremely seriously...We require your undertaking by 4pm on 16 January that you will not publish any information.

How does one deal with these threats? The first thing to understand is that much of the wording in these letters (often including the empty word "CONFIDENTIAL") is designed to intimidate, rather like the letters one receives from a debt collection agency, or when behind with the gas bill. Some of the wording is designed to sound meaningful, or like a formal preliminary "letter before action", but is in fact mere bluster ("LEGAL NOTICE"…"the bank requires by 4pm" etc.). The lawyers may not in fact be hired to initiate a lawsuit: they may be hired to do nothing more than write these threatening letters, for each of which they will charge their client a hefty sum.

On the other hand, of course, the letter may be a genuine prelude to a writ, because of some serious mistake the journalist has made. How do you tell the difference between a hollow threat and a real one? There is a way, and it involves paying close attention to English grammar. Solicitors in the UK are perfectly entitled to give misleading impressions as best they can on behalf of their clients. But what they are not allowed to do by their professional regulators is to tell direct lies. Therefore they will not as a rule inform you that they are going to sue, unless they actually have instructions from their client to do so.

Consequently, this is a piece of key advice. When you receive a lawyers' letter, READ THE LAST PARAGRAPH. This is where, after all the bluster, the lawyer will be obliged to spell out what is going to happen. Observe the grammar very closely. If the lawyer has instructions actually to sue, they will use a formulation in the terms "UNLESS you…then we SHALL" (or similar). Any grammatical construction short of this means they do not have present instructions to issue a writ and are merely trying to frighten you.

In a letter quoted above, for example, the solicitors wrote

Our client will take a breach of his rights extremely seriously.

They added:

In this regard we have instructed leading counsel in this matter to act on our client's behalf should this become necessary (and this letter is written on his advice). Our client will hold The Guardian to account for its involvement in the publication of such material.

The *Guardian* correctly concluded that "to act on our client's behalf", "taking extremely seriously", "holding to account", and "should this become necessary" were phrases indicating that the lawyers did not in fact have instructions to commence a lawsuit. Full details of their client's tax manoeuvrings, together with his explanations, ended up being successfully published without any dire legal consequences at all.

THE HOUSE LAWYER

It may seem from these episodes that law and lawyers simply get in the way of the determined investigative journalist. Worse still, the numerous legal obstacles that appear to arise may be used as an excuse by unenthusiastic bosses to drop a troublesome story. Relationships between the journalist and their own company lawyer can become tense as a result. A less-than-competent in-house lawyer may also be tempted to play safe by raising legal objections to a piece, especially when bullying letters come in. They may try to undermine the story by cross-examining the reporter about their facts. For if an investigation is never published, the lawyer can't get into trouble for having given bad advice about it. A bad lawyer can ensure themselves a quiet life this way, whilst the deeply frustrated investigative journalist is the one who gets the ulcers.

In the best-run media organisations, there is a clear division of roles which helps damp down these conflicts. The reporter should be the person responsible for the accuracy of the facts in a story. If the lawyer signs off on what turn out to be untrue facts, the reporter is then to blame, along with their editor. The lawyer's role is not to usurp the editorial task, claim the power to veto stories, or to carry the can for a cowardly editor. The lawyer's correct role is simply to advise on risk.

Back in the 1970s, *Sunday Times* editor Harry Evans, faced with legal risk on his famous thalidomide exposure, said "I'll go to jail. That's what I'll do. I'll go to jail. Bloody hell, it'd be worth it" [27, p. 155ff]. There was a more recent demonstration of this correct attitude during the Edward Snowden affair, when top secret US intelligence material was obtained by the *Guardian*. Its then editor Alan Rusbridger, privately called in the paper's expert external lawyer, Geraldine Proudler. She advised him that the legal risks of publication included the possibility he would be personally extradited and convicted in America under the US Espionage Act. As he recalls: "This was a story that could land me in jail" [28]. Rusbridger thanked her for her advice, decided the risk was worth it, and took the editorial decision to run with the story. He was not extradited and, despite being British, won an unprecedented Pulitzer prize in the US for the paper.

On a smaller everyday scale, every investigative reporter should understand this same division of responsibilities: if they and their lawyer cannot agree, and there appears to be a risk, then a senior editor must be brought in to make that call. How willing will the editors be to take the lawyer-guesstimated risk? The brute fact is that very few worthwhile stories are entirely risk-free.

The relationship between house lawyer and investigative reporter need not be tense. It can be brilliantly helpful. Many times in my career I was grateful for a smart lawyer who uttered a warning, or spotted an inadvertent piece of dangerous wording and suggested a neat way round it. But a lawyer is not going to be helpful to a reporter unless they have learned to trust them. However, tempting it may be, it is a grave mistake to withhold any background facts because you fear they will make your lawyer nervous. If it all goes wrong and you get sued, your behaviour will have been career-ending. So this is my most solemn piece of practical legal advice: NEVER LIE TO YOUR OWN LAWYER.

AVOIDING THE LAW: INTERBREW

A final, contrarian, case study. As we saw above, playing by legal rules can end with the journalist's head in a noose: Preston discovered this in the Sarah Tisdall case. Sometimes, there is a better way. It can be possible to solve a legal problem by stepping back, thinking laterally, and circumventing the lawyers altogether. Just because paid lawyers see everything in purely legal terms, there is no need for journalists to do the same. A classic example came in 2001, when the *Financial Times*, the *Guardian*, and several other papers were sent documents with information about a potential merger involving Interbrew, the giant Belgian drinks firm. Interbrew's lawyers were aggressive. They obtained injunctions demanding return of the documents, which could have compromised the source. When the *Guardian* refused, the brewers' lawyers dramatically threatened to sequestrate the paper's assets [29].

The newspapers did not have much of a legal leg to stand on, but they had an ethical position to defend.

It dawned on some journalists that, while Interbrew might have been an obscure company to the person in the street, they were in fact the owners of a very well-known brand of beer, Stella Artois. This was mentioned to sympathetic MPs, some of whom decided to start a public campaign with the slogan "Boycott Stella!" It was not very long before it seemed the international company's PR department began to ask questions. Why were some of their own lawyers stimulating protest movements which might impact consumer sales in England? After a short while, the company dialled down its threats. (And many years later, in 2009, the European Court of Human Rights in Strasbourg finally struck down the unjustified injunctions) [30]

Likewise, HSBC's Swiss bank threatened draconian legal action in 2015, its files having fallen into the hands of the International Consortium of Investigative Journalists (HSBC, see Chap. 9). But the ICIJ team in London ensured the bank's public relations team from headquarters were brought in to sit around the negotiating table along with their high-priced external lawyers. Again, it did not take long for commercial good sense to prevail, and the legal threats to be put to one side. Journalism was the winner, and not the lawyers.

REFERENCES

1. Hislop, Ian. 2009. Privacy Law is Censorship by Judicial Process. *Press Gazette*, May 5.
2. Richard, Cliff. 2018. Sir Cliff Richard, OBE v BBC & S Yorkshire Police. [2018] EWHC 1837 (Ch).
3. Reid, Lord. 1968. Conway v Rimmer [1968] AC 910.
4. Leigh, David. 1980. *Frontiers of Secrecy*. London: Junction Books.
5. Robertson, Geoffrey. 2018. *Rather His Own Man*. London: Biteback. *Home Office v Harman (1983) 1 AC 280. Attorney General v New Statesman & Nation Publishing Co. Ltd (1981) QB1.*
6. Ponting, Clive. 1985. *The Right to Know*. London: Sphere.
7. Norton-Taylor, Richard. 1985. *The Ponting Affair*. London: Cecil Woolf.
8. Turnbull, Malcolm. 1988. *The Spycatcher Trial*. London: Heinemann.
9. *R v Felixstowe Justices ex p Leigh (1987) QBD 582.*
10. Leigh, David, David Pallister, Rob Evans, and John Aglionby. 2004. Guardian Victory in Arms Bribe Case. *Guardian*, December 9.
11. Evans, Rob. 2012. Judgment Over Extradition Case is Victory for Open Justice. *Guardian*, April 3. *(Guardian News and Media Limited) v City of Westminster Magistrates' Court* ([2012] EWCA Civ 420).
12. Laville, Sandra. 2016. Certain Family Court Hearings to Take Place in Public in Radical Trial. *Guardian*, December 23.
13. Preston, Peter. 2005. A Source of Great Regret. *Guardian*, September 5.
14. Tesco apology. 2008. Corrections and Clarifications. *Guardian*, September 6.
15. Leigh, David. 1982. Black Jurors to Sue Denning. *Observer*, May 23.

16. ———. 1984. *High Time: The Shocking Life and Times of Howard Marks*. London: Heinemann.
17. Freeman, Simon, and Barrie Penrose. 1997. *Rinkagate: The Rise and Fall of Jeremy Thorpe*. London: Bloomsbury.
18. Wigg, George. 1963. House of Commons. Accessed November 5, 2018. https://api.parliament.uk/historic-hansard/commons/1963/mar/21/journalists-imprisonment#S5CV0674P0_19630321_HOC_512.
19. Newell, Claire. 2018. Sir Philip Green Named in Parliament. *Telegraph*. Accessed November 5, 2018. https://www.telegraph.co.uk/news/2018/10/25/sir-philip-green-named-parliament-businessman-centre-britains/.
20. Davies, Nick. 2013. Phone-Hacking Trial Told Now Safe Held Intimate Details of David Blunkett Affair. *Guardian*, November 7.
21. O'Carrell, Lisa. 2014. Ex-News International Chief Tells Phone-hacking Trial They Had Several Periods of 'Physical Intimacy'. *Guardian*, February 21.
22. Crown Prosecution Service. 2012. Media: Guidance for Prosecutors on Assessing the Public Interest in Cases Affecting the Media. *Legal Guidance*. Accessed November 7, 2018. https://www.cps.gov.uk/legal-guidance/media-guidance-prosecutors-assessing-public-interest-cases-affecting-media.
23. Schillings. 2008. The Leading Law Firm Protecting the Reputations of High-profile Individuals, Corporates and Brands. *Schillings Website*. Accessed November 7, 2018. https://web.archive.org/web/20080803015133/http://www.schillings.co.uk/.
24. ———. 2010. Press Release. *Cision PR Web*. Accessed November 7, 2018. https://pressreleases.responsesource.com/news/49887/schillings-to-participate-on-the-panel-session-at-the-reputation/.
25. Leigh, David, and Owen Bowcott. 2011. Injunction Publicity Backfires on Celebrity Law Firm. *Guardian*, May 24. Accessed January 20, 2019. https://www.theguardian.com/law/2011/may/24/injunction-publicity-backfires-law-firm.
26. House of Commons. 2010. *Press Standards, Privacy and Libel Appendix 1. Culture Media and Sport Committee Report*. London: Stationery Office. Accessed January 20, 2019. https://publications.parliament.uk/pa/cm200809/cmselect/cmcumeds/memo/press/m13102.htm.
27. Knightley, Philip. 1997. *A Hack's Progress*. London: Jonathan Cape.
28. Rusbridger, Alan. 2018. *Breaking News: The Remaking of Journalism and Why It Matters Now*. London: Canongate. (See also Chapter 6.)
29. Dyer, Clare, and Kevin Maguire. Interbrew Drops Threats to Seize Guardian Assets. *Guardian*. Accessed November 7, 2018. https://www.theguardian.com/media/2002/jul/26/theguardian.pressandpublishing/.
30. European Court of Human Rights. 2009. Financial Times Ltd & Ors v UK *(Application No. 821/03)*. Accessed November 7, 2018. https://hudoc.echr.coe.int/eng#{%22dmdocnumber%22:[%2282859859%22],%22itemid%22:[%22001-96157%22].

CHAPTER 6

Dealing with Spies and Spooks

There are many interfaces between investigative reporters and western intelligence agencies. They are not always obvious to young recruits into journalism. But experienced practitioners know their significance. Secretive intelligence agencies, with their seemingly unaccountable powers, often seem to act as a reporter's worst enemies, interfering and trying to bully them. But what is even worse is when they pose as the journalist's friend, planting misinformation on them. Worst of all, because intelligence officers and reporters do similar kinds of work, spies sometime try to recruit journalists as agents or themselves engage in spying whilst pretending to be journalists. This hampers genuine journalism and can endanger people's lives.

Spies as Enemies of Journalists

Many people of all kinds dislike being targeted by investigative journalists. Indeed, who wouldn't? But what makes members of intelligence agencies special is that they can fend off reporters by claiming no-one should be allowed to write about them or their doings. They do this by invoking the notion of "national security".

That is rather a cloudy term: historically in Britain, it was backed up by threats to prosecute journalists under the former clauses of the notorious Official Secrets Act, and by use of a so-called D-notice system to warn them off more informally. Investigative journalists have fought many

© The Author(s) 2019
D. Leigh, *Investigative Journalism*,
https://doi.org/10.1007/978-3-030-16752-3_6

battles over the last 40 years or so to cut down these pretensions to size. Some reporters have recently also set out to document the intelligence agencies' interference with their own profession, in order to shine a badly needed light on it.

The classic attempt to conflate journalism with espionage was the attempt in 1978 to jail expert investigator Duncan Campbell and two of his colleagues, for researching the activities of GCHQ in a then radical magazine, *Time Out* [1]. Under its cover-name, the "Government Communications Headquarters", the UK codebreaking organisation is the counterpart of the National Security Agency (the NSA) in the US, with whom it works in partnership. It operated at the time a large international network of radio intercept stations, manned by the military, and including a base in Cyprus aimed against Middle East countries and the then Soviet states.

From the vantage-point of the modern world, it is difficult to cast one's mind back a few years to the censorship mania of those Cold War times. Hollywood movies are now made without difficulty about the wartime Bletchley adventures of the codebreakers and their guru Alan Turing, the father of modern computing. Ostensibly, the national security rationale for trying to conceal GCHQ's continued existence in the 1970s was that it would otherwise alert Britain's enemies to our success in codebreaking. This was fatuous: real Soviet spies such as Burgess, Maclean, Philby, and Blunt had told the Russians everything of major significance.

What it was really about was the fact that possession of the power to censor always generates bad mental habits. Officials confuse what they would prefer—or even what they would *much* prefer—with what in the words of the European Convention of Human Rights is "necessary in a democratic society". At the extreme, in dictatorships, almost everything is successfully defined as a state secret. In democracies by contrast, investigative journalists will frequently find themselves in conflict with the secret services and their extravagant claims. And this is a good thing.

Campbell & Co fought off the threat of jail, despite being had up in the dock at the Old Bailey as though they were major criminals. Their QC Jeremy Hutchinson and junior Geoffrey Robertson produced embarrassing evidence that GCHQ was not really such a great secret. Robertson recalls:

> Jeremy was soon invited to a dinner party at which he was placed next to a senior figure in MI6, who indicated they would accept a plea to a lesser charge that did not entail prison. [2, p. 239]

There was only one real victim: a young American reporter who had been working with them at *Time Out*, Mark Hosenball. He was solemnly deported by the then Labour government because he had "sought to obtain … information harmful to the security of the United Kingdom" [3]. He was later allowed back into the country and has worked as a prominent US professional journalist ever since.

After this episode of excess, Britain's spies dropped their attempts to have journalists arrested. Instead they turned to the civil laws of confidentiality and contract, in a battle to prevent publication of *Spycatcher*, the ghost-written memoirs of embittered MI5 officer Peter Wright (see Chap. 5). That did not work either, except in a minor way: the British government sought to seize the royalties of Wright's UK-resident ghost-writer, but Wright himself remained untouchable in faraway Tasmania.

Other rogue intelligence officers have subsequently broken cover either to tell stories of malpractice or to air their grievances. David Shayler of MI5 [4] and Richard Tomlinson of MI6 [5] were pursued and jailed in 2002 and 1997 respectively, and attempts were made in 2004 to prosecute Katherine Gunn from GCHQ [6], but the journalists who wrote about them were not prosecuted. Cathy Massiter of MI5 [7], who revealed alarming misbehaviour by her employers on television, was left entirely alone in 1985 along with those who wrote up her stories. In the long run, the British government was obliged to put GCHQ, MI5, and MI6 on a statutory footing for the first time, and publicly to name their directors. One head of MI5, Stella Rimington, even wrote her own memoirs [8].

However, a further major crisis in relations came in 2013, when the renegade NSA analyst Edward Snowden made off with exceptionally top-secret US intelligence files. They detailed among other things, the previously unsuspected contributions being made by Britain to the mass sweeping up of Internet communications. Undersea fibre-optic cables that made landfall in Britain or in the Middle East were being tapped wholesale without lawful sanction. When this material fell into the hands of the *Guardian*, there was understandable fear among the journalists that a re-run of the Duncan Campbell prosecutions of the 1970s was likely. One man, a Snowden intermediary carrying encrypted files, was peremptorily seized in transit at Heathrow airport by the British, and his data confiscated [9]. A plane belonging to the president of Bolivia, and thought to be carrying the fugitive Snowden, was forced down by US action in order to be searched [10].

The *Guardian* editor, Alan Rusbridger, had previously negotiated successfully with US intelligence and state department officials to publish selected Wikileaks disclosures and was hopeful of doing the same over Snowden [11]. But the British reaction to Snowden was more hysterical. A Conservative backbencher, Julian Smith, later promoted to Chief Whip for his services to the government, called for Rusbridger to be punished for treachery [12].

In the end, it appears that compromises were reached. It was observed that the paper did not publish some details, such as the identities of complicit telecoms companies, and the names of Middle East client states. The British agencies also insisted that they be allowed to superintend the ceremonial destruction with hammer and angle-grinder of a *Guardian* hard drive containing the raw data. The images of state bullying went around the world, depicting the journalists as victims. It was nothing but a charade, as the information had already been prudentially shipped out to the custody of the *New York Times*, by the simple low-tech means of sending it in a Fedex parcel.

The upshot was that honour seemed to be satisfied all around. The *Guardian* successfully published the key material: no-one was arrested, and Snowden ended up being provided asylum in Russia.

The Modern Relationship with Intelligence Agencies

This short history of some none-too-successful attempts at bullying may read like a heartening account of retreat and reform. However, the furtiveness continues. Although their director-generals' names are now made public, British editors are still leaned upon not to identify individual intelligence officers.

Editors are also manipulated in other ways. The spooks still do not operate general press offices as do the police and other government departments. Instead they specify an individual "trustie" journalist, one in each media outlet, to whom they are prepared to talk unattributably. No-one else gets access. The terms of the deal are that information supplied will never be attributed directly to the intelligence services. If you break these conditions, you are cut off. The system is supplemented by periodic discreet lunches and dinners between agency directors and editors themselves—Top Chap dining with Top Chap.

It is an undesirable system of power without responsibility. When it transpired that MI6 officers had indeed been implicated in the "rendition" and torture of Islamist suspects, the *Observer*'s Peter Beaumont wrote an angry account of how an anonymous briefing system had been abused:

> The official denials are what our readers get to see ... What readers don't get to see is another kind of to-and-fro. The direct appeal to editors and reporters. The insistence that our secret services "don't do this kind of thing", are bound by rules, by UK, EU and international law, are "crown servants", and in any case are bound by a sense of decency. Except, as it is now quite clear, it was all a bloody lie. [13]

VETTING OF JOURNALISTS

Recruits to British journalism are regularly checked out by the intelligence agencies. This is another method of controlling them. The BBC, thanks to its history as a state broadcaster, appears to have the worst record in this respect. Official archives now reveal that, at least into the 1980s, the BBC adopted a deliberate policy of lying about the fact that, ever since the 1930s, all its would-be journalistic recruits had been covertly referred to MI5. A retired brigadier was even installed in a back room at Broadcasting House with the title "Special Assistant to the Director of Personnel", to liaise directly with the security service. Those considered politically undesirable were blacklisted in secret, with no opportunity to appeal or correct mistakes. If journalists were already employed inside the BBC, they were blocked from future promotion by a small "christmas tree" symbol discreetly stamped on their personnel file [14].

It would be naïve to imagine that national newspaper editors do not do something similar. (Although the late Tony Howard, then deputy editor of the *Observer*, did to his credit authorise the first full-scale newspaper exposure of BBC vetting in 1984, co-written by the present author.) [15]

What lesson should investigative journalists draw from this knowledge? At the very minimum, they should understand that if they make direct attacks on MI5, MI6, and GCHQ, they are going to attract the ire of these agencies, and there may be career repercussions which are not altogether visible. They may have their phones tapped. They are unlikely to find themselves approved for "sensitive" media posts such as defence correspondent, or to be in line for a knighthood. On the other hand, some military and intelligence correspondents, such as the veteran

Richard Norton-Taylor of the *Guardian*, have maintained their integrity and indeed been severe in their criticisms of the spies from a leftist perspective. It has not harmed them, because they have earned respect by fair reporting over the years. We in the west are not yet living in a Stalinist dystopia, with a Stasi informer around every corner.

Vigilance is, nevertheless still required. In 2017 Britain's legislative updating organisation, the normally innocuous Law Commission, suddenly slipped out proposals that would have once again made it possible for journalists who write about intelligence in the UK to be criminally convicted of espionage [16]. The intelligence agencies had suggested to them again that journalists who distributed secret information should be punished as spies even if they did not have a "purpose prejudicial to the safety or interests of the state", as the present law requires.

The intention was to make it easier to lock up Alan Rusbridger and his fellow-journalists, the next time an Edward Snowden came along. No such new law had yet been drafted by 2018, but it is unmistakably there on the intelligence agencies' agenda. The censoring impulse does not go away.

SPIES AS FRIENDS OF JOURNALISTS

At least journalists know where they stand when the intelligence agencies seek to bully them into silence. The relationship is even more dangerous for the truth, however, when the spooks and spies pose as their best friends. Intelligence agency propaganda can be planted on journalists, who agree to disguise its origin from their readers. An active programme by the secret agencies to influence what appears in the British press, used to be called, if publications by various defectors can be believed, "I/Ops". That is an abbreviation for "Information Operations" [17].

Black propaganda—false material where the source is disguised—has been a tool of British intelligence agencies since the days of the Second World War, when the Special Operations Executive got up to all kinds of tricks with clandestine radio stations, to drip pessimism and undermining rumour into the ears of impressionable German soldiers.

Post-war, this unwholesome game mutated into what might much of the time be more fairly called grey propaganda—material that was not necessarily untrue, but heavily "slanted". A cold war unit was set up under the vague acronym IRD, standing for "Information Research Department", and financed from the British "secret vote". Its task was ostensibly to plant anti-communist news stories abroad, in the press of the third world, often using secretly controlled Middle East news agencies. IRD's lurid tales of Soviet drunkenness and corruption sometimes leaked back to confuse the readers of the British media [18].

A vivid example of the way these techniques expanded to meet the exigencies of the hour came in the early 1970s, when Northern Irish readers of the *News of the World* scandal-sheet, not normally a vehicle for foreign policy analysis, were treated to a front page splash, headlined "Russian Sub in IRA plot sensation". It came complete with an aerial photograph, purportedly of a Soviet conning tower awash off the coast of Donegal. As those at the paper were later to concede, the story was a fabrication supplied by an official of the IRD, whose disinformation brief at the time was to stigmatise the Catholic bombers of the Irish Republican Army as agents of international communism [19].

British introductions to IRD were made discreetly; one distinguished liberal journalist recalls how he was taken to lunch at a London club by his retiring predecessor to pass him on to his IRD "contact". All journalists were told as little as possible about the department. So-called background briefing material was sent to their homes under plain cover. IRD correspondence was marked "personal" and carried no departmental markings. Recipients were told documents were "prepared in the Foreign Office primarily for members of the diplomatic service, but are allowed to give them on a personal basis to a few people outside the service who might find them of interest... they are not statements of official policy and should not be attributed to HMG, nor should the titles themselves be quoted in discussion or in print. The papers should not be shown to anyone else and they should be destroyed when no longer needed".

It was not until 1978 that investigative journalists succeeded in exposing the awkward fact that their colleagues' work was coloured by IRD activities. British writers on IRD confidential mailing-lists turned out to include two Labour journalist MPs. There were also three writers connected with the *Financial Times*; five from the *Times*; two from the *Observer*; five from the *Sunday Times*; five from the *Telegraph*; six from the *Economist*; one from the *Daily Mail*; two from the *Mirror*; one from the *Sunday Mirror*; and one from the *Express*. Other journalists were informally blacklisted as politically undesirable or had assistance withdrawn if they became politically embarrassing [20].

Some journalists in the post-war years made a career out of being spoon-fed all sorts of politically sympathetic material from behind the intelligence arras. The most notorious was the late Harry Pincher of the *Daily Express*, who changed his by-line to the more sonorous "Chapman Pincher" and regaled his readers with hints that trade union leaders, Labour politicians, and even a former head of MI5 itself, were really Soviet agents. It was Pincher that left-wing historian EP Thompson famously referred to when he railed against a kind of "*official urinal where high officials of MI5 and MI6 ... stand side by side patiently leaking*" to "*self-important and light-witted*" journalists [21].

A rare demonstration of how cautious journalists need to be when taking unattributed material from the spies was documented in 1995. Readers of the *Sunday Telegraph* were presented with a dramatic tale about Saif Gaddafi, son of the then despotic ruler of Libya, and his alleged connection to a currency counterfeiting plan. The story was written by Con Coughlin, the paper's chief foreign correspondent. He attributed its key quotes to a "British banking official". In fact, the story had been given to him by officers of MI6, who, it transpired, had been supplying Coughlin with material for years. They did not let him take away copies of documents.

Saif Gaddafi sued in London for libel, apparently affronted by the suggestion that he was no more than a common criminal. The *Sunday Telegraph* could not, of course, stand up their story, regardless of whether or not it was true. In an effort to defend the lawsuit, they finally decided to admit who their source was.

In a statement which entered the public domain in the course of a lengthy judgement given in the court proceedings [22], the paper explained how a private lunch had been arranged by the paper with the then Conservative foreign secretary, Malcolm Rifkind. Coughlin was invited along. Informed by Rifkind that countries such as Iran were trying to get hold of hard currency to beat sanctions, Coughlin was then briefed in more detail by an MI6 man—his regular contact.

Some weeks afterward, he was introduced to a second MI6 officer, who spent several hours with him and handed over extensive details of the story about Gaddaffi's son. Although Coughlin asked for evidence, and was shown purported bank statements, the legal pleadings make clear that he was dependent on MI6 for all the discreditable details about the alleged counterfeiting scam. He was required to keep the source strictly confidential.

Throughout the formal submissions, the *Telegraph* attempted to preserve an unconvincing fig leaf over its sources by referring only to a "Western government security agency". But the case was soon quietly settled with a payment of some money to Gaddafi for his legal fees, and a grovelling apology. The paper said:

> The Sunday Telegraph has accepted not only that there is no truth in these allegations, but that there is no evidence to suggest that there is any truth in them, and they have agreed to apologise to the claimant [Mr Gaddafi] in this court and in the newspaper. [23]

So, unusually, an MI6 exercise in planting a story was laid bare. There was no suggestion that Coughlin was dishonest in his work. He was a perfectly conscientious journalist who clearly tried to substantiate his facts and undoubtedly believed in their truth. But nevertheless, those facts may not have been correct. And many would think he was unwise in falsely attributing the material to a "British banking official". His readers ought to have known where his material was coming from. When the *Sunday Telegraph* got into expensive trouble with the libel case, they seem, after all, to have suddenly found it possible to become a lot more explicit about their sources.

I would not want to sound too holier-than-thou about these matters. I did once personally, to my knowledge, also become involved in an MI6-inspired story. In August 1997, the then *Observer* foreign editor's MI6 contact supplied him with intelligence information about an Iranian exile in Britain. This man was running a pizza business in Glasgow: but he was also attempting to lay hands on a sophisticated mass spectrometer which could be used for measuring uranium enrichment—a key stage in acquiring components for a nuclear bomb. We were supplied with a mass of apparently high-quality intelligence from MI6, including surveillance details of a hotel meeting in Istanbul between our pizza merchant and people involved in Iranian nuclear procurement.

I should make clear that we did not publish merely on the say-so of MI6. We went off to Glasgow ourselves, and confronted the pizza merchant. Only when he admitted that he had indeed been dealing with representatives of the nuclear industry in Iran did we publish an article [24]. In that story, we made it plain that our target had been watched by western intelligence. Nevertheless, I felt uneasy, and vowed never to be sucked into such an exercise again. Although all parties, from the foreign editor downward, behaved quite scrupulously, we had gone too far. We had been obliged to conceal from our readers the full facts and had ended up, in effect, acting as government agents.

A remorseful journalist who later gave a relatively full account of his exploitation by intelligence officers on both sides of the Atlantic was David Rose of the *Observer* and subsequently the *Mail on Sunday*. His former colleague, the award-winning investigative reporter Nick Davies, acidly concluded of Rose at the time: "He has all the self-confidence of great reporters, but less of the judgment" [25, p. 339].

As home affairs editor of the *Observer*, Rose was proposed in 1992 to be the personal link between the paper and MI6 by his then editor, Donald Trelford. Over lunch, this new intelligence friend told Rose that while MI6 "had always had a few, very limited contacts with journalists and editors, it now felt the need to put these arrangements on a broader and more formal basis" [26]. Rose gave his connection the pseudonym "Tom Bourgeois" in his published magazine article:

> If I wanted to quote or paraphrase anything Bourgeois said, I would have to use a circumlocution so vague as to make it impossible for any reader to realize that I had spoken to someone from the Office at all.

In the run-up to the military invasion of Iraq in 2003, Rose began to publish a drumbeat of *Observer* articles implying he had intelligence sources. Typical was a so-called Observer Focus Special of 11 November 2001 headlined:

> THE IRAQI CONNECTION: After a month-long investigation, David Rose reports on the links between Saddam and the 11 September hijackers.

In reality there were no such links. The piece's phraseology included:

> Senior US intelligence sources say …Parts of British intelligence had reached the same conclusion….A top US analyst—a serving intelligence official—told The Observer……..CIA sources have confirmed ……The senior US intelligence source said.

In his subsequent *mea culpa*, Rose wrote:

To my everlasting regret, I strongly supported the Iraq invasion. I had become a recipient of what we now know to have been sheer disinformation about Saddam Hussein's weapons of mass destruction and his purported "links" with al-Qaeda.

Spies as Journalists; Journalists as Spies

The line between journalism and spying is quite blurred. My former colleague Farzad Bazoft was a young Iranian exile in London, who had been taken on as a freelance by the *Observer*, in somewhat obscure circumstances. On an official journalistic visit to Saddam Hussein's Iraq, he was discovered taking soil samples at a possible chemical weapons plant that had been in the news. The Iraqis hanged him as a spy [27]. His remains and a small memorial can be found today at the "journalists' corner" in Highgate Cemetery.

Was Farzad a spy, pressured into working for the British intelligence agencies, or was he just an over-zealous reporter desperate to make his mark? [28]. He was probably completely innocent, but in a way, the answer is irrelevant. Either way, he ended up dead. The use of journalists as spies, or the use by spies of journalistic cover: these are facts, and they cause journalists to be put in danger, whether or not any particular accusation is true.

In the US, the 1960s and 1970s saw a raft of disclosures that the CIA (along with MI6) was secretly funding magazines and other publications: and that it had scores of other journalists on its books who were covertly working for the intelligence agency as "assets".

In Britain, the *Observer* had a reputation for its particular links with the intelligence agencies. The notable MI6 officer Kim Philby was positioned with a job there before his exposure as a KGB double-agent and his subsequent flight to Moscow. Some others on its staff also had histories with the espionage organisation: editor Donald Trelford writes of his assumption that the paper's late correspondent Gavin Young had MI6 as his "other employer" [29].

The distinguished writer Neal Ascherson, on the other hand, used to entertain listeners with his comic story of MI6's vain attempts to recruit him by means of a homosexual hand on the knee. Trelford himself confided in his memoirs that he had "done a few jobs for MI6" whilst a youthful editor of a paper in what was then Nyasaland. He travelled to Rhodesia several times during the period of Ian Smith's Unilateral Declaration of

Independence and reported back to the then MI6 regional head of station—although he emphasises that he did nothing for them at the *Observer* subsequently.

And even the thriller author Frederick Forsyth says he "ran errands" for MI6 whilst at the Reuters news agency [30]. None of these incidents are surprising. Journalism is a trade of finding things out. So is espionage.

But the tactic of manipulation which gives special concern, however, is that spies on the staff of intelligence agencies are tempted to pretend to be genuine journalists. During the wars following the break-up of Yugoslavia, the MI6 officer Richard Tomlinson, by his own account, spent 6 months in 1993 travelling around war-torn Croatia and Serbia trying to recruit informants, under the guise of being a British reporter.

The intelligence writer Stephen Dorril published allegations later that the *Spectator* magazine had unknowingly been used as journalistic "cover" by no fewer than three MI6 officers working in Bosnia, Belgrade, and Moldova [31]. Tomlinson, who was to be jailed for such indiscretions, was also the likely source for Dorril's disclosure that an MI6 officer was the author of two controversial *Spectator* articles that appeared in early 1994 under the pseudonym "Kenneth Roberts" [19]. They were datelined Sarajevo, and "Roberts" was characterised by the magazine as working with the UN in Bosnia as an "adviser".

British soldiers were on the ground as UN "peacekeepers", but anyone who read "Roberts'" articles might have begun to wonder whether it was not a better policy for them to go home and leave the attacking Serbs a free hand. The first article on 5 February rehearsed arguments for a withdrawal, pointing out that all sides committed atrocities. The second piece complained, baselessly, about "warped" and inaccurate reporting by other journalists, including the BBC's Kate Adie [19].

The most dismaying allegation floated by Tomlinson was that he had heard tell within MI6 of "a national newspaper editor" who was used as an agent, and had received up to £100,000 in covert payments, accessed at an offshore bank, via a false passport obligingly supplied by MI6 itself. This claim set off a hue and cry. But with no outcome. Newspapers employ many "editors"—they have, for example, education editors; they have environment editors; they have defence editors (not, I should say, that I have any evidence against any individual members of these categories).

Tomlinson's allegation could be true. It could be false—who knows? The trouble with accepting stories from secret agents is that, unlike conscientious investigative reporters, they are often not at all reliable.

DEALING WITH SPOOKS AND SPIES

DO

STAND UP TO BULLYING

BE AWARE OF SURVEILLANCE

REMAIN SCEPTICAL

DON'T

MAKE THEM YOUR ENEMIES

TRUST YOUR COMMUNICATIONS

LIE ABOUT SOURCES

RUN ERRANDS

REFERENCES

1. Campbell, Duncan. 2015. GCHQ and Me. *The Intercept.* Accessed November 8, 2018. https://theintercept.com/2015/08/03/life-unmasking-british-eavesdroppers/.
2. Robertson, Geoffrey. 2018. *Rather His Own Man.* London: Biteback.
3. Harris, of Greenwich Lord. 1977. Mr Agee and Mr Hosenball: Deportations. *House of Lords.* Accessed November 8, 2018. https://api.parliament.uk/historic-hansard/lords/1977/feb/16/mr-agee-and-mr-hosenball-deportations.
4. Guardian. 2002. Shayler Jailed for 6 Months. *News Section.* Accessed November 8, 2018. https://www.theguardian.com/media/2002/nov/05/pressandpublishing.davidshayler1.
5. BBC. 1997. Ex-MI6 Man Jailed Over Memoirs. *BBC News.* Accessed November 8, 2018. http://news.bbc.co.uk/1/hi/uk/40704.stm.
6. Norton-Taylor, Richard, and Ewen MacAskill. 2004. Spy Case Casts Fresh Doubt on War Legality. *Guardian.* Accessed November 9, 2018. https://www.theguardian.com/uk/2004/feb/26/freedomofinformation.iraq.
7. Massiter, Cathy. 1985. MI5's Official Secrets. 20/20 Vision. Accessed November 9, 2018. https://www.concordmedia.org.uk/products/mi5s-official-secrets-1099/.
8. Rimington, Stella. 2001. *Open Secret: The Autobiography of the Former Director-General of MI5.* London: Hutchinson.
9. Bowcott, Owen. 2016. Terrorism Act Incompatible with Human Rights, Court Rules in David Miranda Case. *Guardian.* Accessed November 9, 2018. https://www.theguardian.com/world/2016/jan/19/terrorism-act-incompatible-with-human-rights-court-rules-in-david-miranda-case.

10. BBC. 2013. Bolivia President's Jet Grounded in Snowden Search. *BBC News*. Accessed November 9, 2018. https://www.bbc.co.uk/news/av/world-latin-america-23166146/bolivia-president-s-jet-grounded-in-snowden-search.
11. Rusbridger, Alan. 2018. *Breaking News: The Remaking of Journalism and Why It Matters Now*. London: Canongate.
12. Lewis, Julian. 2013. National Security (The Guardian). Accessed November 9, 2018. https://hansard.parliament.uk/commons/2013-10-22/debates/13102269000003/NationalSecurity(TheGuardian).
13. Beaumont, Peter. 2018. I Tried to Expose the Truth About MI6 and Torture But Was Lied to. *Observer*, July 1.
14. Reynolds, Paul 2018. The Vetting Files: How the BBC Kept Out 'Subversives'. *BBC News*. Accessed November 9, 2018. https://www.bbc.co.uk/news/stories-43754737.
15. Leigh, David and Paul Lashmar. 1985. The Blacklist in Room 105. *Observer*, August 18.
16. Law Commission. 2017. Protection of Official Data. Consultation Paper. Accessed November 9, 2018. https://www.lawcom.gov.uk/project/protection-of-official-data/.
17. Lashmar, Paul. 2013. Urinal or Conduit? Institutional Information Flow Between the UK Intelligence Services and the News Media. *Journalism*, January 30.
18. Lashmar, Paul, and James Oliver. 1998. *Britain's Secret Propaganda War: A History of the Foreign Office's Information Research Dept, 1948–77*. London: Sutton.
19. Leigh, David. 2000. Britain's Security Services and Journalists: The Secret Story. *British Journalism Review* 11 (2): 21–26.
20. ——— 1978. Death of the Department That Never Was. *Guardian*, January 27.
21. Thompson, EP. 1978. A State of Blackmail. *New Statesman*, November 10.
22. Gaddafi v Telegraph Group Ltd [1998] EWCA Civ 1626, [2000] EMLR 431.
23. Tweedie, Neil. 2002. Gaddafi's Son Settles for Apology in Libel Case. *Telegraph*. Accessed November 9, 2018. https://www.telegraph.co.uk/news/uknews/1391457/Gaddafis-son-settles-for-apology-in-libel-case.html.
24. Doyle, Leonard, Jonathan Calvert, and Robin McKie. 1997. Iran Bomb Plot Foiled in Britain. *Observer*, August 31.
25. Davies, Nick. 2008. *Flat Earth News*. London: Chatto & Windus.
26. Rose, David. 2007. Spies and Their Lies. *New Statesman*, September 27.
27. Fazad Bazoft was hanged on March 15, 1990.
28. Vulliamy, Ed. 2003. Proved Innocent. *Observer*, May 18.
29. Trelford, Donald. 2018. *Shouting in the Street*. London: Biteback.
30. Forsyth, Frederick. 2015. Frederick Forsyth Reveals MI6 Spying Past. *BBC News*. Accessed November 9, 2018. http://www.bbc.co.uk/news/entertainment-arts-34101822.
31. Dorril, Stephen. 2000. *MI6: 50 Years of Special Operations*. London: Fourth Estate.

CHAPTER 7

Conspiracy Theories

An investigative journalist is someone who wants to expose hidden wrongdoing. But, as I have repeated more than once in this book, the trade is a game of Blind Man's Buff. A reporter rarely has possession of all the facts, or even most of them. Instead, they have to play a guessing game and formulate a case-theory which will enable them to ask the right questions and reach the right destination. They have to use their imagination.

Sometimes only imagination will help them get the story: on World in Action, we were able to expose Jonathan Aitken as a lying politician because we used our imaginations to deduce that his wife must have been taking their daughter to a school in Switzerland, not in Paris paying his hotel bill as he claimed—and that led us on an eventually successful hunt for the evidence which stood up our hypothesis [1]. Case-theory comes first: hard evidence should follow.

But sometimes ambitious reporters have over-active imaginations. A proneness to conspiracy theories is the *déformation professionelle* of investigative journalists. It is tempting to join up the dots into a particular picture, despite the lack of real knowledge, and then chase after an exciting hypothesis. Many people with motives of their own will promote such conspiracy theories to the gullible reporter. How do you test them? There are useful methods. If we look at some striking conspiracy theories that should never have found their way into print, we will see that they have certain warning signs in common.

© The Author(s) 2019
D. Leigh, *Investigative Journalism*,
https://doi.org/10.1007/978-3-030-16752-3_7

THEORY ONE: THE DEATH OF KENNEDY

When I arrived at the *Washington Post* as an eager young British reporter on a fellowship, the first thing editor Ben Bradlee told me to do—undoubtedly with a twinkle in his eye—was to find out who really killed Kennedy. A British investigative writer, Anthony Summers, had just published a thick book with the single-word title: "CONSPIRACY". On the book's jacket was written in large letters:

> It is certainly possible that a renegade element in US intelligence manipulated Oswald ...That same element may have activated pawns in the anti-Castro movement and the Mafia to murder the President. [2]

Ever since the day US President John Kennedy was shot with a sniper rifle in Dallas back in 1963, conspiratorialists had been in the field. The shooter, a confused loner called Lee Harvey Oswald, was not interesting enough for the traumatised American public. They wanted more. There was such a plethora of books demanding "Who killed Kennedy?" that it spawned a crop of parodies. One such was called "Dr Who Killed Kennedy". (Referencing a popular British TV science-fiction series, its sub-title was "The Shocking Secret Linking a Time Lord and the President"). My personal favourite was "Elvis Killed Kennedy".

Following Bradlee's instructions, I set off for the retirement communities of Florida to interrogate some of the grizzled CIA veterans implicated by Summers in his CIA-Cuban-Mafia scenario. I came back a week or so later and deflatedly told Bradlee "I've found out who killed Kennedy: it was Lee Harvey Oswald all the time". The pursuit of the conspiracy theory had been tiring and pointless. There was no hard evidence behind it of any kind. "Certainly possible" and "may have" were not meaningful phrases. Only later did it dawn on me that this did not actually matter much for the author, who had a book to market. All that was likely to concern him was that he cut through the everyday noise with his bold claims and got a considerable amount of media attention.

THEORY TWO: THE DEATH OF JONATHAN MOYLE

Some years on, I was very startled to read one day in the *Daily Mirror* an investigation headlined "MURDER in Room 1406" [3]. Proclaiming "We can reveal the sinister truth", the paper's writers told the story of a young British helicopter pilot called Jonathan Moyle who wrote for an aviation magazine. He had gone to a conference in Chile, and had been found dead in his hotel room, hanging from the door of the wardrobe. At the time, the media had been full of tales that a Chilean firm, Cardoen, might have been supplying under-the-counter weaponry from Chile to Saddam Hussein's Iraq.

Joining the dots, the *Mirror* team decided this must have been the secret scandal that Moyle was covertly investigating. And furthermore, his hanging had occurred in the very same month, March 1990, when Iraq had brutally and publicly hanged another UK journalist (Farzad Bazoft, see Chap. 6), for investigating Saddam's chemical weapon supplies. It all fitted together! As the paper told its readers:

> People who knew Moyle believed he was killed because he was on the brink of exposing arms dealings with Iraqi dictator Saddam Hussein.

I was surprised to see this story, because we had actually investigated the Jonathan Moyle case for World in Action, a little while earlier. I had spent some time with his grieving parents, who believed in this murder thesis. They were understandably desperate to find a context that might give a dignified meaning to their son's death.

We did not take the imaginative approach of joining the dots, but went on a more routine search for concrete evidence. We engaged a local journalist in Chile to make inquiries as to what exactly had happened. He was able to fax over copies of the original Santiago police report. It had photos of the room and a description of the body. He had been found hanging with a rope around his neck. The rope was padded by one of his own shirts wrapped around it.

This single hard fact instantly exploded the conspiracy theory. For the only purpose of padding a noose would be to make it more comfortable. An assassin would not trouble to make the noose more comfortable. This led us eventually to a massive casebook published by the FBI in Washington, called "Auto-Erotic Asphyxiation". From its grisly illustrated examples, we discovered that it was all too common for people to accidentally die whilst seeking sexual gratification by hanging themselves. At a point of hypoxia—oxygen deprivation—there comes sexual release.

Sophisticated practitioners would suspend themselves by a pulley arrangement they could hold on to, so that if they lost consciousness, they would automatically release their hold and fall safely to the floor. It seemed poor Jonathan Moyle, however, might have been something of an amateur in this regard.

We dropped the story.

THEORY THREE: THE DEATH OF HILDA MURRELL

This was an investigation published at length in the normally very respectable pages of the *Guardian*, blaming MI5 for the death of an old lady. Over nearly 4000 words, the paper printed extracts from a book written by the freelance journalist Judith Cook and published by the equally reputable firm of Bloomsbury [4]. The dead woman, retired professional rose-grower Hilda Murrell, had allegedly been the March 1984 victim of a rural break-in. She had been sexually assaulted and her body was found some distance from her cottage. But the Cook version concluded starkly:

> The official story said that a burglary had gone tragically wrong.... Now new evidence ties the threads of the mystery together. There was a conspiracy. [5]

What led the conspiracy theorists to join up the dots were two associated facts. The first was that Hilda Murrell had been a dedicated campaigner against the nuclear industry in the days of the Thatcher government, and during the aftermath of the Falklands war. In the course of the fighting to re-take those remote islands, the invading Argentine cruiser, the General Belgrano, was sunk by a British nuclear submarine in murky circumstances. The torpedoing by HMS *Conqueror* cost the lives of more than 300 hapless young Argentine conscripts and was immensely controversial. In 1984, the rumbling controversy even provoked one official, Clive Ponting, to defy the Official Secrets Act and reveal that the Belgrano had not in fact been sailing towards British forces, as had been falsely claimed (see Chap. 5).

The second factor latched on to by activists was that Hilda Murrell had a nephew, ex-Commander Rob Green. He had actually been working in naval intelligence at the very time the British submarine *Conqueror* had been ordered to sink the Belgrano! He had since left the navy and shared her anti-nuclear sentiments. The inference was irresistible. Clearly, Green possessed incriminating documents. Equally clearly, he must have passed them on to his activist aunt. He himself claimed to have come under suspicion of doing just that. It followed, as dot joined inexorably up to dot, that the intelligence agencies would have been secretly tasked to get back papers dangerous to the Thatcher regime. And from there, it was surely only a short step to the contemplation of a political killing. It was all just like the movies!

Judith Cook wrote for the *Guardian*: "A retired MI5 officer, often used as a consultant by the media, was casually asked about the Murrell murder. Freelance operatives had, he said, been sent in and they had panicked when the old lady returned unexpectedly. Their MI5 handler had been severely reprimanded" [5].

This was the nearest the entire saga came to offering a fact. And it was not one to be relied upon. The "source" was an anonymous person, claiming to be a retired intelligence officer, and possibly taking money from the media. He might well have been a confidence trickster, because con-men make their living by telling people things that they passionately *want* to believe. The social scientists call it "confirmation bias".

One of the frequent features of conspiracy theories is that they live on indefinitely because nothing can be proved one way or the other. The Murrell-MI5 conspiracy, however, was unusual. More than 20 years after Hilda Murrell's death, the truth finally came out. After new advances in DNA testing, a teenage criminal, Andrew George, was proved to have in fact abducted the 78-year-old campaigner after she had disturbed him burgling her house. Burglary had been, of course, the original much-derided "official story". George, who was 16 when he stabbed the old lady and left her to die, was jailed for life. As the *Daily Telegraph* laconically put it in the headline on its brief court report: "Conspiracy theories laid to rest by Murrell conviction" [6].

THEORY FOUR: THE DEATH OF DIANA

Beautiful princesses are the inhabitants of fairy stories. The conspiracy theory about Princess Diana's death was just such a fairy story. It used to be presented regularly on Monday mornings in huge screaming headlines in the *Daily Express*. One classically evidence-free front page said "DIANA: POLICE CANNOT RULE OUT MURDER" [7].

Diana, the estranged wife of Prince Charles, died in a car crash in Paris in 1997. She and her current boyfriend, Dodi Fayed, were being pursued by paparazzi photographers when their Mercedes, driven by a hotel security man, collided at high speed with an underground pillar. All the occupants were killed and their driver proved to have a lot of alcohol in his blood. The conspiracy theory that was elaborated in subsequent months was that Diana had been ambushed. It was said that some witnesses had seen a mysterious white Fiat Uno nearby, which could have driven into the Mercedes' path. There was also a suggestion that the British intelligence services could have deployed blinding lights to cause the driver to veer off the road and crash.

The reason for such an assassination? Dodi's father, the wealthy Egyptian owner of Harrods, Mohammed Fayed, was among those who asserted that Diana had been murdered by MI5, the Duke of Edinburgh, or other agents of the British royal family, either because they could not tolerate her plan to marry a Muslim (which she had never said she intended to do) or because she was pregnant by Dodi Fayed (which she was not).

As it happened, I was on duty at my paper the weekend Diana crashed and died. As shocked as anyone, I started to look into the circumstances. What had occurred—as was subsequently confirmed at the inquest—was that Diana and Dodi had aborted their original travel plans because of harassment by the paparazzi on motorbikes. The photographers were chasing shots of the celebrity couple that they could sell.

Pursued by the paparazzi, the pair had fetched up instead at the Paris Ritz, also owned by Fayed. Dodi phoned his father in London for advice. The hotel's security man Henri Paul was summoned from the bar (where he had apparently been downing shots) and ordered to lose the photographers by driving Diana and Dodi off in another car, in a new direction.

Just as with similar cases, the discovery of just one concrete fact was quite enough to explode this particular conspiracy theory. It was perfectly simple. There could not have been an ambush of any kind with mystery cars lying in wait. For it was established that the couple had, at the last minute, in this way changed their planned route. Any ambushers would not have been lying in wait in the right place.

Some kindly souls assumed that in propagating conspiracies, Dodi Fayed's father was unhinged by grief. However, conspiracy theories, even the most preposterous ones like his, can get into circulation for more rational reasons. First of all, why did the *Daily Express* fan the story? The clue is in the appearance of those Monday headlines. Monday mornings have traditionally the slowest sales of the week, because few newsworthy events happen on Sundays. But the *Express* could put 20,000 or so on to its circulation by running a big splash about Diana. Their enthusiasm to promote Fayed's allegations was not because they were gullible. But it might be because they were cynical.

And as for Fayed, there were also rational aspects to his wild theories. They perhaps served to divert attention in his own mind from the fact that it was on his advice the drunken Henri Paul had been ordered out to drive his own son and Diana to their deaths.

Any investigative journalist who dispassionately looked into the death of Diana at all would have thus seen that there was hard evidence on the one hand, and more than one understandable motive to fantasise on the other. They would have been able to reject the conspiracy theories decisively. And in fairness to the journalistic community, that is what most of them did.

THEORY FIVE: THE DEATHS FROM 9/11

The horrifying attack by Islamists on the twin towers in New York on 11 September 2001 again detonated conspiracy theories. Truly grotesque rumours surfaced in the media—that the hijacked planes had never really been flown into the World Trade Center, for example, and that the collapse of the towers was in reality a deliberate demolition organised by the CIA. In a popular alternative scenario, it was the Israelis who were to blame, having covertly warned all the Jews who worked in the building to stay away that day.

In the West the flames were fanned by unstable attention-seekers such as the renegade MI5 officer David Shayler, who announced that his spy background enabled him to pronounce that 9/11 was an "inside job" [8]. One might have thought no-one could take such talk seriously: but I was jolted some months afterwards when I was invited to Egypt to give a lecture on investigative reporting. My audience were well-educated and youthful journalism students, many of them apparently sophisticated young women. A majority of them asserted that they believed in these theories.

Once again, the key to evaluating such allegations lies in an examination of motive. The 9/11 conspiracy theories served a psychological purpose. They were diversions promoted by those who could not process the truth—that Muslim radicals had behaved in a barbarically murderous fashion for which there could be no excuse. It was easier to turn the facts inside out and blame traditional enemies—the Israelis or the Americans—regardless of the lack of evidence. One might feel disheartened as a journalist at the sheer strength of such psychological compulsions, which seem to have so much more power than do mere facts. But at least one can learn to avoid the waste of time and journalistic energy that might be involved in the pursuit of such shadows.

THEORY SIX: THE DEATH OF DR KELLY

A Liberal Democrat member of Parliament, Norman Baker, put his name in 2007 to a book called "The Strange Death of David Kelly" [9]. The title was a play on the 1935 work by popular historian George Dangerfield called "The Strange Death of Liberal England". In reality, the only strange thing about Dr Kelly's death was the bizarre conspiracy theory that became attached to it.

Dr Kelly was a security-cleared British government scientist, by all accounts a mild-mannered man, who became sucked into the savage political combat between a right-wing journalist then working for the BBC and a left-wing journalist working for the then Blair government. The row over Prime Minister Tony Blair's part in the misbegotten 2003 invasion of Iraq was one of the most bitter of the period.

The BBC journalist Andrew Gilligan rather casually alleged on air that the government had deliberately "sexed-up" a dossier purporting to show that Iraq possessed so-called weapons of mass destruction. It had been published despite the fact that the relevant intelligence material at the time appeared to have definitively said no such thing (and despite the fact that, as events proved, no "WMD" had ever existed).

The Prime Minister's spin doctor, the former tabloid journalist Alastair Campbell, retaliated by launching aggressive attacks on the BBC for airing such claims. In the course of these denunciations, and further probing inquiries by parliamentary committees, Dr Kelly found himself exposed as Gilligan's source for the "sexed-up" allegation [10]. He had been on a BBC roster of science contacts which had been provided to Gilligan when he joined the Today programme.

Shortly afterwards, Dr Kelly, who was 59, was found dead in woods near his home. It seemed he had cut his wrists, and the inquest verdict was suicide. But a conspiracy theory began to gain traction among some parts of that very large section of the public, right across the political spectrum, who were incensed that Britain had been taken to war on a false prospectus. Newspapers even published suspicious letters from doctors saying there had not been sufficient blood to justify the suicide finding. The implication of all the suspicion and protest was that Kelly had not in fact committed suicide, but had in fact been targeted—perhaps by "British intelligence", the regular scapegoat. One newspaper splash headline bluntly came out with it. "WAS KELLY MURDERED?" [11]

This particular conspiracy theory was quite perverse. Again it could be easily exploded. No-one had the least motive for murdering Dr Kelly in order to "silence" him. He had already said what he had to say, and it was common ground by then that the technical facts alluded to in the so-called dodgy dossier had proved to be wrong. The argument raging was a political one as to whether the intelligence services themselves had exaggerated the facts, or whether Blair, Campbell, and their circle had deliberately inflated the intelligence advice received in order to deceive the public. Kelly could not shed any further light on that issue.

On the other hand, there was ample motive for Kelly to commit suicide, exactly as per the inquest verdict. He was, it seemed, a sensitive and honourable man, not used to the limelight and appalled by the Iraq invasion. He had been betrayed and dragged into a fierce political battle not of his making. The results of his exposure as a source were proving catastrophic. His government employers, the British Ministry of Defence, were now taking disciplinary action against him for illicitly talking to journalists. This could lead to the loss of his security clearance, the loss of his livelihood, and his personal humiliation and disgrace. It was sad and unfair, but far from surprising, that he should seek a way out.

THEORY SEVEN: THE JULIAN ASSANGE "HONEYTRAP".

Assange, the creator of Wikileaks, the data leaking site, faced an unpleasant threat to his status as a counter-cultural hero when two women in Sweden accused him of sexual misconduct in 2010. His response was to suggest that there was a conspiracy against him. The idea was amplified by his band of disciples, their social media outlets, and by his lawyers.

His associates talked of a plot by "crazy feminists ... sending a young man into a honeytrap" [12]. Others went further. British newspapers printed the words of Assange's own solicitor alleging a CIA conspiracy. The lawyer said:

> We saw the smirking American politicians yesterday. The honeytrap has been sprung. Dark forces are at work. After what we've seen so far you can reasonably conclude this is part of a greater plan. [13]

Assange allowed this idea to float: he told the BBC, "I have never said that this is a honeytrap. I have never said that this is not a honeytrap" [14]. The term honeytrap, popular in espionage thrillers, refers to the way a target can be tricked into a sexual encounter, filmed, and subsequently blackmailed or pressurised.

The dismayed professional journalists—who up to that point had been working in collaboration with Assange—investigated the Swedish circumstances on the ground. They found a less picturesque story. The essence of the women's complaints was that they had consensual sex on separate occasions, but he had acted against their will by not using a condom. When he refused to get checked for HIV at a clinic, they made good on a threat to go to the police. Events escalated from there. Assange left town and resisted all Swedish attempts to extradite him, eventually jumping bail in Britain and taking refuge in the Ecuadorean embassy, where he was to remain for more than 5 years before being eventually arrested [15].

No evidence ever came to light of a conspiracy to frame him sexually, by the CIA, the "feminazis" of Sweden, or by anyone else. The lawyer Geoffrey Robertson eventually disclosed that Assange had confided in him at the time, whilst strolling through Regents Park in London, that the women had merely been—in Assange's opinion—"petulant" [16, p. 246]. We can safely say there never was any honeytrap.

Here again, calm examination of motive and a forensic approach to the facts were all that were needed to explode the theory.

How to Deal with Conspiracy Theories

There are three common features that cause all these false conspiracy theories to find their way into print. The first is an outrageously loose attitude to evidence. Because some events happen simultaneously or in the near time frame, it does not mean that they are connected by cause and effect. But we can see that, time and again, journalists are tempted to join up the dots and make a picture that exists only in their own imaginations.

The second frequent factor is confirmation bias. The journalists are driven by a variety of political or ideological beliefs, either overtly or without realising it. They *want* to see a particular explanation for events that suits those beliefs, and they cherry-pick bits of information that seem to bear out their presuppositions. They don't have open minds.

Third and finally, there is simply over-excitement. Journalists are handed conspiratorial explanations and think they would make a wonderful story. They don't stop long enough to enquire whether their sources have axes to grind and are peddling these conspiracy theories for dubious motives of their own.

Real conspiracies do of course exist in the world. Watergate, the benchmark of modern investigative journalism, was itself a full-scale conspiracy by President Nixon and his aides to commit a crime and then cover it up (see Chap. 2). It is certainly a central job of all investigative reporters to try and unearth the conspiratorial behaviour, big and small, which so often conceals wrongdoing. But to do so, they need to learn the means of distinguishing between genuine conspiracies and empty fantasies. Real evidence must always come first.

DEALING WITH CONSPIRACY THEORIES

DO

STICK TO THE EVIDENCE

KEEP AN OPEN MIND

EXAMINE MOTIVES

DON'T

JOIN UP THE DOTS!

REFERENCES

1. Harding, Luke, David Leigh, and David Pallister. 1999. *The Liar*. London: Guardian Books.
2. Summers, Anthony. 1980. *Conspiracy*. New York: McGraw-Hill.
3. Clarkson, Wensley. 1998. MURDER in Room 1406. *Mirror*, February 26.
4. Cook, Judith. 1994. *Unlawful Killing: The Murder of Hilda Murrell*. London: Bloomsbury.
5. ———. 1994. Inside Story. *Guardian*, September 17.
6. Britten, Nick. 2005. Life for Burglar Who Left Peace Campaigner to Die. *Telegraph*, May 7.
7. Palmer, Richard, and John Twomey. 2005. Diana: Police Cannot Rule Out Murder. *Express*, May 23.
8. O'Neill, Brendan. 2006. Meet the No Planers. *New Statesman*. Accessed November 10, 2018. https://www.newstatesman.com/politics/politics/2014/04/meet-no-planers.
9. Baker, Norman. 2007. *The Strange Death of David Kelly*. London: Methuen.
10. History of the BBC. Iraq, Gilligan, Kelly and Hutton 2003. *The Hutton Report*. Accessed November 10, 2018. https://www.bbc.co.uk/historyofthe-bbc/research/culture/bbc-and-gov/hutton.

11. Isabel, Oakeshott and Hugh Dougherty. 2004. Was Kelley Murdered? *London Evening Standard*, January 27.
12. Shamir, Israel. 2010. Assange: The Amazing Adventures of Captain Neo. *Counterpunch*. Accessed November 10, 2018. https://www.counterpunch.org/2010/08/27/assange-the-amazing-adventures-of-captain-neo-in-blonde-land/.
13. Razaq, Rashid, Craig Woodhouse, Martin Bentham. 2010. Dark Forces at Work to Take Assange to US, Says Lawyer. *London Evening Standard*, December 8.
14. Humphrys, John. 2010. Transcript: The Assange Interview. *BBC Today Programme*. Accessed November 10, 2018. http://news.bbc.co.uk/today/hi/today/newsid_9309000/9309320.stm.
15. Harding, Luke, and David Leigh. 2013. *Wikileaks: Inside Julian Assange's War on Secrecy*. London: Guardian Books.
16. Robertson, Geoffrey. 2018. *Rather His Own Man*. London: Biteback.

CHAPTER 8

Bad Practice and Good Practice

In the canon of fictional representations, most movies depict the investigative reporter as a hero and desirable role model. But there are some exceptions. A 2007 Hollywood thriller called *The Bourne Ultimatum* was directed by Paul Greengrass, an ex-World in Action producer, and it contains a sly cameo portrait. In the very first reel, an eager young *Guardian* journalist in London goes off to meet a confidential source in the hope of a hot story. Things are not at all what they seem, the journalist is assassinated, and that's the end of him. The film proceeds with the adventures of the indestructible Jason Bourne, an ex-CIA killer who is a real tough guy, not a naïve idiot who gets himself shot.

An intriguing if now less-remembered *noir* British political thriller was also made in 1986, called *Defence of the Realm*. Directed by David Drury, the film depicts a workaday Fleet Street world of bad tabloid journalists, who are only too willing to peddle political smears and act as mouthpieces for crooked proprietors. Against this milieu, it sets another more honest young investigative reporter, played by the photogenic Gabriel Byrne. With great determination, the Byrne character uncovers a government plot to conceal a nuclear air crash, and he boldly defies a sinister tribunal of UK intelligence officials ("I take it then, that you are a believer in Freedom of Information?" "Yes, I am!"). They respond by arranging a bomb which explodes in his flat. And that's the end of him too.

Silly as this denouement was, the movie-makers had obviously researched the newspaper landscape. They incorporated one very useful

© The Author(s) 2019
D. Leigh, *Investigative Journalism*,
https://doi.org/10.1007/978-3-030-16752-3_8

journalistic tip: the protagonist copied his documents and had them mailed to other media outlets all over the world. Even after his death, his exposure story lived on as a result. Exploiting those traditionally potent visual images, the movie showed thundering presses rolling unstoppably at the *New York Times*, the *Frankfurter Allgemeine* and *Le Monde*. It is an important fact that time and again, journalists have been able to circumvent censorship or political pressure by collaborating with other reporters in other jurisdictions. There's nothing silly about that.

But otherwise, I felt quite exasperated with Gabriel Byrne's portrayal when I saw the movie. He didn't seem smart. The most successful investigative reporters I know do not go in for unnecessarily aggressive showboating and defiance. They are quieter and more observant. When the water is full of sharks, why start splashing and shouting? Furthermore, the investigative reporter character ended up dead. In my book, that is evidence of journalistic failure.

The relevance of these movie fictions is that they paint in a melodramatic style what is a real truth: the work of an investigative journalist, if not carried out carefully, can be dangerous. I personally always feel embarrassed when reporters from developing countries ask if my life has ever been threatened. In the states of the west, and particularly in the UK and the US, probing journalists are by and large very unlikely to be assassinated, run over, or beaten up in jail. They might get embroiled in a nasty lawsuit, or even lose their jobs. But they don't usually die. The same is not true of journalists trying to work in Latin America, Asia, Russia or Africa.

Assassinated Journalists: Guerin, Politkovskaya, Galizia

Sometimes deaths do happen even closer to home.

Reporter Veronica Guerin, driving her red Opel coupe, stopped at a light on the outskirts of Dublin on 26 June 1996. A gunman on the back of a following motorbike shot her six times. There was widespread shock in Ireland and internationally. The mother of a six-year-old boy, Guerin's crime investigations for the *Irish Sunday Independent* had made her unpopular with the underworld, and she had been repeatedly threatened. Prime Minister John Bruton called it "an attack on democracy", his words memorialised by the International Press Institute when designating her a "World Press Freedom Hero" [1]. After her death, a number of drug gangsters were eventually imprisoned and the Irish government sought to crack down on organised crime, bringing in powers to seize the assets of drug dealers. A movie was made about her, starring Cate Blanchett, which received mixed reviews [2].

Anna Politkovskaya at 48 was among the best-known investigative journalists working for *Novaya Gazeta* in 2006. As she came out of the lift in her Moscow apartment block, a gunman stepped forward and fired four shots into her chest, shoulder, and head. A mother of two, she was a fearless opponent of Putin and of Ramzan Kadyrov, the brutal pro-Kremlin puppet ruler of Chechnya [3]. The Russian FSB intelligence agency had been hacking into her emails, according to leaked National Security Agency files published by the Intercept website in the US [4].

While five individuals, including three Chechens, were eventually convicted of her murder, the Russian authorities did not seek to identify who was behind them. It was one of 36 reported killings of journalists during the two decades of Putin's government [5].

Daphne Caruana Galizia, a professional journalist in Malta, drove away from her home in this Mediterranean island on the afternoon of 16 October 2017. One of her three adult sons described hearing the distant blast as a remote-controlled bomb went off under the driver's seat. He rushed out of the house and found her remains. In Galizia's popular blog, called Running Commentary, and in newspaper columns, she had long excoriated local politicians, attacking money-laundering; corruption; the sale of passports; smuggling; and organised crime [6]. In her last post, she wrote: "There are crooks everywhere you look. The situation is desperate" [7].

The Daphne Project was subsequently launched—a collaboration of 18 media organisations, including the *Guardian, Reuters, Le Monde*, and the *New York Times*. They pledged to continue her work. As a result a great deal of international attention was focused on allegations of corruption in this previously obscure EU mini-state. Although three purported hitmen were arrested, those behind the assassination remained unidentified a year later [8].

The Daphne Project response was inspired by a Paris-based investigative reporters' network called Forbidden Stories [9]. Their group in turn echoed the way the venerable Investigative Reporters and Editors (IRE) network grew up in the US in the 1970s. A reporter from Phoenix, Don Bolles, was killed in a similar car bomb in 1975. His murder left unfinished an inquiry into fraudulent land sales. As a result, 38 journalists from 28 newspapers and television stations from all over the US decided to work together collaboratively to probe corruption in Arizona. The Missouri-based IRE is still going strong [10].

Those three assassinated women, Guerin, Politkovskaya, and Galizia, were particularly brave. I don't want to demean their courage. And everyone must decide on their own crusades. But I wouldn't want anyone to think that a necessary qualification for investigative journalism is a reckless willingness to put your own life on the line. Journalism should not usually be an arena in which to demonstrate how driven or intrepid you are prepared to be. Is it better for the cause of truth, perhaps, to live to fight another day?

OVER-ENTHUSIASM: THE *TIMES* AND LORD ASHCROFT

Recklessness then is an unwelcome personality trait for a would-be investigative journalist. So is simple over-enthusiasm. The story of how the once-staid *Times* of London tried to embark on "target journalism" in 1999 demonstrates its sometimes-disastrous consequences. The newspaper, by then under the ownership of Rupert Murdoch, printed as part of a campaign a dramatic piece headlined: "DRUGS AGENCY HAS ASHCROFT ON ITS FILES" [11].

Michael Ashcroft was a powerful and colourful figure. He was a businessman who grew up in the freewheeling offshore jurisdiction of Belize, in Latin America, where he operated a bank. He ruffled many feathers among British Tories by tipping large donations into the Conservative party, and gaining political influence in London as a result. He became party treasurer and was made a member of the House of Lords.

What the *Times* had discovered, however, was that the US Drug Enforcement Agency intelligence files contained a number of references to Ashcroft. Those DEA file entries indicated his private plane had been used for a number of flights in Latin America linked to a suspected drug-runner, and his Belize bank operated some accounts for suspects. The bare facts about the file contents were quite correct. But they gave the misleading impression that Ashcroft himself was a suspected drug-runner. His plane had been chartered, in quite a routine way, to a number of other people. His bank had very many customers. The DEA's raw intelligence files did not actually carry any implication that Ashcroft was a criminal, but the *Times* story possibly did.

Ashcroft was furious. He said: "Now I can add the *Times* to my list of enemies" [11]. As he wrote in his memoirs, "I employed lawyers to scrutinise every word written about me" [12]. He set about getting his revenge, with no expense spared. The first step was to sue the paper and its then editor, Peter Stothard, for libel under the old unreformed British defamation law, where the journalists would have to prove the truth to legal standards, not only of the underlying facts, but of all the unpleasant implications a judge would discern. It was going to be a costly and uphill legal struggle to prove Ashcroft was really a drug baron.

The *Times'* barrister recalls, "As we were arguing hammer and tongs in the courtroom, we were passed a note from our solicitors, saying that Ashcroft had met Rupert [Murdoch] on a golf course in Florida and that they had decided to settle" [13]

Ashcroft's price for agreeing to drop the case did not include an apology. But the paper had to pay its own heavy legal costs and was obliged to say, "The Times is pleased to confirm that is has no evidence that Mr Ashcroft or any of his companies have ever been suspects of money laundering or drug -related crimes" [14]. Stothard did not long continue as editor. Following an episode of ill-health, he moved into editing the *Times Literary Supplement*, a bookish backwater.

But Ashcroft had only just begun his revenge. Having employed researchers to delve into all his political opponents, he used his great wealth to publish a book denouncing them, called "Dirty Politics, Dirty Times". Tom Baldwin, the reporter who had written some of the *Times* articles, was the particular target of wounding abuse: "I found not only that Baldwin was a binge drinker but also that he was a habitual user of cocaine, …The MP told me 'Tom Baldwin is a clever man, but he is not an honest man'" [12, p. 91ff].

The enraged businessman also determined to trace the source who had revealed the contents of his DEA files. He demanded the US drug agency launch its own inquiry into the leak. In due course a DEA agent called Jonathan Randel was exposed. He had had dealings with a freelance journalist who first marketed the story to the *Times*. This was a criminal offence. Ashcroft recorded: "I was extremely pleased when I was told that Randel had been imprisoned" [12, p. 198]. His revenge was complete.

Emotionalism: Lord McAlpine and the BBC

Emotional over-engagement is another psychological trap for the investigative reporter. Particularly when sex abuse is the subject, common sense seems to disappear. The temperature rises to boiling-point. To falsely accuse people of a horrible crime that is ultimately hard to prove or disprove can be unforgivably destructive. On the other hand, to ignore the disclosures of a victim of abuse can be even more immoral. It betrays the victim all over again. Investigative reporters thus find themselves picking their way along an exposed mountain ridge with an abyss on either side. A slip one way or the other can be deadly.

This was cruelly demonstrated during the great paedophile witch-hunt that careered off through the landscape of British journalism in 2012, leaving many professional casualties behind. We detailed in an earlier chapter how two very effective investigative journalists on BBC Newsnight, Liz McKean and Meirion Jones, succeeded in revealing that the celebrity broadcaster Jimmy Savile was also a brazen sexual predator, exploiting his teenage audiences and his ready access to hospitals and the like for his "charity work". Savile had been a darling of the Conservative administration of Mrs Thatcher when she was prime minister, and she got him a knighthood (see Chap. 4).

From a journalistic point of view, the good news for McKean and Jones as they set to work was that Sir Jimmy had recently died. This meant that there were no legal dangers about identifying him. Despite some protest campaigns by the relatives of well-known people, in Britain you cannot libel the dead. (My colleague Peter Chippindale and I used to fantasise in our cups that there was only one way to defeat the ruthless millionaire exploiters of British libel law. A "libel hit squad" could hire itself out to assassinate such litigants: their lawsuits would all die with them).

The bad news for the Savile journalists was, of course, that their findings were extremely embarrassing to their own employer. Savile had been a celebrity presenter for years on high-profile BBC programmes—not only "Top of the Pops", but also on "Jim'll Fix It", a show which provided youngsters with some of their dearest wishes. A lengthy tribute programme to the recently deceased entertainer was being scheduled for the coming Christmas.

Investigating the misdeeds of one's own organisation is always a recipe for trouble. In the case of the BBC, there was also the particular structural difficulty of working in a TV environment. A fraction of the broadcaster's staff laid claim to journalistic values: but the larger part of the BBC did not. It was primarily in the business of corporate survival and popular entertainment, not investigative journalism. Newsnight's bosses failed to run the story. The upshot was that the Savile exposure ended up being taken elsewhere; the BBC was denounced for a scandalous cover-up; and Newsnight's two journalists were effectively forced out of their own jobs in the backwash of the affair.

What happened subsequently, however, was even worse. Having leaned over backwards to conceal Savile's wrongdoing, those involved with Newsnight proceeded to lurch over too far the other way. They swallowed a completely mistaken accusation that a top political figure was a sex abuser. Their target was the Conservatives' party treasurer, the rotund figure of Alistair McAlpine, a scion of a prominent British family construction firm. It was part of a cloud of allegations that the Tory administration was riddled with paedophiles.

The original Savile case may have been an example of good journalism being thwarted by bosses. But the subsequent McAlpine imbroglio was a saga of bad journalistic mistakes.

The starting-point for analysis of those mistakes is one of the transfixing spectacles of the Savile scandal. This was the sight of the BBC director-general, George Entwhistle, being publicly grilled and denounced for a cover-up by a parliamentary committee, chaired by veteran Conservative MP John Whittingdale [15].

The opposition Labour party's deputy leader, Tom Watson, saw what was going on in the committee room. Watson was collecting sensational allegations from those who approached him, and he was not averse to stirring the political pot. The following day, 24 October, he stunned the public by gravely telling the House of Commons that he had "clear intelligence suggesting a powerful paedophile network linked to Parliament and No. 10" [16].

There was actually less to this sensational accusation than met the eye. Among the things Watson had heard was that the parliamentary inquisitor Whittingdale was himself related to a sex abuser. This turned out to be true, as far as it went. His half-brother, a former prep school master called Charles Napier, who had an earlier conviction, was eventually to be reinvestigated and convicted again of 21 such offences against young boys [17].

It was also true that Whittingdale himself constituted a "link" of a sort to No 10, the Prime Minister's residence. He had once served as an aide there to Mrs Thatcher. These meagre facts did not quite add up to the vast dot-joining paedophile conspiracy at the top of the British state at which Tom Watson was hinting.

It was, however, quite effective politics. The temperature rose to a fever-heat. Unaware of what relative trivia lay behind Watson's Commons allegations, a memory stirred in another investigative journalist, Angus Stickler. He recalled a sex abuse allegation which had seemed to be connected to the Tory party. A former inmate of a north Wales children's home, Steven Messham, had, many years before, made similar charges. Stickler consulted his own boss, Iain Overton. Overton was the newly appointed editor of a small non-profit group in London called the Bureau of Investigative Journalism. Overton took the idea to Newsnight.

The BBC programme was still in disarray over Savile. Staff were reeling from the charge that they had covered up the Savile sex abuse story. Here, it must have seemed, was a providential opportunity to make amends and restore Newsnight's journalistic reputation.

The apparent witness, Messham, was tracked down and interviewed. Traumatised, and as much a victim in the end as anyone, he appeared to finger McAlpine, as required. Everything was done at high speed—too high a speed perhaps to make adequate checks—and by 2 November, the item was ready to go. No-one seems to have even taken the elementary step of showing Messham a picture of the alleged abuser.

The BBC lawyers would not let McAlpine be identified by name, but Overton was not deterred from publicising what he knew. He tweeted: "If all goes well we've got a Newsnight out tonight about a very senior political figure who is a paedophile". Overton also let fall the actual name of McAlpine at a dinner in front of other intrigued journalists. The Commons Speaker's wife, Sally Bercow, tweeted, "Why is Lord McAlpine trending? *innocent face*". It was all around town that Lord McAlpine was in the frame [18].

I was working on the *Guardian* at the time, and I can remember my feeling of dismay at what we feared was a straightforward case of mistaken identity. Alistair McAlpine was a metropolitan figure who had absolutely nothing to do with north Wales, where Messham had been abused. He did have a relative with a similar name and an estate in that area who was also completely innocent. It was possible that boys from the North Wales home had been sent there on occasion to work on the grounds. It was even possible that someone other than a McAlpine, but connected with the estate, had abused one or more of the boys and Messham knew about it in a garbled version.

But what was certain was that in accusing the Tory peer, Newsnight had got hold of the wrong end of the stick. Our own lawyer, Gill Phillips, had taken the precaution of preserving a transcript of an original public inquiry into the North Wales home. Despite a fog of asterisks and pseudonyms, it was clear that Messham had testified at the time, and it became equally clear that he in fact had no concrete evidence whatever against Alistair McAlpine.

The situation was very ticklish. We gathered in the *Guardian* editor's office to argue about it. If we went ahead and printed McAlpine's name, even in the context of exonerating him, would he want to sue us for libel? Some thought he might—after all, he was a Conservative and we were a left-leaning paper, so he might think we were slyly trying to taint his reputation.

On the other side of the argument, some were reluctant to take up the cudgels on the Tory McAlpine's behalf: one well-meaning executive said, in an all too common attitude, "Surely we should support the victim?" In the end, fidelity to the evidence did win the day, and we printed what we had found. The entire McAlpine allegation promptly collapsed.

A subsequent BBC inquiry report determined, "The combination of the Newsnight Report and online speculation had led to Lord McAlpine being incorrectly identified as Mr Messham's abuser. This has been a grave breach which had been costly to all concerned" [19].

If anything, that was an understatement. Within a week, George Entwistle was gone: "In the light of the unacceptable journalistic standards of the Newsnight film broadcast on Friday 2 November, I have decided that the honourable thing to do is to step down from the post of director general" [20].

Ian Overton, the editor of the Bureau of Investigative Journalism resigned too. The Bureau's reporter Angus Stickler departed. The BBC's acting head of news was moved to a "non-news" job. McAlpine was paid £185,000 for being defamed. Sally Bercow was also sued for libel for her tweet and had to apologise and pay damages. In what seemed to be the BBC equivalent of being exiled to run a Siberian power station, Peter Rippon, the Newsnight editor who had first suppressed the Savile exposure, was sent to build the BBC's online News Archive.

Nor did the chapter of investigative disasters even end there. The paranoia over sex abuse that had infected the world of journalism continued at an "investigative website" called Exaro. Its editor, a professional journalist called Mark Watts, was credited in the media with intending "to return to Fleet St's golden age" [21]. With his motto of "Holding Power to Account", he and a stable of other former professionals gave house-room to two more purported victims of high-society sex abuse, known by the pseudonyms "Darrell" and "Nick". Police set up elaborate investigations into their allegations and carried out raids on houses, whilst Exaro came to function as their cheerleader.

A characteristic piece reads: "Exaro revealed...detectives had seized video that places a former Conservative cabinet minister at one of several parties where men sexually abused boys" [22]. Top people were subject to false accusations by various journalists not just of indecency but sometimes also of torture, rape, and even murder. They included former Prime Minister Edward Heath; former Home Secretary Leon Brittan; ex-Field Marshal Lord Bramall; and ex-Tory MP Harvey Proctor.

The journalists had hitched themselves to the wrong wagon. For the saga culminated with the arrest of "Nick" in 2018 on charges of perverting justice and fraud. It transpired that he had obtained £22,000 compensation for the abuse he said he had suffered [23]. Exaro was closed down.

Journalists with the Wrong Temperament

Recklessness, over-enthusiasm, and emotionalism: these are certainly undesirable character traits for an investigative reporter. But there are plenty of other personal disqualifications, too. Many people are keen on journalism as a career for reasons which virtually guarantee they will fail as public interest investigators. These are the narcissists who crave big by-lines, exotic travel, political opportunities, and friendly acquaintance with celebrities. The fact is, you don't—and you shouldn't—make many friends as an investigative journalist.

Most unsuitable of all, perhaps, will be those people who want to be writers. Fine writing is not the kind of prose that investigative journalists deploy much of the time. Instead, they are obliged to write very often in a kind of code, cramped and fenced-in by the demands of libel law and the need to pick apart various forms of deceit and concealment

---

INVESTIGATIVE BAD BEHAVIOUR

RECKLESS

OVER-ENTHUSIASTIC

OVER-EMOTIONAL

EGOCENTRIC

The picture may look bleak. But are there then positive traits that are more likely to turn you into a successful investigative journalist who can avoid these pitfalls? The answer is "yes", very definitely. People do, of course, succeed in this demanding trade. To do so, however, you need to be cantankerous, in order to stand up to pressure, but biddable enough to work with others. You need to be imaginative, to work around obstacles and think yourself into an opponent's shoes. But you must also be as pedantically methodical as a librarian.

These amazing qualities are seldom found in one person. So investigators often succeed when they band together in pairs, or in small teams. Woodward and Bernstein of Watergate fame are probably the most well-known journalistic pair, although they then went on to have separate careers.

I've always found there are strong advantages to a two-person team: some of my own most productive periods as a journalist were when I worked in partnership with my colleagues Paul Lashmar at the *Observer*, and later with Rob Evans at the *Guardian*. The reasons are not very difficult to see. My partners both repaired weaknesses in my own approach. For example, they were highly organised, where I was not. I once got so behind with my expenses claims that I was reduced to giving Paul 10% if he would fill them in for me...He also headed off some of my more embarrassing wild goose chases.

A partnership provides someone to talk to. This is not as banal as it may sound: when so much in the journalists' game of blind man's buff turns on lateral thinking and the development of an imaginative case-theory, it is extremely helpful to have a colleague in the office with whom one can debate and think aloud. Two heads are very often better than one. Allied to this is a moderating effect: your partner can add a realistic splash of cold water to your more reckless or unrealistic schemes.

They will also often provide emotional support. Again, this is not so trivial an aspect as one might imagine. An investigative project often involves day-by-day dealings with outside contacts who are unco-operative, surly, openly hostile, or even threatening. Yet the need for security often limits the openness that is possible with friends or office colleagues. Your editors and bosses tend in my experience to be not very interested in your problems. They would rather hear about your solutions. Under these circumstances, to have a supportive partner to whom one can frankly confide, can be very useful in keeping the spirits up.

There is a final, organisational point. A journalistic team of two is relatively easy to co-ordinate. Each can generally keep abreast of what the other is doing without too much difficulty. A team of three will double the difficulties. With every additional person on the team, the task of co-ordination becomes exponentially greater until, in the end, someone has to be hired whose job is merely to co-ordinate all the others. It's better, perhaps to remain nimble.

To some extent, however, my preference for working in pairs is just a matter of temperament. There are some brilliant, if rare, investigative journalists who have been loners by nature. Nick Davies of the *Guardian* is a loner: virtually single-handed, he cost the Murdoch media empire millions and closed down the *News of the World* by exposing the scandal of phone-hacking [24]. Sy Hersh of the New Yorker was a celebrity one-man operation who exposed the My Lai massacre during the Vietnam war [25]. Andrew Jennings, working alone for Panorama, exposed corruption at the Olympics and in international football against the open hostility of virtually every other British sportswriter [26]. The virtues of joint working—debate, support, division of tasks—can feel like tiresome impediments to some very successful journalistic personalities: they don't want to be in a structure that will slow them down.

> ### THE IDEAL INVESTIGATOR
> **CANTANKEROUS**
> but
> **BIDDABLE**
> **IMAGINATIVE**
> but
> **PEDANTIC**

INVESTIGATIVE GOOD PRACTICE: WORKING IN TEAMS

As an alternative to working in pairs, full-scale team working has now become a relatively fashionable way of structuring media investigations. It is a technique whose use has ebbed and flowed with the fortunes of various media outlets. Harry Evans in the 1960s launched the concept in Britain with the famous *Sunday Times* Insight Team—it had a large budget and some highly distinguished reporters as members, including Philip Knightley, Elaine Potter, and Bruce Page.

With Evans' departure, this unit lingered on at Murdoch's *Sunday Times*, doing less valuable work and sometimes using questionable methods. The *Observer* set up a rival team in the 1980s, with a much smaller budget and a core membership of just two people—myself and a researcher, Paul Lashmar. It did not survive the disarray into which the

Observer fell in later years. The prominent TV teams of the 1990s, at This Week and World in Action, were also disbanded with the demise of those programmes, leaving only the venerable BBC Panorama still in operation.

The twenty-first century saw the revival of team journalism at Alan Rusbridger's *Guardian*, with a group that did large-scale work on, for example, corporate tax avoidance; the Wikileaks disclosures of US military and diplomatic dispatches; offshore finance; and Edward Snowden's intelligence disclosures.

This unit grew out of two significant developments in the field of investigative journalism, which will be analysed in detail in a following chapter. One was technical—the accumulation of large electronic databases in the world led, inevitably, to the leaking of some of them, and the need to develop new means to search and analyse what were relatively gigantic quantities of information.

The other development was structural—with the decline of conventional print media came a rise in cross-border collaborations by investigative journalists, often in concert with non-profit foundations such as the International Consortium of Investigative Journalists.

The technological shift has had an impact on individual investigative journalists. To take part in the most important projects, a reporter now has to be prepared to work in a group—often a cross-border team. The most successful of these teams do not use the old *Sunday Times* model, which had a relatively large set of permanently employed reporters, and a sizeable budget.

Under that structure, the team would then, in effect, sit about trying to think of something to investigate. It is cheaper, more realistic, and more effective to assemble ad hoc teams, depending on the story and the nature of the material—teams which will then largely disperse afterwards. Projects become story-led rather than department-led.

To deal with the Afghan and Iraq "war logs", for example, one of the earliest big data troves which came from a US database leaked by Private Chelsea Manning, the *Guardian* pulled together a team in London with three quite different elements—a small number of core editors co-ordinating the search and writing process; a set of *Guardian* specialist writers brought back from Afghanistan and the Middle East who understood the contexts; and a group of collaborators from other overseas media, including the *New York Times* and Der Spiegel [27]. The team coalesced: then afterwards, it split back into its component parts.

To make all this work requires diplomatic and people skills, as those of us involved were to learn—sometimes painfully. A good investigative reporter nowadays is someone who can swim in all waters.

INVESTIGATIVE GOOD BEHAVIOUR

LEARN TO CO-OPERATE

FIND PARTNERS

KEEP A LOW PROFILE

STAY ORGANISED

BE A DIPLOMAT

REFERENCES

1. IPI. 2000. Veronica Guerin, Ireland World Press Freedom Hero. Accessed November 11, 2018. https://web.archive.org/web/20120318032106/http://www.freemedia.at/awards/veronica-guerin/.
2. Veronica Guerin. 2003. Director Joel Schumacher. Touchstone Pictures.
3. Parfitt, Tom, 2006. The Only Good Journalist... *Guardian.* Accessed November 11, 2018. https://www.theguardian.com/world/2006/oct/10/russia.media.
4. Biddle, Sam. 2016. Top Secret Snowden Document Reveals What the NSA Knew About Previous Russian Hacking. *The Intercept.* Accessed November 11, 2018. https://www.documentcloud.org/documents/3247784-Anna-Politkovskaya-Intellipedia-Redacted.html#document/p1.
5. Kurmanaev, Anatoly. 2018. Russia Criticized for Handling of Anna Politkovskaya Probe. *Wall Street Journal.* Accessed November 11, 2018. https://www.wsj.com/articles/russia-criticized-for-handling-of-anna-politkovskaya-probe-1531828270.
6. Garside, Julia. 2018. A Bomb Silenced Daphne Caruana Galizia But Her Investigation Lives on. *Guardian.* Accessed November 12, 2018. https://www.theguardian.com/world/2018/apr/17/a-bomb-silenced-daphne-caruana-galizia-but-her-investigation-lives-on.
7. Galizia, Daphne Caruana. 2017. There are crooks everywhere you look. *Running Commentary.* Accessed November 12, 2018. https://daphnecaruanagalizia.com/2017/10/crook-schembri-court-today-pleading-not-crook/.
8. Atwood, Margaret. 2018. A Year After Her Murder, Where Is the Justice for Daphne Caruana Galizia? *Guardian.* Accessed November 12, 2018. https://www.theguardian.com/commentisfree/2018/oct/16/murder-justice-daphne-caruana-galizia-malta.

9. Accessed November 12, 2018. https://forbiddenstories.org/about-us/.
10. ——, 2018. https://www.ire.org/about/history/.
11. Baldwin, Tom, and Andrew Pierce. 1999. Drugs Agency Has Ashcroft on Its Files. *Times*, July 17.
12. Ashcroft, Michael. 2009. *Dirty Politics, Dirty Times*. London: Biteback.
13. Robertson, Geoffrey. 2018. *Rather His Own Man*. London: Biteback.
14. Times. 1999. Ashcroft Affair: Statement on the Settlement. *Times*, December 9.
15. Whittingdale, John. 2012. DCMS Committee. Accessed November 12, 2018. https://www.parliament.uk/business/committees/committees-a-z/commons-select/culture-media-and-sport-committee/news/121023-bbc-and-js-ev/.
16. Watson, Tom. 2012. Prime Minister's Questions. *House of Commons*. Accessed 12 November 2018. https://publications.parliament.uk/pa/cm201213/cmhansrd/cm121024/debtext/121024-0001.htm.
17. News Agency Report. 2014. Charles Napier Admits String of Historic Sex Offences Against Boys. *Telegraph*. Accessed November 12, 2018. https://www.telegraph.co.uk/news/uknews/law-and-order/11238339/Charles-Napier-admits-string-of-historic-sex-offences-against-boys.html.
18. Sherwin, Adam. 2013. Twitter Libel: Sally Bercow Says She Has Learned 'The Hard Way'. Accessed November 12, 2018. https://www.independent.co.uk/news/uk/crime/twitter-libel-sally-bercow-says-she-has-learned-the-hard-way-as-she-settles-with-tory-peer-lord-8630653.html.
19. BBC Trust. 2012. Newsnight: McQuarrie Report. Accessed November 14, 2018. https://www.bbc.co.uk/news/uk-20784534.
20. Entwhistle, George. 2012. Statement from George Entwhistle. *BBC Media Centre*. Accessed November 14, 2018. https://www.bbc.co.uk/mediacentre/statements/george-entwistle.html.
21. Plunkett, John. 2012. How Mark Watts of Exaro Aims to Return to Fleet Street's Golden Age. *Guardian*. Accessed November 14, 2018. https://www.theguardian.com/media/2012/sep/30/mark-watts-exaro.
22. Conrad, Mark. 2014. Met's VIP Paedophiles Probe Turns into Murder Investigation. *Exaro*, January 11.
23. Dodd, Vikram. 2018. Man Who Said He Was Victim of VIP Child Sexual Abuse Ring Charged. *Guardian*, July 8.
24. Davis, Nick. 2014. *Hack Attack: How the Truth Caught up with Rupert Murdoch*. London: Chatto & Windus.
25. Hersh, Seymour M. 1972. Cover-up. *New Yorker*, January 22
26. Jennings, Andrew. 2015. Fifa, Sepp Blatter and Me. *BBC Panorama*. Accessed November 14, 2018. https://www.bbc.co.uk/programmes/b06tkl9d.
27. Harding, Luke, and David Leigh. 2013. *Wikileaks: Inside Julian Assange's War on Secrecy*. London: Guardian Books.

CHAPTER 9

Cross-border Collaboration

THE INTERNATIONAL CONSORTIUM OF INVESTIGATIVE JOURNALISTS

Chuck Lewis, a visionary US TV journalist, was one of the people who started a revolution—and I was lucky enough to be there during its early days. He launched an approach that transformed the practice of investigative journalism over the ensuing 20 years; and it has been a very exhilarating experience. But it means that we have all had to learn to operate in a new way.

I first heard of Lewis around the turn of the millennium, whilst I was working as an editor in London for the *Guardian*. I got a letter from America inviting me to join his newly invented "International Consortium of Investigative Journalists". The letter reassured me rapidly that no payment of money was required. Instead, he said, it would be a means of giving work to experienced reporters.

Any doubts I had dissolved when I recognised my two listed fellow founder-members from the UK as highly distinguished practitioners. One was Duncan Campbell—the veteran Scottish-born investigator who has helped expose government intelligence agency eavesdropping over two decades, in the teeth of more gagging injunctions and Official Secrets Act prosecutions than most (see Chap. 6). And the other was Australian-born Phillip Knightley, whose fame rested on breaking open the Kim Philby scandal for the old pre-Murdoch *Sunday Times*. His then newly published autobiography "A Hack's Progress", was already a classic [1].

© The Author(s) 2019
D. Leigh, *Investigative Journalism*,
https://doi.org/10.1007/978-3-030-16752-3_9

A free plane ticket to Boston followed on from Lewis's letter, with an invitation to spend a weekend at Harvard helping set up the ICIJ scheme. At the university hall in Cambridge, Massachusetts, Lewis had collected together a crowd of around 50 other investigators from all over the world. Some I'd heard of, some I hadn't. A large and powerful woman with flashing eyes proved to be Yevgenia Albats from Moscow. The wiry figure next to her at the buffet table was Yossi Melman, then the brilliant intelligence specialist from the Hebrew-language Tel Aviv daily, *Ha'aretz*. There was a polite environmental journalist from Japan and an impressively bearded bruiser from Panama. I already knew people like Campbell and Knightley could be belligerent in their separate ways. And altogether, this was a very unlikely collection of people to get together in one room. Their general stance of conflict with the authorities seemed likely to generate a quantity of truculence in the air that could rise way off the scale. How on earth was anyone going to get them to agree about anything?

At the time, I thought Lewis' mission statement for the donor-funded ICIJ sounded optimistic, and, to be honest, even a touch self-righteous. His plan was "to conduct investigative projects across nation-state borders on the premise that an enlightened populace is an empowered populace". This one-time producer on CBS's flagship programme 60 Minutes set out to strike a high-minded note in promoting his aims:

> For decades, people around the world have seen or heard news of global events simultaneously, from political and economic scandals to wars and natural disasters. But the commercial demands of the news industry have often meant that such information is brief, disjointed, and confusing.

His grand scheme was that "ICIJ and its cadre of international journalists investigate major global issues that affect us all". [2] Underlying the inspirational rhetoric was a brutal fact. Regular journalism had a lot of catching up to do. Newspapers and broadcasters had been working to an old model in which the news was essentially domestic (with occasional excursions to inspect the doings of foreigners). But the world had already turned global and was becoming much more so.

The clothes on people's backs came from Vietnam or China. The factories in which they worked were owned by the Japanese and imported their components from Romania or Slovakia. The money they spent on buying things was sluiced offshore through tax havens and secrecy jurisdictions in

Dublin, Luxembourg, and the British Virgin Islands. Tanks and planes they built were sold to Middle Eastern potentates via bribes paid into Swiss banks, recirculating funds those rulers got from global sales of oil— its brokers sending tankers steaming continuously round the world, looking for ports where they might unload at the best rates. African email conversations were routed by US tech companies through servers in Finland, whilst being intercepted en route beneath the oceans by British intelligence agencies.

To confront all these globalised developments, ICIJ was a collaborative spin-off from Lewis's little existing non-profit parent body, the Center for Public Integrity. This was already based in an office in Washington DC and had published domestic US investigative reports since its inception a decade before. The centre's work included "The Buying of the President", a useful study of the intersection of money and politics in the American campaign system.

But to splice together a heterogeneous crowd of foreign journalists and find a way for them to work jointly—this was a much more tricky exercise. Some had staff jobs on their own local papers or TV channels and wanted scoops for their own organisations. Others were freelancers, who needed sources of income rather than vague protestations of goodwill to the world. Journalistic stances and standards varied wildly.

What Lewis understood, however, was that the power of Internet links was changing everything. His group of what he saw as a potential worldwide order of dedicated "Jedi Knights" [3, p. 18] would be linked together by secure email, would be able to pool their knowledge, and could publish simultaneously across national borders, using local media partners to amplify their impact.

Lewis's scheme managed to tap into something psychologically interesting—the sense of camaraderie and the love of detective work that it seems bind investigative reporters together the world over. It also offered a professional means by which everybody could win.

By the time of the second ICIJ international conference—at Stanford University the following year—Maud Beelman, a veteran foreign correspondent for Associated Press, had been hired as operations director. The ICIJ's first big global investigation was finally under way, in conditions of secrecy. It brought together some, though not yet all, of the distinctive elements that were to characterise future cross-border collaborations.

BIG TOBACCO AND BIG DATA: THE BAT INVESTIGATION

Our first investigation did involve Big Data, as would many of its successors. But this initial multinational project was primitive: there was no database. Instead, the data resided in a physical warehouse in an English country town, housing a mountain of paper. The global tobacco multinational, BAT, had settled a US lawsuit brought by the state of Minnesota, on condition that they made their internal company files available to researchers for a period of 10 years. Dismayed, BAT had persuaded a judge only to allow access via an archive near their British headquarters in Guildford. And they did not help inquirers understand what the contents of their records might signify. But these obscure files covered their operations in virtually every country on the globe.

Funded by a donor foundation, Beelman recruited Duncan Campbell in Britain as a consultant. "We had to be granted a place" Campbell says: "BAT lawyers constantly introduced rules. They would say there were a maximum of six places available. Or only one organisation at a time was allowed in. Then, suddenly, all the available places were booked up for weeks ahead. The staff there were clearly told to be polite but everything was as difficult as it could be". At one point, tobacco campaigners enlisted the original Minnesota state lawyers to threaten BAT with a return to court and a revocation of their special dispensation to set up a depository out of US jurisdiction. BAT then grudgingly complied. A six-month process resumed of scanning BAT indexes of thousands of documents, ordering up potentially interesting files, and trying to interpret their contents.

The journalists succeeded in proving that BAT executives had been colluding in the worldwide smuggling of cigarettes. The company could make just as much money from wholesaling smuggled products as it did from marketing heavily taxed legitimate ones—sometimes indeed a lot more money—as smugglers could penetrate markets and countries from which the tobacco giant was officially barred. Naturally, these facts were strenuously denied by people at the firm. But the reporters succeeded in piercing through a screen of euphemisms used to speak of smuggling in the documents—"DNP product" (for "Duty Not Paid"); "General Trade"; or "Transit".

In a classic episode of cross-fertilisation, Campbell came across a regular sales destination in the Guildford depository files named "San Andresitos". It seemed likely to be in Latin America, but he could not trace it on any map. Beelman in Washington then consulted a third team member from Colombia, Maria Teresa Ronderos. She laughed. "San Andresitos" was in fact the local slang for the black market [4]. As the *Guardian* put it: "This was a group of investigative reporters whose newsroom was the world" [2].

Just as the journalistic team was cross-border, so, unprecedentedly, was the method of publication. The *Guardian*, the first mainstream partner to give credibility to the enterprise, printed a 3000-word story in English [5]. Simultaneously, Maria Teresa Ronderos ran a Spanish-language version in her Colombian magazine, La Nota. ICIJ launched the parallel story on their Washington-based website, and Channel 4 news followed it on British TV. The *Guardian* joint by-line was unusual for a British daily paper: it read "By Maud S Beelman; Duncan Campbell; Maria Teresa Ronderos; Erik J Schelzig", thus crediting two ICIJ employees; a British freelancer; and a Latin-American magazine editor.

Significantly, the ICIJ as yet had no mainstream US partners on this project. The initial attitude of such established Anglophone outlets as the *New York Times* was uncomprehending, not to say disdainful. As the business model upheavals of the twenty-first century gathered speed, that media attitude was to change. People began to understand that togetherness was a necessary new way of doing things.

FARMSUBSIDY.ORG

Over the next few years, the idea of cross-border collaboration began to spread more generally. A creative Brussels-based journalist, Brigitte Alfter, organised a Europe-wide project to reveal the identity of the thousands of beneficiaries of European Union subsidies—payments supposedly meant to aid the continued survival of small peasant farmers.

The story began in 2004, when two Danish journalists got hold of some names relating to Denmark. The European Commission turned down a freedom of information request by Alfter for data from the whole of the EU. She and others retaliated by founding Farmsubsidy.org. The online network helped domestic journalists throughout Europe to make country-by-country requests, in order to get access to the data that way. Alfter says: "The Farmsubsidy.org team created a win-win: the team's techniques were useful for journalists on the national level to do a story they otherwise did not have the skills for, and the Farmsubsidy team could compile the European data set pieced together through national freedom of information requests" [6]. The upshot was the discovery that the biggest beneficiaries of EU cash across Europe were not peasant farmers, but in fact aristocrats, politicians, and big agribusiness.

At around the same time, the *Guardian* in London began running a series of investigations into the arms giant BAe. This was a much looser style of cross-border collaboration, simply setting up a series of bilateral transactions with fellow-journalists in the BBC and in Sweden, South Africa, Romania, and Tanzania. These links ranged from the mere sharing of information to—in the more elaborate Swedish case—also taking part in an undercover "sting" using a Briton as actor. At the same time, the *Guardian* collaborated with British police authorities and also with activist NGOs. The UK government's covert involvement with bribery in arms sales was detailed in one initial large dataset which underpinned the investigation. This was, once again, data of a primitive kind—it consisted of a physical store of typed paper documents held in Britain's national archives, in a bunker near the famous botanical gardens at Kew (see Chap. 3).

Big Data Leaks: Hacking and Searchability

In 2010, a new development arrived. This was the advent of electronic Big Data Leaks. They changed the journalistic game. The Internet was by now bringing vast online datasets into being, compiled by governments, intelligence agencies, and businesses. As they came into existence, of course, they could be leaked—and leaked with lightning speed across national borders. It was a technological change which kicked the practice of collaborative journalism up several gears. Crucial to this renewed thrust were two novel phenomena—hacking and searchability.

A hacker is, to put it bluntly, a person who knows how to steal electronic information. The skills required are very different from those of the old-fashioned whistleblower, who only had to know how to photocopy sheets of paper. The US leaker Daniel Ellsberg back in 1971 Xeroxed the 47 volumes and thousands of pages of the secret Pentagon Papers one by one, taking a long time and lots of effort to do it [7].

Now files that were bigger than that by many orders of magnitude could be loaded onto a disc, or a tiny USB stick, or magically downloaded from the ether itself in no time at all. A problem with this new phenomenon was that hacker skills seemed too arcane for ordinary journalists to master—and yet it would turn out that the hacker temperament was often very different from that of the professional reporter who would end up having to rely on them.

Searchability, on the other hand, was an astonishing new quality which investigative reporters could indeed easily use for themselves. With the help of pieces of software, some more elaborate than others, the journalists could make huge datasets speak to them. Using keywords and phrases, they could interrogate the files for information and discern novel patterns, despite the fact that no human could ever actually read such enormous masses of material from beginning to end.

These new techniques did not make the conventional journalistic mindset obsolete—on the contrary, it meant that it was more important than ever to have a journalistic understanding of what questions it might be in the public interest to ask. It also meant that investigative journalists had to learn the shortcomings of data—that it could be "dirty", and limited by the behaviour of the original compilers. Some "data journalists" were in the future to find it all too easy to be dazzled by datasets. They would have to learn all over again the truth of the statisticians' motto: "Garbage in, garbage out".

Wikileaks

Wikileaks was the first really big data leak. The files came from a disaffected US soldier, Chelsea Manning, who called herself a "hacktivist". The US military, who were after all the original progenitors of the idea of the Internet, had by now built an elaborate and worldwide online system called SIPRNET (Secret Internet Protocol Router Network). Even a junior intelligence analyst like Manning could access it. From a remote desert outpost in Iraq, she worked out how to use her computer terminal to scrape and download this classified military material on to a disc of her own. Then she walked out of the army building, uploaded her haul back on to the civilian Internet, and sent it, re-encrypted, to "a crazy white-haired Aussie who can't seem to stay in one country very long" [8, p. 78].

This Aussie was Julian Assange, a hacker who had pioneered the notion that mass data leaking could change the world. Having stumbled on ways of breaking into international communications, he and a small group of supporters set up "Wikileaks". Their idea was that hackers could post their purloined raw material online, and crowd-sourced explanations would interpret it all. The leaks would be uncensorable and legally untouchable, as they would be uploaded from servers in faraway places. The encrypted leaks would be untraceable back to their source, of whom even Assange himself would always be unaware.

This concept was never to work out in practice the way Assange originally envisioned it, but Private Manning decided she wanted to join his
crusade. One of the first pieces of material she sent over was a hair-raising
piece of video footage she had found in an army legal file.

Assange himself was awestruck by it. I met him for the first time in
Norway, in March 2010 at an investigative journalists' conference where
he had been invited to speak. Late at night, he could not resist coming up
to my hotel room in the little town of Tonsberg, locking the door, and
playing over the footage. I was shocked too by what I saw. It was the video
and audio from an Apache helicopter gunship hovering invisibly a kilome-
tre up in the sky over Baghdad, as its heavy machine-gun blasted a group
of people around a van in one of the city streets. The .50 calibre bullets
scattered them like rag dolls. The footage was the more shocking because
two innocent children were wounded, whilst among those killed were a
Reuters war photographer and his driver.

Assange wanted to be his own journalist. He called a press conference
in Washington DC, played the leaked video file, and labelled it "Collateral
Murder". Although he caused a sensation, he did not get the political
reaction he wanted. This was partly because of his browbeatingly tenden-
tious title: the victims had in fact been killed by mistake. It was clear from
the recorded conversations that the helicopter crew wrongly believed they
were firing on armed insurgents.

Nick Davies of the *Guardian* eventually persuaded Assange it would be
a better idea to share the rest of Private Manning's material with the
much-derided "MSM" (for "mainstream media"). This would make better sense of the leaks and market them to the world.

The result of his negotiations was a series of joint exposures in the
Guardian; the *New York Times*; and Der Spiegel. Eventually, *Le Monde* in
France and El Pais in Spain were to join the MSM consortium as well.
These investigative stories analysed large databases detailing every significant military event involving US and allied forces, both during the invasion of Iraq and during the relentless fighting in Afghanistan. They also
detailed the contents of a third database, containing the texts of thousands
of US diplomatic cables sent back to Washington from nearly every
embassy in the world, and classified up to "secret" (a fairly high level,
although by no means the highest).

The *Guardian*'s eventual front page headlines, written over four
months, give a flavour: "MASSIVE LEAK OF SECRET FILES EXPOSES
TRUE AFGHAN WAR" (26 July 2010); "SEE NO EVIL: SECRET

FILES SHOW HOW US IGNORED IRAQI TORTURE" (23 October) "250,000 LEAKED FILES THAT LAY BARE US VIEW OF THE WORLD" (29 November).

But to reach this point of successful publication involved new difficulties for investigative journalists. The challenges came in three areas—technical, operational, and ethical.

SOFTWARE, DECODING, AND DATA VISUALISATION

Technically, the first Wikileaks problem was that the documents were enormous—a daunting total, in those days, of 1.65 gigabits. The second problem was that they also seemed incomprehensible. The Iraqi and Afghan data, in particular, was written in clipped military jargon, spattered with unknown acronyms. By recruiting reporters to the team who had been out working in those countries during the fighting, in particular *New York Times* specialists who had been embedded with US troops, we were eventually able to penetrate the SIGACT ["significant activity"] reports, scribbling translations of acronyms on a whiteboard as each in turn was identified. A big breakthrough came, for example, when "EKIA" was decoded as "Enemy Killed in Action", giving us the means to start a body-count.

The large size of the data dumps was a problem once again to be solved by enlarging the team. All the SIGACTS and all the diplomatic cables were written in a rigid bureaucratic format. Date, time, geographical co-ordinates, signatures, embassy locations, outcomes, casualties, narrative text—all appeared in the same place, in the identical style, in every document. So we could recruit tech engineers, who could write automated scripts that would re-cast this material into searchable databases.

We were naïve, initially. One of our first attempts was to populate the Afghan data into a simple Excel spreadsheet. It came out at 60,000 different rows of material. Our colleagues from Der Spiegel, we eventually discovered, were using a similar spreadsheet, but with not 63,000 but 92,201 entries. Why the discrepancy? It turned out that we had been using an early version of Excel, with limited capacity. When it reached the figure of 60,000, it simply stopped. Without telling us. We had accidentally deleted a big chunk of our own data.

Eventually, however, we were provided with a proper database. We could then search for every cable from a particular country, for example; or every landmine explosion on a particular date; or indeed, for every incidence of purported EKIA. Many of the casualties were officially classed by those who wrote them up afterwards as "Enemy", even though contemporary accounts of some notorious incidents suggested that many of the dead were in fact innocent civilians. It made the data often suspect. This was our first attempt to grapple with data journalism, and we had to learn to make journalistic judgments about history and provenance, not just gleefully manipulate the figures.

Working with Wikileaks data was really an upside-down form of journalism. Conventionally, an investigative reporter is told a story of wrongdoing, and then tries to find the documents to prove it. Here, we were provided with a vast mass of documents to start with, and then had to try and find out if there were stories in them. The basic technique was straightforward searches of key words—for example, to collect all the details of "KIA" and study each incident where there were admitted civilian deaths—(civilians proved to be coded as "WHITE", with local afghan forces coded "GREEN").

Once the jargon was understood, some further stories presented themselves. We were able to collect, for example, all incidents of "BLUE ON WHITE". This revealed every occasion on which, to the knowledge of the US, allied British forces killed civilians. Such incidents had never previously been publicly reported. Using these revelations, we were then able to press the British ministry of defence for further details, using FOI requests and researching military blogs. This revealed further stories.

One particular unit, for example, was revealed by this analysis to have shot up unusually large numbers of civilians whilst on patrol in Kabul. Further research showed the fault may have lain with their commanders—the unit were switched at short notice to urban patrolling with insufficient training. Terrified of bombs, they opened fire on any civilian vehicle that approached their convoys too closely.

People who don't know anything about it sometimes assume "leak journalism" is an easy alternative to "real" journalism. They imagine that public interest exposures are simply handed over on a plate. In fact, the process of making sense of such leaked data can require even more than the usual kinds of hard work.

It also requires a different approach to the technical problems of layout. By the time Private Manning's data landed on our screens, new methods of online presentation were well advanced. A project could include what we called "multiple points of access"—hyperlinks through to images of original documents; video mini-documentaries; podcasts; animations. The

Guardian had indeed by now reached the point of employing a full-time "data visualiser". With his help, we experimented with new ways of making such data speak.

One of the most ambitious was a project to reveal the true course of the fighting in Afghanistan by plotting every single one of the hundreds of roadside bombs (IEDs or "Improvised Explosive Devices") that wreaked such havoc. Thanks to the great detail in the data, we could plot the IED blasts not only on a map of the endangered roads, but also by date and time, and number and type of victims. With one click of a mouse the visualisation could be set running, and would reveal the ebb and flow of bombing over five years as, by and large, everything got not better, but worse. This visualisation offered a unique way of understanding an otherwise invisible war. But, of course, it also required yet another addition to our interdisciplinary, international team, cloistered in their secretive London "war room". These technical projects are not cheap or simple.

SIMULTANEOUS PUBLICATION AND TENSIONS WITH PARTNERS

The operational problems with the Wikileaks data were also considerable. All big and sensitive cross-border collaborations need careful management. The first rule is generally that all media partners must publish more or less simultaneously. This has two purposes. The first is to protect each publisher from being individually pressured or gagged. This was particularly important when dealing with classified US government documents.

The second purpose—equally vital—is to stop any one outlet from scooping the others. That would not only cause rancour, but also collapse any future collaborations. It can be imagined how tricky simultaneous publication was to organise when the partners operated in different time zones. Furthermore, *Le Monde* came out in the afternoon, while the other papers published in the morning. Der Spiegel meanwhile, was a German magazine that only published once a week...

The most white-knuckle moment came in fact with Der Spiegel. They printed copies of the magazine and distributed them around Europe on trucks under strict embargo. But a railway bookstall in Basel started to sell them early. A tweeter purchased a copy, was intrigued, and started to re-post the contents online. There was panic. Everyone else's deadlines were pushed forward and the day was narrowly saved.

There were plenty of other managerial issues involved. We were trying to strike novel agreements between a group of international media who had not operated before as journalistic partners. It only worked because of high-level co-operation at the editorial level, notably between Alan Rusbridger of the *Guardian* and Bill Keller of the *New York Times*. While individual investigative journalists may have a sense of common purpose about cross-border stories, these kinds of big projects can only succeed if there is interest and commitment at the very top. For some reporters at media new to the game, that may involve educating editors.

By and large, the mainstream media worked well together, with a relatively smooth set of professional understandings. What was more difficult was to work with Assange, the Wikileaks hacker, who had a different agenda. He certainly understood that it was to his benefit to ride on the back of the worldwide publicity that MSM newspapers could generate. But he could not resist the temptation to try and "discipline" them, primarily by drip-feeding the material which had fallen into his hands.

One of my own particularly tricky tasks as co-ordinator of the London end of this project, was to manage Assange. This involved putting him up in my house when he flew into London with nowhere to stay—and persuading him to hand over all Manning's remaining files. The situation was further complicated when an Icelandic former colleague of Assange fell out with him and handed over a rival copy of all the data to a freelance British journalist, Heather Brooke. She too had to be brought into the partnership.

The question of who had control of the files became a struggle: it erupted into a sulphurous row when Assange tried to prevent the *Guardian* sharing the material, as previously agreed, with the *New York Times*: he objected to a critical piece the US paper had published about his quarrels with his own staff. Assange also objected to the newspapers printing detailed complaints of sexual misbehaviour made against him by two women in Sweden: he was seeking, by contrast, to promote the self-interested idea they were part of a CIA conspiracy against him. It took a lot of diplomacy to keep the show on the road for the time it took to publish.

Self-Censorship

Journalists don't, however, publish everything they know. They do self-censor. This is partly guided by the industry codes of ethical practice. These are drawn up by voluntary regulators such as IMPRESS or IPSO for newspapers; by state regulators such as OFCOM for the BBC and other broadcasters; and by in-house codes for employees of individual papers, such as the *Guardian*. To take simple examples, British media generally will not publish detailed methods of suicide or identify vulnerable children.

Sometimes, however, it gets more complicated. The Iraq and Afghanistan war logs in particular contained details of military attacks from which it would be possible for anyone with local knowledge sometimes to work out which individuals had given information to the Americans. To all the US and European journalists, it was obvious that we didn't publish such details. There seemed to be a clear moral duty not to endanger other people's lives.

There was also a practical virtue to saying so loudly and clearly. Faced with accusations that we were breaking laws and aiding what could be said to be in effect military treason, we wanted to identify ourselves as good citizens, acting carefully and in the public interest. This also meant we were not willing to give free access to the material to scores of strangers around the world, even if they said they were journalists.

None of these concerns resonated very much with Julian Assange. In his counter-cultural moral universe, the whole point of Wikileaks was to publish big data leaks in their entirety. This would "free information", fully empowering the citizens alongside the elite, and upending the structures of political control. It was also a commonplace view in hacker circles that the MSM, in thrall as they were to US imperialism, already spent far too much of their time censoring the truth.

Arguing with the journalists about the likely fate of US informants, Assange memorably said: "If they get killed, they've got it coming to them. They deserve it" [8, p. 111]. In the end, he did dump out all the data via his own Wikileaks operation. As far as we know, nobody did die. But the debate revealed an ethical chasm between us.

And relations irreparably soured. Assange's biographer, Andrew O'Hagan, recorded what the Australian said of myself: "What a sleazy cocksucker. Who does he think he's talking to?" [9]. When the *Guardian* journalists wrote a history of the whole affair, Assange's reaction was abusive. He wrote that it was a "toxic, biased book. Published and written by people we have had a bitter contractual dispute with for years, whose hostility is well known" [10].

There was a subsequent movie about Wikileaks, *The Fifth Estate*, starring Benedict Cumberbatch as Assange. But he was equally violent about

that: "Distorted truth about living people doing battle with titanic opponents... A work of political opportunism, influence, revenge and, above
all, cowardice" [10].

Assange eventually retreated into a back room in the small Ecuadorian
embassy in London, claiming political asylum. He was to spend more than
5 years there in flight from the US and from Swedish authorities over the
sex allegations, until his expulsion and eventual British arrest. He appeared
to have been exploited by Putin's Russia in 2016 to circulate hacked emails
embarrassing to presidential contender Hilary Clinton in order to promote the election of Donald Trump. This largely marked his political eclipse.

Was the correct conclusion from the Wikileaks saga that investigative
journalists and hackers simply don't mix? Or were there to prove to be
other collaborative models that would work better for journalism in the
new era of mass data leaks?

Offshore Leaks

Evidence that other, more successful, models could be devised soon followed. There was a renaissance by the then venerable International
Consortium of Investigative Journalists. This was thanks to another
Australian of a very different character, Gerard Ryle. Ryle is a highly professional journalist of Irish extraction, a former deputy editor of the
Canberra Times and an investigative editor at the Sydney Morning Herald.
In [DEL1911 DEL] 2011, he agreed to move to Washington DC with his
wife and take over the donor-funded ICIJ. He transformed it with a series
of massive projects that revealed an entire universe of offshore tax avoidance and money-laundering. Ryle's acquisition of large caches of leaked
data enabled him to build cross-border collaboration on a truly global
scale, that eventually came to recruit scores of journalists. It also changed
the political weather.

I was one of those who gathered at Kiev in the Ukraine in October
2011, when Ryle unveiled his initial plans to his ICIJ circle. We met
behind the scenes of the conference organised by GIJN (the Global
Investigative Journalists Network). Ryle had been publishing work in
Australia on tax avoidance. As a result, he was in contact with a whistleblower who had supplied him with years of data scraped from the internal
files of two firms who specialised in setting up shell companies in the
British Virgin Islands.

The BVI is a Caribbean mini-state, still controlled at arm's length by the British who had first colonised it. It derives much of its income from the sale of financial secrecy. A BVI entity would not disclose any accounting information or reveal the identity of its true owners; its offshore-controlled bank account, whilst a vehicle for some perfectly legal "tax-haven" manoeuvres, was also an ideal channel for money-laundering; illegal tax dodging; or financial crime.

Ryle's preliminary sampling of his data revealed the astonishing scale of a financial universe that was inaccessible to conventional business journalists. The two BVI incorporation firms had set up more than 100,000 companies. And they in turn represented only about 10% of the booming BVI offshore industry. The *Guardian* and the BBC agreed to work jointly with Ryle to find technical means of cracking the content and bringing it to light. Subsequently, the ICIJ partnered with a further wide range of local journalists in countries all over the world to expose the offshore activities of their particular citizens. It took more than a year of work before the first British media partners were in a position to publish.

Once again, the problems this kind of journalism faces can be broken down into technical, operational, and ethical issues.

Offshore Leaks: Software Solutions

The Wikileaks data dump had confronted the journalists with 1.65 GB of rigidly structured material that was relatively straightforward to automate into a database. With the offshore material, when a large portable hard drive thumped on to my desk in London from the hands of a Fedex courier, its contents were much more dismaying. They totalled a staggering 200 GB. Furthermore, the material was wildly unstructured. Its variety of formats included account ledgers; Excel spreadsheets; images of passports; and copies of messages in obsolete email applications. Some of the material stretched back 30 years.

Our salvation this time was a sophisticated platform of Australian origin called Nuix. Ryle negotiated a deal with the manufacturers to let us experiment with this extremely expensive software, which was used by law enforcement agencies to process complex case-files. The manufacturers claimed that their engine could ingest email and other formats and make them instantly searchable "across a virtually unlimited quantity of unstructured data". Their boasts proved correct—or at least they proved correct when the *Guardian* went out to buy a much more powerful machine than its ordinary newsroom terminals. It took many hours for the new computer to digest this huge assortment of other people's correspondence. But the results were worth it.

Once we broke into the data, there were then the predictable problems in understanding what we were reading. The BVI companies frequently took their instructions in turn from intermediaries—"wealth management" firms in London, Russia or Hong Kong—who generally did not mention the true identities of their customers. If one tracked all the correspondence, sometimes, however, a name or a true address would slip out. But often the identity of the "beneficial owner" would remain a mystery, despite all our efforts. Sometimes messages about a property purchase would reveal its whereabouts: sometimes not.

Occasionally, the BVI companies would make half-hearted attempts to establish the true ownership of the entities they were setting up—but the identity documents with which they were supplied were just as likely to be themselves proxies or relatives, behind whom a Russian or Indian oligarch could continue to hide.

Much as with Wikileaks, it was not enough for the journalists to break into another world: they then had to learn to understand the language that was being spoken, and play detective. But we found enough devastating information to justify the effort. As Ryle wrote, the final tally successfully laid bare an extraordinary range of people using these offshore hideaways, with customers from 170 territories all over the world:

> They include US dentists and middle-class Greek villagers as well as families of despots, Wall Street swindlers, Eastern European and Indonesian billionaires, Russian executives, international arms dealers and a company alleged to front for Iran's nuclear-development programme. [11]

One of the glories of searchability was that we were able to identify and expose a hired squad of sham company directors, many of them impecunious Britons living in obscure spots outside UK jurisdiction—Nevis, Dubai, Cyprus. "Nominee directors" allow their name to be used on registers, and they sign all the official company documents for hundreds or even thousands of offshore entities. But in fact, they do not control the companies and their bank accounts: the first pieces of paper they sign are an undated letter of resignation, and a "power of attorney" giving all their rights to the company's real owner. These sham directors are simply acting as fronts for secretive flows of money.

Another trick the database enabled us to expose was the sale and purchase of expensive London property, tax free. If a London house was bought in the name of an anonymous entity registered offshore in the BVI, it could be traded without incurring stamp duty—the tax on property purchases which can run to thousands of pounds. The house would never officially be sold—instead, the shares in the offshore company that owned it would simply be transferred to a new owner. Furthermore, the house could avoid UK inheritance tax if the owner died, and UK capital gains tax if it was sold at a profit. The manoeuvre was very popular: eventually, thousands of London houses were traced that had been bought in this way.

OFFSHORE LEAKS: TIMING AND ETHICS

Compared to the formidable technical problems, the other issues were relatively easy. The timing of publication proved awkward, because the second tier of local journalists recruited by ICIJ at a later stage were not ready to publish in a synchronised way with the *Guardian* and the BBC. In the end the British media, who had spent more than a year already on the project, went ahead in 2012, whilst the international group essentially followed up the next year.

Eventually, ICIJ learned from this episode: they re-structured procedure to enable them to do all their own preliminary in-house analysis in Washington DC. It could then be distributed simultaneously. ICIJ was also able to set up its own centralised database, to which all the partners could have remote online access through an elaborate system of passwords. By then, ICIJ had established so much international credibility that it was no longer so dependent on the goodwill of conventional media partners. Everyone wanted to be allowed to join in.

The final list of collaborators on the Offshore Leaks project included *Le Monde* in France, *Süddeutsche Zeitung*, and *Norddeutscher Rundfunk* in Germany, as well as the *Washington Post*, the Canadian Broadcasting Corporation (CBC), and 31 other media partners around the world. A role was played by no fewer than 86 journalists from 46 countries.

The ethical dimension was easier than with Wikileaks. No-one's life was potentially at stake, although some of the BVI customers we identified were liable to face unwelcome attention from their local tax or law enforcement authorities. We were, of course, obliged, both ethically and legally in Britain, to trace every individual we were planning to expose and give them the opportunity to explain why they apparently operated an offshore company. This took up a lot of time and energy: but it was inescapable.

ICIJ worked across jurisdictions, and its own publishing operations in Washington DC were largely legally fireproof against gagging injunctions thanks to the US First Amendment's constitutional protections. But all its international partners were, of course, subject to their own domestic laws. In practice, this means that ICIJ texts would be written to comply with the most onerous information laws of its partners—and in practice, this generally meant the laws of the British.

Although we often faced angry reactions and threats from our targets' lawyers when we confronted them before publication, this did not usually come to actual lawsuits: our hand in Britain was strengthened immeasurably by the fact that publication by ICIJ in the US could never be stopped. This is one of the beauties of cross-border collaboration.

LEAKS IN JERSEY, LUXEMBOURG, BAHAMAS, SWITZERLAND, PANAMA

Ryle and his team followed up the success of the "Offshore Leaks" project by obtaining a leaked series of new collaborative exposures from the offshore world. These were of ever-increasing magnitude. There were 50,000 names, many of them British, from the Kleinwort Benson "wealth management" firm in Jersey in the Channel Isles—another one of the City of London's offshore operations.

Next came "Luxleaks", a leak from international accountants PWC. This may have been a mere 28,000 documents, small enough to put on a memory stick, but it had seismic political effects. It showed that the firm was devising bespoke schemes under which big companies could get cheap tax deals from Luxembourg, by purporting to route their European profits through this EU micro-state of a mere 600,000 inhabitants. The former prime minister of Luxembourg, Jean-Claude Juncker, was now president of the European Commission itself. The business journal Bloomberg called on him—unavailingly—to resign:

> Juncker, you could say, made his country rich by picking the pockets of other countries, including those of the European Union he is now mandated to serve. [12]

From a practical journalist's point of view, there were two particularly striking aspects of Luxleaks. One was that it marked a growing trend for investigative reporters in one country to see the value of approaching an international group with their files. The prominent French journalist Edouard Perrin originally got hold of the rich material, and put out some stories with French and British TV. But his international impact—and the resources available—were greatly increased by ICIJ joining in.

Secondly, Perrin and his whistleblower sources faced legal attacks, having taken on one of the rich and powerful "Big Four" global accountancy firms. The house of a source was raided by French police, on allegations of theft and disclosure of trade secrets. But the co-ordinated publication by ICIJ in 26 countries strengthened Perrin's own legal hand. He told fellow-journalist Brigitte Alfter:

> "Since we were all indicted in the weeks after LuxLeaks broke, for us to be able to go to court with all that had been published, it's all ammunition that we could use in court. It was very helpful. I had that in mind even before we got in trouble. The louder you get the better...When you go and see the investigating judge, I felt I was not alone. We had well known media around the world, that could give the story unheard of leverage. The echo was enormous. If I had do it again, I'd do it again." [4]

Ryle and ICIJ went on next to crack open the activities of a Swiss bank. This time it was reporters from *Le Monde* in France who decided to share their riches with other journalists. The files had passed from a Swiss whistleblower, Herve Falciani, to the French tax authorities—who had done very little with it. This was no doubt for reasons of political embarrassment connected with the French names that appeared on the list.

The material had then found its way to *Le Monde* [13], who realised it had global possibilities—and indeed needed global resources that would unlock it. The data was a series of 30,000 customer records at a Swiss bank operated by the giant British firm, HSBC. The clients came from all over the world and the files revealed their identities, their interactions with the bank and the amounts in their accounts. Like the British Virgin Islands, Switzerland's stock-in-trade is financial secrecy—Swiss bankers can go to jail for revealing any of this information. As a result, their banks are magnets for tax-dodgers, corrupt politicians, and criminals.

Following a joint meeting of the intended collaborators in Paris, the *Guardian* led on the British end of operations: this was where HSBC was headquartered. I was called in by the paper to run a team assembled from business reporters, the core investigative team and outside experts. Our remote link to ICIJ was this time through their own online database.

Searchability was once again the key: it enabled us to demonstrate potential wrongdoing by the bank's officials. We were able to extract lists of customers from Britain and high-tax countries in Scandinavia, who would leave the bank in Geneva, and head home with their briefcases bulging with "bricks" of untraceable cash in their local currencies.

Similarly, we were able to collate files showing that when the EU sought to impose a general withholding tax on Swiss accounts, the bank systematically offered to help its customers circumvent it by switching their money into new accounts in the name not of individuals, but of offshore companies. People in the bank were well aware that it was a haven for tax-dodgers.

The most delicate task we carried out in London for ICIJ was to negotiate with HSBC. It demonstrated once again that, for investigative reporters, finding things out is only half the problem. The other half is the problem of successful publication. As soon as we asked a long list of customers why they had Swiss accounts, those alarmed clients rushed for their own lawyers. The bank's hired legal team began to utter ferocious threats to the *Guardian* and the ICIJ, trying to prevent publication. In dealing with this, we were to benefit from basic survival lessons learned over years of investigative journalism.

> *KEY SURVIVAL LESSONS*
>
> **UNDERSTAND YOUR OPPONENT'S THOUGHT-PROCESSES**
>
> **LITIGATION IS NOT THE ONLY WAY TO DEAL WITH LAWYERS**
>
> **COLLABORATION IS A SHIELD**

We realised that many of the account-holders were protesting to the Swiss bank that the bankers were not keeping secret their financial information, as advertised. This carried the implied threat that they could sue HSBC for failed security if we published. The bank was therefore trying to protect itself from its own angry customers by in turn, threatening us. The answer was not necessarily to embark on a legal fight to the death with HSBC: it was to reassure the bank.

We explained carefully to HSBC that we were happy to promise not to disclose any details of their individual customers—unless we found actual evidence of wrongdoing. From the bank's point of view, this was indeed reassuring. They could promise legitimate customers that nothing would be made public. The selected crooks and tax-dodgers that we proposed to identify, on the other hand, would not at all be likely to put their heads above the parapet by launching public lawsuits.

As for the bank's own position, we were able to explain to HSBC's public relations team that they would not save the bank's reputation by getting a UK legal gagging injunction against the *Guardian*. On the contrary, that would merely provide a bigger and better story—about the attempt at a cover-up—and it would be unstoppably published all round the world by ICIJ and their other foreign partners. Surely, it would be much better for the bank to say how shocked they were to discover unsavoury goings-on by their customers, and promise to tighten up...? They saw the point.

A culminating batch of ICIJ exposures—the Panama Papers and a year later the 2017 Paradise Papers—were again sparked by European journalists who realised that international collaboration was the key to exploiting hot material. This time it was two German reporters from *Süddeutsche Zeitung*, who turned over an enormous trove of 11.5 million leaked files to Gerard Ryle. It was never clear who was the original hacker who broke into these records, They were of the type western tax and intelligence authorities had by now shown themselves as willing to buy for quite large sums of money, for purposes of their own.

Eventually more than 370 journalists from 78 countries worked on aspects of the story. The Panama records belonged to Mossack Fonseca, a law firm based in one of the world's most notorious secrecy jurisdictions, and they unveiled the most comprehensive picture to date of a huge, hitherto hidden, global industry, fuelled by what were often large and respectable banks and legal firms.

The ICIJ team wrote at the head of their exposure story when they launched it in 2016: "A massive leak of documents exposes the offshore holdings of 11 current and former world leaders and reveals how associates of Russian President Vladimir Putin secretly shuffled as much as $2 billion through banks and shadow companies. The leak also provides details of the hidden financial dealings of 128 more politicians and public officials around the world" [14]. This was "the largest media collaboration ever undertaken", as Ryle correctly said.

EDWARD SNOWDEN LEAKS

ICIJ's impressive success showed that by banding together, investigative reporters could effectively analyse data leaks and take on some of the world's most powerful financial actors. The Snowden case showed that it was also possible in this way to break open secrets that were even more difficult and dangerous: those of a major intelligence agency.

Edward Snowden worked for America's NSA—the National Security Agency—a giant secret surveillance organisation that, in concert with allies in Britain, Canada, New Zealand, and Australia, eavesdropped on the world. In the summer of 2013, Snowden bailed out of his job in the US and headed for what he believed to be a safe haven in Hong Kong. Declaring "I can't allow the US government to destroy privacy and basic liberties", he proposed to make public the extraordinarily lawless schemes the NSA and its allies had developed to spy on the Internet [15].

He turned over some of his material to the *Guardian*. It consisted of files, memos, and presentations he had managed to download, all of which were highly classified, according to both US and British law. Operations such as the one code-named TEMPORA, for example, involved the British breaking into undersea fibre-optic cables and scooping up huge quantities of passing data, which they then sought to filter and reduce to manageable dimensions, whilst sharing the product with their major customer—the United States. Because Internet traffic criss-crossed the world on these submarine cables, the implication was that no electronic message was safe anymore.

The investigative headaches this project gave the journalists can, once again, be separated into technical, operational, and ethical issues.

CODE NAMES AND INFORMATION SECURITY

In terms of searchability, the Snowden files were quite manageable. They were not particularly big, and the data was not nearly as messy as offshore company records. Most of it consisted either of simple text or of PowerPoint presentations. But the huge technical problem was to decode what the words meant. Every operation, private corporation, and technique was given a code name, but with the exception of a handful of projects on which Snowden had briefed us, such as TEMPORA, we did not possess a dictionary. Our whistleblower was no longer in position to give us advice—he was at first in hiding in Hong Kong, and eventually in Russia. Contact with him by any sort of electronic means was out of the question. Some of the code names and jargon could be eventually decoded by laborious searches and cross-checking for occasional slips by memo authors that gave something away. But much remained mysterious.

In past data projects, information security had not been the highest priority. We would lock the door of our "war room", of course—and we would frequently communicate by encrypted email. But now, our dangers shot up to a different level. The NSA and its British partner, GCHQ—as we could see all too clearly—were in the business of intercepting anything and everything.

We had a learning curve about mobile phones. Buying "burner" pay-as-you-go phones that were unregistered and could be discarded was good enough for drug dealers, but not for us. Every mobile phone had to be left outside a meeting room. And not taken to outside destinations where it might function as a geographical locator. There was a belief that you could safely put your phone in the fridge—as a metal box it would form a "Faraday cage" that could block signals. But no-one was absolutely sure.

Alan Rusbridger, the *Guardian* editor, described the precautions taken in internal guidelines that he posted up to control journalists working on the material. He was emphasising the care being taken by the *Guardian* to stop the Snowden data falling into the wrong hands—but those wrong hands did of course include the British and US governments:

The documents are stored on five computers. None of the computers have ever been used before. None is linked to, or ever has been linked to, the internet. None is part of any network. This is to mitigate the risk of malware, phishing or hacking attacks. No outside electronics are allowed into the room where information is accessed. We have ... positioned someone outside the door of the room as well as hiring additional security for the building. The documents are stored solely in encrypted file containers. Each requires two complex passwords to access, and no one individual knows both. This means at no time has any one person alone been able to have access to the files. Only a very small pool of editors and reporters has had any access to the files. There is a master key to the database held by a senior editor with a password known only to two people. This unlocks a final password. A portion of documents directly relating to and evidencing stories we have produced are kept on a heavily-encrypted USB stick. This requires only one password to access as it has been used to prepare documents for redaction on the limited occasions where this is considered necessary to evidence our journalism.

ARRESTS AND HARD-DRIVE DESTRUCTION

The inability to use email, phone calls, or any other form of electronic communication, meant that the *Guardian* ended up spending a fortune on plane tickets. The network of individuals handling the story over several months was exceptionally far-flung. Snowden was sitting in a hotel room in Hong Kong. We had to send a reporter there. The journalists who had initially received his leaks were an independent film-maker, Laura Poitras, who was based in Berlin, and a freelance writer, Glenn Greenwald, then employed as a *Guardian* US columnist. He lived in Brazil, and his editors worked out of New York. The *Guardian*'s headquarters were, of course, in London. We also eventually worked in partnership with two other US outlets, the non-profit Propublica and the *New York Times*. Every communication had to be done physically. Every document had to be couriered. This was not only expensive: it was, of course, also tiring and slow.

With Snowden, Greenwald and Poitras, the *Guardian* was also back in bed with counter-cultural activists who were not ultimately under the paper's control. Would the differences of perspective end in tears once again, as with Assange? There was indeed, a bit of tension: Greenwald felt at one point suspicious of the *Guardian*'s resolve, and eventually parted company with the paper to set up his own outlet, the Intercept, backed by eBay founder, Pierre Omidyar.

But this friction was minor. The only real problem came over security: Greenwald's domestic partner in Brazil, David Miranda, was caught by the British at Heathrow airport carrying a hard drive with an encrypted copy of the data on it. The UK's intelligence agency promptly confiscated it, citing anti-terrorist laws. This was not fatal: there were back-ups in existence. The *Guardian* had also taken the precaution of physically sending a copy to the *New York Times*, to hold in case the British paper was raided. These were complicated and troublesome ways of managing a story. But they worked.

ETHICAL ISSUES

In its efforts to stem Snowden's disclosures, the British and US authorities freely flung around accusations against the investigative reporters involved. A Conservative politician, Julian Smith, spoke of treachery: he told the Commons that the *Guardian* "has threatened the security of our country, and stands guilty today, potentially, of treasonous behaviour" [16].

Britain's top security adviser, Oliver Robbins, in submissions to the courts played the (evidence-free) card that intelligence officers could be killed, saying the government "was certain that disclosure of this type of information could cause grievous harm to national security and counter-terrorism operations, as well as posing a direct threat to life of UK government employees" [17]. The British tried to stop more publication via the so-called Defence Advisory (DA) system, in which editors were confidentially beseeched to keep silent. Rival newspapers in Britain were indeed more inclined to denounce the *Guardian* than to support it.

The *Guardian* was only able to maintain its position against a blizzard of abuse, because of a rigorously thought-out approach to the public interest. Snowden himself said that he did not want the paper to publish details of anti-terrorism work. The paper was highly selective in what it did publish. The editor, Alan Rusbridger, was willing to talk off the record to officials in the Washington White House, and in Whitehall: there was a measure of negotiation. The *Guardian*'s security precautions were designed, among other things, to show how responsible was the paper's behaviour.

One of its (largely symbolic) compromises was to agree that government officials could supervise the smashing-up of a hard drive containing the full data, so that it could not fall into terrorist hands. These journalistic strategies were sound: neither the British nor the US government proved willing to make themselves even more unpopular by arresting the journalists and charging them with espionage. Rusbridger's triumph was cemented when—unprecedentedly for a British organisation—it won a Pulitzer prize in the US [18, p. 301ff].

BIG DATA LEAKS: CONCLUSION

But the Snowden saga demonstrated in the starkest way possible the questions, both ethical and technical, implicit in all these Big Data leaks. Raw dumps of computer-generated data are a new phenomenon. They generally contain two kinds of information—material that ought to be made public, and material that ought not. Who is capable of separating one from the other? The answer so far, has been heartening. Investigative journalists have demonstrated that, by and large, they can learn how to do it.

The price paid has been to accept a big change in their working methods. The investigative reporter who wants to operate in this new world has to be willing to co-operate with overseas reporters from other organisations; with hackers and other activists; with non-profit campaigners; with journalists in other types of media; with tech engineers; with data visualisers and graphic designers; and above all, with media outlets who have the time and money to fund complex collaborations.

As has been a repeated theme of this guide: the space available for the lone maverick with a hunch is shrinking.

REFERENCES

1. Knightley, Philip. 1997. *A Hack's Progress*. London: Jonathan Cape.
2. Leigh, David. 2000. Today's Remarkable Revelations About British American Tobacco Owe Their Genesis to a Group of Investigative Reporters Whose Newsroom is the World. *Guardian*, January 31.
3. Lewis, Charles. 2018. Global Teamwork: The Rise of Collaboration in Investigative Journalism. *Reuters Institute for the Study of Journalism*. Accessed November 15, 2018. https://reutersinstitute.politics.ox.ac.uk/risj-review/global-teamwork-rise-collaboration-investigative-journalism.
4. Alfter, Brigitte. 2019. *Journalism Across Borders: A Step-By-Step Guide to Transnational Reporting*. London: Routledge.
5. Beelman, Maud et al. 2000. How Smuggling Helps Lure New Generations of Smokers. *Guardian*, January 31.
6. Farmsubsidy.org. 2017. Farmsubsidy.org at a Glance. Accessed November 15, 2018. https://farmsubsidy.org/about/.
7. Ellsberg, Daniel. 2002. *Secrets: A Memoir of Vietnam and the Pentagon Papers*. New York: Viking.
8. Harding, Luke, and David Leigh. 2013. *Wikileaks: Inside Julian Assange's War on Secrecy*. London: Guardian Books.
9. O'Hagan, Andrew. 2014. Ghosting. *London Review of Books*. Accessed November 15, 2018. https://www.lrb.co.uk/v36/n05/andrew-ohagan/ghosting.
10. Assange, Julian. 2013. Letter to Benedict Cumberbatch. *Wikileaks*. Accessed November 15, 2018. https://wikileaks.org/First-Letter-from-Julian-Assange.html.
11. Ryle, Gerard. 2013. Secret Files Expose Offshore's Global Impact. *ICIJ*. Accessed November 15, 2018. https://www.icij.org/investigations/offshore/secret-files-expose-offshores-global-impact/.
12. Editorial Board. 2014. Jean-Claude Juncker Needs to Go. *Bloomberg*. Accessed November 15, 2018. https://www.bloomberg.com/view/articles/2014-11-09/jeanclaude-juncker-needs-to-go.
13. Davet, Gérard, Fabrice LHomme, and Serge Michel. 2015. Swissleaks: The Backstory of a Worldwide Investigation. *Le Monde*. Accessed November 15,

2018. https://www.lemonde.fr/evasion-fiscale/article/2015/02/08/swiss-leaks-the-backstory-of-a-worldwide-investigation_4572334_4862750.html.
14. Ryle, Gerard. 2016. Giant Leak of Offshore Financial Records Exposes Global Array of Crime and Corruption. *ICIJ*. Accessed November 15, 2018. https://www.icij.org/investigations/panama-papers/20160403-panama-papers-global-overview/.
15. Harding, Luke. 2014. *The Snowden Files*. London: Guardian Faber.
16. Smith, Julian. 2013. Intelligence and Security Services Debate. *House of Commons*. Accessed November 16, 2018. https://hansard.parliament.uk/Commons/2013-10-31/debates/13103154000001/IntelligenceAnd SecurityServices.
17. Robbins, Oliver. 2013. First Witness Statement. Miranda v Home Secretary QBD CO/11732/2013. Accessed November 16, 2018. https://archive.org/stream/781973-r-miranda-v-home-secretary-oliver-robbinss/781973-r-miranda-v-home-secretary-oliver-robbinss_djvu.txt.
18. Rusbridger, Alan. 2018. *Breaking News: The Remaking of Journalism and Why It Matters Now*. London: Canongate.

CHAPTER 10

Fake News in Mainstream Journalism

Guy Rais and the *Telegraph*

Investigative journalists in the twenty-first century face a difficulty that is not often talked about in conventional textbooks. This is the increasing difficulty they have in actually being believed. People speak about "fake news" in the era of social media as though the invention of stories was something new. But mainstream media themselves have, of course, a long record of polluting the water supply of news with reckless inventions.

I have a personal confession to make. There was a legendary reporter in the Fleet Street where I worked as a young journalist—the late Guy Rais of the otherwise staid *Daily Telegraph*. With his dated moustache and fund of outrageous anecdotes, he was an old-fashioned fireman, sent off by the news desk to cover whatever random news happened to be breaking in the world. The story about him that we all repeated delightedly to each other concerned the Paris air show of June 1973.

It was well after lunch on that—normally peaceful—summer Sunday shift, when a news agency "flash" clattered off the London teleprinters. The supersonic Russian rival to Concorde, the Tupolev 144, had exploded at the French air show. It had crashed on to people's houses. Rais was bundled on to the next plane. In those pre-Internet days, he had but a few hours to find eyewitnesses before the looming print deadline.

© The Author(s) 2019
D. Leigh, *Investigative Journalism*,
https://doi.org/10.1007/978-3-030-16752-3_10

But Rais came through. The next morning's front page carried this dramatic account:

> M. Bernard Malfois was walking towards his fiancee's when the force of the explosion threw him on to the road, bruising his shoulder. 'I had heard this noise of a plane and almost immediately there was a tremendous explosion in the air. The force threw me off my feet and when I recovered from the blast, houses around me had almost disintegrated. For a few seconds there was an uncanny silence. Then people came running from everywhere. Many of them had miraculous escapes as they crawled from the wrecked houses. Some were bleeding from their wounds and I saw one man with his right arm dangling by his side. It seemed to have been almost severed.' [1]

The punchline of the legendary tale was that many months later, Rais received a letter from the French military authorities investigating the crash. They wrote that it seemed the *Telegraph* reporter had very brilliantly found the sole eyewitness to the moment of the aerial explosion. His evidence was going to be vital, so if Mr Rais would be so good as to supply M. Malfois' particulars …

The intrepid reporter by his own account then turned this dismaying news to his own advantage. He spent many expenses-paid days in the French countryside, searching without avail for the elusive M. Malfois. In the end, the pursuit was quietly dropped. Why this anecdote constitutes a personal confession for me is that we (often hard-pressed) reporters found his story of falsified facts to be extremely amusing. That was the roguish Fleet Street culture.

But of course, there are many examples of this kind of thing, which are not in the least funny.

THE *DAILY MAIL* AND "ANOTHER HUMAN RIGHTS FIASCO!"

The *London Daily Mail* ran a print front page with this splash headline on 15 December 2017. As so often with that type of paper, the news story sought to instruct its readers just what to think—in this case that an Iraqi terrorist had made fools of the British taxpayer. The headline text explained:

> Iraqi 'caught red-handed with bomb' wins £33,000—because our soldiers kept him in custody for too long.

This so-called human rights fiasco was blamed on the machinations of left-wing lawyers. But the truth was quite different. The published judgement from the UK High Court had found unequivocally that the Iraqi concerned was perfectly innocent, had been the victim of a false accusation, and was compensated primarily for having been beaten and brutally mistreated. The facts were the opposite of what the *Mail* had decided to splash as its main story of the day [2]. It was a good example of prejudice masquerading as investigative journalism. The effect was to whip up unmerited hostility towards a range of minority or "elite" targets—Arabs, Muslims, human rights lawyers, and judges.

There were protests. Five days later, the *Mail* attempted to get away with publishing a brief "clarification" on page 2. It said

> The secondary headline to an article on 15 December ('Another human rights fiasco!') reported the claim of arresting soldiers that Abd Al-Waheed had been 'caught red-handed with bomb', and that he had been awarded £33,000 for being kept in custody 'for too long'. We would like to make clear that the judge found that the soldiers' claim was a false embellishment and, as was stated in the article, the £33,000 was the total compensation awarded to Mr Al-Waheed for several breaches of the European Convention on Human Rights: £15,000 for beating, £15,000 for inhuman treatment, and £3,300 for unlawful detention. We are also happy to clarify that, although British troops suspected Mr Al-Waheed of being involved in bomb-making, a review committee found he was not and—after that decision was unlawfully overturned—he was retained in custody for another 33 days.

There were further protests. Published at the bottom of page two a month later, came a second "clarification". It was headlined in rather obscure terms: "Iraqi abuse claims: Abd Al-Waheed". Eventually conceding the *Mail*'s allegations had been downright false, the statement added the undoubtedly weasel words: "We apologise if any contrary impression was formed".

Academic commentator Professor Brian Cathcart, who was among the protestors, said that one was obliged to read through the whole statement carefully, to find the *Mail*'s actual concession that "another of its front-page stories designed to crank up hatred towards Muslims was no better than a fiction" [3].

Continuing protestors finally took their complaints to the industry-funded self-regulatory body, IPSO. Despite the flagrant nature of the *Mail*'s behaviour, IPSO neither imposed fines, nor required any specific disciplinary action be taken against the then editor Paul Dacre or members of his staff. The paper claimed in mitigation that "notes" had been sent to seven individuals telling them not to do it again. No-one was otherwise punished despite the fact that the story "seriously misrepresented" a court judgement and the paper had published "seriously misleading information on an important subject". IPSO only asked that its adjudication be published with a line at the bottom of the front page directing attention to the full text on an inside page [4].

The editor of a major paper which publishes a false front-page splash on a sensitive topic ought to be sacked. But British downmarket editors don't get sacked for misleading their readers. The former British tabloid editor Roy Greenslade is among those who speculate that browbeatingly false journalism of this kind not only damages trust in the mainstream media, but ultimately does something even more serious: it helps destroy trust in the very notion of objectively reliable facts.

> Part of the problem seems traceable to the way news and comment have been conflated in our mainstream media outlets ... The result has been blatant bias. It is an understatement to call it spin. Heavily angled stories and headlines are the norm... Once all news is identified as fake, then its fakeness becomes a matter of degree. [5]

If truths are distorted to comply with an ideological attitude, as in the *Mail* story, such political framing weakens the credibility of journalistic disclosures in general. People start to feel that "it's all politics". And it is, of course, only a short step from there to what President Trump's aide once memorably termed "Alternative facts" [6].

THE SUNDAY TIMES AND MICHAEL FOOT

There is nothing new about journalistic recklessness. Back in 1995, the Murdoch-owned *Sunday Times*, then edited by John Witherow, melodramatically alleged that Labour politician Michael Foot was secretly in the pay of the Soviet Union. The front-page headline blared: "KGB: MICHAEL FOOT WAS OUR AGENT". They said his code name was Agent Boot.

The scholarly left-winger sued: the paper retracted and paid over more than £100,000 to persuade him to drop the case [7, p. 284ff]. After Foot died, Witherow, by now editor of sister paper, the *Times*, reheated the allegations. He was safe from the laws of libel and could say what he liked, whether or not it was justifiable [8].

The Agent Boot espionage story—and the political weight that was put on it—showed an inattention to real evidence. Such facts, as there were, boiled down to one single word: lunch. In the 1960s, a Russian press attaché lunched with Foot about once a month at the MP's favourite Soho restaurant, the Gay Hussar. In this prominent spot, it seems Foot, who edited the left-wing paper Tribune, would chat about current affairs.

Michael Foot was no fan of the Soviet Union at the time, unlike a few other radical Labour MPs. In 1968, for example, Foot denounced Russia for sending in tanks to crush the Prague spring [9]. Much later, in 1980, he became Labour party leader for three years—at which point he also became a major domestic political target.

The allegation against Foot came solely from a defector, Oleg Gordievsky. This KGB officer had told his new MI6 handlers, by way of a dowry, that he had seen old files detailing attempts over 20 years to culti-vate the "progressive" Foot. He said the press attaché at lunch in the 1960s had really been a KGB officer. The files said Foot had been given money at the time, and, at their very first meeting with Foot at the Tribune offices, "KGB officers posing as diplomats slipped £10 into his pocket" [9].

One can leave aside for the moment the large fact that Foot did not actually possess any secrets. He was a mere backbencher and journalist. The evidence on which the story was based—a draft of Gordievsky's mem-oirs—was legally worthless. Gordievsky had a book to sell. He said he had once seen a file. But such a file was itself merely evidence that somebody had once written down such claims and sent them to Moscow in a report.

The paper made some effort to check. An ex-KGB officer in Moscow confirmed there could have been a file on Foot called BOOT. He denied it subsequently. This did not corroborate the file's contents.

Most seriously, the paper did not seem to have considered a fact of which Gordievsky himself was well aware. The defector admitted later to his biographer, Ben McIntyre, that such KGB officers as Foot's purported handlers were often lazy, incompetent, and crooked. He said they busied themselves "fiddling their expenses". Because the role of the men in the field was to cultivate contacts, recruit informants, and target possible agents, they had in effect "an invitation to corruption".

Gordievsky added, devastatingly: "Most officers simply invented their interaction... falsified bills, made up their reports and pocketed their allowances" [9].

There is evidence to support Gordievsky's bleak view of such intelligence reports. A defector from the sister Czech agency, Josef Frolik, painted a similar picture in his own memoirs. Frolik recalled how a colleague treated them all to expensive sessions in London night clubs: "Jan Koska had invented an 'English policeman' who cost Prague £1,500 in bribes to cover Koska's drinking bills" [10].

In other words, the 1960s "Agent Boot" secret reports back to KGB headquarters could have been little more than optimistic expenses claims.

Foot said, "As far as I know I've never met the KGB in my life". It was not disputed that the cash-strapped Tribune had accepted some paid adverts from Soviet organisations. And his lawyer later suggested that maybe "KGB agents would sometimes attend fundraising parties for Tribune ... and leave a contribution" [7]. But this was a far cry from the evil picture that was being painted of Foot and his motives. He protested "The idea behind that wicked headline was to suggest that I had been prepared ... to serve a hideous Stalinite dictatorship".

He drew a distinction between legitimate investigative journalism and the journalism of the smear: "[Witherow] implies in his headlines that I am a traitor to my country... if this type of journalism is to go unchallenged, the disease will afflict our whole public life" [11].

ROLLING STONE AND THE "GANG RAPE"

The group looked at each other in a panic. They all knew about Jackie's date that evening at Phi Kappa Psi, the house looming behind them. "We have got to get her to the hospital," Randall declared. The other two friends, however, weren't convinced. "Is that such a good idea?" countered Cindy ... "Her reputation will be shot for the next four years." Andrew seconded the opinion. The three friends launched into a heated discussion about the social price of reporting Jackie's rape, while Jackie stood behind them, mute in her bloody dress.

This was the novelistic picture which journalist Sabrina Erdely conjured up for the US magazine *Rolling Stone* in 2014, in a now-deleted article headlined: "A Rape on Campus" [12].

Readers would never have guessed from her I-was-there prose style that the reporter had not even ever spoken to the three friends to whom she gave pseudonyms. Neither had she been told the identity of Jackie's supposed date; nor indeed had she ever been allowed to see the supposedly "bloody dress" which rounded off the rhythm of her paragraph so graphically. "Jackie" had recounted in rich detail to the journalist how she had been brutally gang-raped by seven unidentified men at a University of Virginia fraternity house—but her own identity was also withheld from the readers.

The subsequent post-mortem and litigation, after the *Rolling Stone* story fell apart, were educational. The magazine commissioned an inquiry by academics at the Columbia Journalism Review and published the findings [13]. There was also a successful libel suit by a university administrator who was accused in the piece of having an uncaring attitude towards "Jackie". It threw up a further mass of testimony and emails [14].

From all this, it transpired that Jackie had fabricated the rape story. Initially, she may have done so to get sympathy and attention, but subsequently the tale took on a life of its own. The well-meaning reporter who contacted Jackie two years on, seeking evidence of rape culture on campus, fell prey to a syndrome that all investigative journalists know and fear—the story became too good to check.

The Columbia inquiry was unsparing of the journalists' lack of professional standards:

> The editors and Erdely have concluded that their main fault was to be too accommodating of Jackie because she described herself as the survivor of a terrible sexual assault.

Expressing scepticism, the inquiry pointed to evidence that the journalists in fact did not want to press her too hard at the time for fear of losing her co-operation. "A Rape on Campus" was, they said:

> A story of journalistic failure that was avoidable. The failure encompassed reporting, editing, editorial supervision and fact-checking. The magazine set aside or rationalized as unnecessary essential practices of reporting ...The published story glossed over the gaps in the magazine's reporting by using pseudonyms and by failing to state where important information had come from.

In these cases, the *Mail, Sunday Times,* and *Rolling Stone* thus perpetrated three very different types of "fake news". But they do have a common element. In each case, the journalists and their organisations were certainly displaying commercial opportunism. They could make sales and indeed make reputations, by stirring up public rage against so-called terrorists, traitors, and rapists. But that was not the crucial factor. What these misbegotten stories have in common is that their authors were blinded by prejudice. A more polite term would be "confirmation bias". They saw what they expected to see, because it fitted in with their pre-existing beliefs, and they disregarded evidence that might compete with that.

HITLER DIARIES, JANET COOKE, STEPHEN GLASS, JAYSON BLAIR, JACK KELLEY, CARLTON TV

Other more deliberate frauds litter the history of media faking. One of the most infamous was the forged "Hitler Diaries", purchased by tycoon Rupert Murdoch in 1983 and published in the UK in the *Sunday Times*. Brian MacArthur, one of the executives innocently involved, recalled: "What suckers we all were...The discovery of the Hitler diaries offered so tempting a scoop that we all wanted to believe they were genuine" [15].

Another fake, this time in the *Washington Post*, won a Pulitzer prize before being exposed in 1980.

> Jimmy is 8 years old and a third-generation heroin addict, a precocious little boy with sandy hair, velvety brown eyes and needle marks freckling the baby-smooth skin of his thin brown arms.

This was how young reporter Janet Cooke began her heart-wrenching tale. The Pulitzer award was her undoing: the publicity threw up discrepancies in her CV. Very soon, she had to return the prize. She wrote a confession that "Jimmy's World" was a fabrication: "I never encountered or interviewed an 8-year-old heroin addict". Her career was over. More recently, she wrote wryly to an ex-colleague, "Essentially, I've spent the last 30 years waiting to die" [16].

There has been quite a list of other US journalists who have succumbed to the temptation to plagiarise or invent. A prolific writer for the *New Republic* in Washington DC, Stephen Glass, was discovered to have made up much of his entertaining material. The magazine concluded that 27 of 41 pieces written between 1995 and 1998 contained fabrications. Glass fended off suspicion: as one commentator wrote, "because of the remarkable industry he applied to the production of the false backup materials which he methodically used to deceive legions of editors and fact checkers" [17].

In the ultra-respectable *New York Times*, in 2003, 27-year-old Jayson Blair was similarly exposed after a surprisingly long career of dishonest news reporting. The paper wrote, self-laceratingly: "Mr. Blair repeatedly violated the cardinal tenet of journalism, which is simply truth. His tools of deceit were a cellphone and a laptop computer—which allowed him to blur his true whereabouts—as well as round-the-clock access to databases of news articles from which he stole" [18].

The paper's then editor Howell Raines, did not survive the scandal.

Foreign news is even easier to fake than domestic stories. USA Today's foreign reporter, Jack Kelley, was revealed to have spent much of his stellar career simply making things up. The paper reported glumly that he "fabricated substantial portions of at least eight major stories, lifted nearly two dozen quotes or other material from competing publications...He used a snapshot he took of a Cuban hotel worker to authenticate a story he made up about a woman who died fleeing Cuba by boat. The woman in the photo neither fled by boat nor died, and a USA TODAY reporter located her this month" [19].

In Britain, an award-winning investigative film called The Connection demonstrated that mainstream fakery is not confined to print. The camera too can lie. The Connection was broadcast by the commercial channel Carlton TV. Its director Marc de Beaufort constructed an hour-long programme which purported to follow a drug mule as he swallowed heroin packages and flew with them from Colombia into London.

De Beaufort's researcher subsequently went sour on him and started to talk. As a result, the *Guardian* was able to publish a lengthy exposé, maintaining, "The true story of Carlton's programme is one of lies, broken promises and the lust for ratings, fame and prizes". The paper said that the "mule" had not really swallowed any heroin, the drug-smuggling plane trip had not taken place as alleged, and those involved had been paid actors. The British TV regulator agreed, and fined Carlton £2 million [20].

THE SPREAD OF MISINFORMATION

So we should quite rightly feel some scepticism towards everything that is presented to us in the media. As well as the kind of factual misreporting we have detailed here, consumers of journalism are often also fed a toxic diet in more general ways. Political propaganda; misleading advertising; cynical "reputation management" by PR firms; false stories planted by intelligence agencies or mischievous hackers in Macedonia; worthless "clickbait"; the deliberate "invention of uncertainty" by big business interests seeking to confuse people about the effects of tobacco or climate change—the list is long of the ways that speech in the media is perverted until it no longer gives much of a reliable picture of the world.

There has been, as we know, a huge technological shift. Nowadays there is virtually instantaneous and universal circulation of words and video by a myriad of uncontrolled online groups. This leapfrogging over the slow "dead tree" media has worsened matters. It has tended to destroy a hierarchy of credibility that existed before.

A newspaper like the *New York Times* or the *Financial Times* is a physical product—a ubiquitous brand that is respectable in appearance, signals its history as a cultural gatekeeper, and is carried under their arms by high-status individuals. When the London *Times* in the early 1960s ran its advertising campaign with the slogan "Top People Read the Times", it was referencing a real-world landscape of businessmen and government officials who did the *Times* crossword on commuter trains or in gentlemen's clubs. The image contrasted strongly with that of the tatty pamphlets in which neo-Nazis or religious fundamentalists peddled their ideas, or the low-grade paper on which the tabloids printed screaming headlines which no-one took very seriously.

Nowadays, on the screen of an iPhone, it all looks the same.

Dominant search engines such as Google use algorithms which, for all their claims of sophistication, throw up garbage in the same manner as credible information. On social media such as Twitter, researchers are beginning to demonstrate that, in the absence of gatekeepers, false stories and rumours spread more successfully than genuine ones. This may happen, it is speculated, simply because lies are inherently more novel and exciting:

> We found that falsehood diffused significantly farther, faster, deeper, and more broadly than the truth in all categories of information … Many more people retweeted falsehood than they did the truth … Although we cannot claim that novelty causes retweets or that novelty is the only reason why false news is retweeted more often, we do find that false news is more novel and that novel information is more likely to be retweeted. [21]

"Lügenpresse": The Lying Press

The media's own poor record and the opportunities for unscrupulous actors to game the new online system thus combine to make investigative reporters vulnerable to political attack. Their opponents not only seek to discredit their findings, but also even set out to delegitimise independent journalists' very entitlement to ply a trade as countervailing voices in society.

Donald Trump became notorious during his 2016 presidential campaign for calling the media "enemies of the people" and throwing around the phrase "fake news". But his own family of immigrants would have been more familiar with the equivalent term in their native German: "*lügenpresse*". The expression's literal meaning is "lying press", and it has an ugly history.

The German magazine Der Spiegel constructed a graph of the frequency with which the term has reared up in German writing [22]. It first emerged around 1848, the "Year of Revolutions", as a term of abuse for liberal and democratic newspapers. There were surges of mentions vilifying the foreign press during Germany's wars of 1870 and 1914–18. But a great spike in the frequency line appeared in the 1930s as an anti-democracy slogan. In Spiegel's words "The Nazis ... used the term to agitate against Jewish and leftist newspapers".

With Hitler's defeat, the phrase subsided in Germany until about 2014. Then the anti-immigrant group Pegida adopted it once more. They were seen marching through Dresden in order to denounce Germany's mainstream media by chanting this old Nazi slogan [23]. Violent anti-Muslim demonstrators in the former East German town of Chemnitz, attacked journalists, whilst shouting it too. By October 2016, Trump enthusiasts had picked it up and were videoed chanting the word at a US rally [24]. Far-right Trump supporter Richard Spencer denounced what he called "the mainstream media—or perhaps we should refer to them in the original German, *lügenpresse*" [25].

The political effect of toxifying the media wholesale in this fashion is to open the way to a form of gaslighting. Absent credible journalism, truth can easily be made to seem like lies, lies to seem like the truth. A populist politician like Trump has an abusive relationship with the electorate, constantly destabilising their perception of reality. Among a blizzard of evident falsehoods, he notoriously insisted that more spectators had turned out for his Washington inauguration than ever before, despite photographs proving the contrary. In September 2018, he calmly denied that 3000 people had died in the Puerto Rican hurricane. He said his enemies had made up the figure to make him look bad.

When a tape emerged of his infamous "grab them by the pussy" remarks about women, he stated "I said it, I was wrong and I apologise". But Marty Baron, editor of the *Washington Post*, the paper that was a target of many of Trump's attacks, recounts the way that subsequently, when the true details had been somewhat forgotten, the president privately started to circulate the idea that the "pussy" tape was in fact a forgery [26].

Trump is not the only national strongman to play this game. In Russia too, President Putin not only tells lies but similarly even revels in doing so. Yale history professor Timothy Snyder, in his 2018 study of Russian proto-fascism, documents a pattern of what he calls "implausible deniability". When a Russian missile team in Ukraine shot down a civilian aircraft—Malaysian plane MH17—Putin's official propaganda at first proposed that the attack had in fact been a bodged attempt by Ukraine's own forces to assassinate Putin himself. By day two, Russian TV was voicing the even more surreal idea that the CIA had sent a ghost plane filled with corpses overhead to provoke Russian forces [27].

The same contemptuous attitude towards reality was demonstrated in 2018 when the British authorities managed to identify two Russian secret agents who used a bottle of nerve agent to poison both Russian spy defector Sergei Skripal and some innocent passing Britons.

The pair of accused assassins were produced on Russian state television to give evidently scripted interviews. They claimed with straight faces to be architecture enthusiasts, who had made a special tourist trip together to England from Moscow merely in order to view the famous cathedral in the "wonderful town of Salisbury", the provincial spot where Skripal had been living [28].

As a historian, Snyder finds this behaviour particularly frightening. "To abandon facts is to abandon freedom," he writes, "If nothing is true, then no one can criticize power because there is no basis upon which to do so. If nothing is true, then all is spectacle" [27].

But he is not, of course, the first to make this point about the ways of tyranny. George Orwell, in "1984", describes how his dissident protagonist, Winston Smith, signals his eventual submission. "It was as though some huge force was pressing down upon you … Persuading you, almost to deny the evidence of your senses. In the end the Party would announce that two and two made five, and you would have to believe it" [29].

POLICING OTHER JOURNALISTS

So how, in this world of doublespeak, can you make your own investigative journalism believed? Here are four fairly straightforward answers. The first is that investigative journalists have a duty not only to avoid lying, but also to police the production of lies by their colleagues. Many of the examples of fake journalism detailed here only came to light thanks to dogged investigation by other journalists. This kind of house-cleaning does not make you popular: the *Guardian* was attacked at the time by its TV counterparts for seeking to expose the bogus Carlton documentary. Investigative reporter Nick Davies was subject to what his editor calls a "wall of lies, dissembling, obstruction, threats and smears" for exposing criminal behaviour at Murdoch's *News of the World* [30]. But honesty must start at home.

It is, perhaps, too much to hope for that young wannabe journalists will also keep off the payroll of media organisations with a track record of low ethical standards. I was lucky in my own career—I never found myself working for the Murdochs or the Rothermeres, for example, which would have put severe strains on my personal conscience. On the other hand, as recounted earlier in this guide (see Chap. 4), I did once find my then paper, the *Observer*, taken over by a villainous proprietor. I was able nevertheless cheerfully to carry on working for him for several years, freely publishing what I believed in. The media environment in a marketised society is inevitably corrupt. But so it is also in a state-run society. It is sometimes possible nevertheless to find space everywhere to carry out honest journalism—at least for a while.

CALLING OUT LIES

Journalists should be rigorous investigators of the lying use of words by others. Reporters are wordsmiths by trade, and they ought to take an interest in exposing all the varieties of fake speech which are used to bamboozle the public. Instead of simply taking shorthand like a news stenographer, a key job of an investigative journalist should be publicly to decode weasel words. One small example of such is the way whistleblowers in schools and hospitals and victims of sexual harassment are made to sign intimidatory non-disclosure agreements (NDAs), the misleading small print of which is in fact legally unenforceable. Another type of fake speech is found in the bullying letters from lawyers and debt collectors who have no real intention of ever going to court.

Jeremy Paxman, the BBC Newsnight TV interviewer, gained some notoriety when he quoted the famous former operating principle of distinguished *Times* reporter Louis Heren: "Why is this lying bastard lying to me?" [31].

It sounds brutal. But it is often a useful initial question for an investigative reporter to ask themselves. Chief executives are coached to deliver smooth public relations messages, and politicians get elaborate "media training" to avoid actually answering questions. The behaviour of these people should be a target not just of challenge during interviews, but of regular linguistic analysis by journalists. Orwell, again, was among the first to do this work, detailing the way political language "is designed to make lies sound truthful and murder respectable, and to give an appearance of solidity to pure wind" [32, p. 252ff].

In Britain, the BBC and other media outlets have eventually grasped the need for public education. "We all have a duty to instil public confidence in professional journalism" the BBC Director-General Tony Hall said in a 2018 speech. "We're using the fundamental principles of journalism to teach critical thinking. Sending our reporters into schools to teach pupils about how to spot fake news…Jaws literally dropped when we discussed the reasons why people might pump out disinformation" [33].

In the wake of Donald Trump's exceptionally untruthful election campaign, some newspapers and TV began actually to call out the lies one at a time. It was remarkable that the decision to do so was seen as a novelty.

Reporting Transparently

Investigative journalists need to cement their credibility with the public by open disclosure of their reporting methods. Working as they now often do in an intellectually hostile environment, it is a bad idea for reporters to try to continue their old habits of citing obscure "sources" and retailing anonymous quotes which could very easily be invented.

But a piece of journalism does not necessarily demonstrate its integrity by the dull boasting which sometimes accompanies an exposure piece— "We interviewed 273 individuals, and a team of 32 reporters travelled 2082 miles to produce this investigation". The end result can still be unreliable. Heavily edited multinational compilations of the kind that used to appear in US magazines like Newsweek painted a picture of events that—to those actually involved in them—often seemed subtly wrong.

What will genuinely help writers to demonstrate their honesty are the technical facilities of the Internet. Online viewers can click through to see instant details of cited books and articles. They can see video of speakers actually uttering quotes. They can often also click through to images of original documents obtained by the reporter. The process of inserting all these links into an online article is very tedious (and can't be replicated in print). But the investigative journalist needs to do it patiently, because it provides reassurance to the public.

Building an Honest Brand

Serious investigative journalists in an online age need to reinstate a hierarchy of believability. They have to train viewers and readers to recognise that they are at the top of such a hierarchy, and conspiracy theorists with websites are way down at the bottom. This is, of course, easier said than done and is always going to be a slow process.

Individual reporters can only make a limited contribution to brand-building by the organisations and outlets for which they produce material. But there are some useful things they can do. One is to sign up to professional networks. If you build enough of a reputation, you can be invited to join a grouping such as the Washington-based International Consortium of Investigative Journalists (ICIJ) or one of its regional equivalents such as OCCRP in the Balkans or the EIC in western Europe. This will add something to your standing. The National Union of Journalists applies a professional standards code to its members [34].

On a personal level, it is valuable to be open to admitting mistakes. Investigative journalists can't help making mistakes sometimes—it's always Blind Man's Buff! But to openly admit and publish accounts of errors in fact tends to add to a journalist's credibility, rather than diminish it. This is a lesson that has been understood by some highly credible media organisations. Taking entirely at random the *New York Times* regular corrections column for 1 April 2018, it reads:

> A photo caption with an article on the cover this weekend about renovations misidentifies a woman in Niskayuna, N.Y., who had a problem with her contractor. She is Terri Goldman, not Terry Goldman.

An article about Cuba on March 18 misstated the year in which President Barack Obama visited that country. It was 2016, not 2015.

The 52 Places Traveler column last Sunday, about San Juan, P.R., misstated the number of people in Puerto Rico without electricity. As of February, the number was more than 900,000, not 400,000.

This fulsome correction of apparently minor errors carries several unspoken but very useful subtexts. Those silently reassuring messages say "We care about accuracy to the point of fanaticism". They also say "What we print is important. Errors go with the territory. But most of our errors are tiny and you shouldn't worry about them too much". And finally, they also convey the implicit message "We are quite unlike our trashy rivals".

The task of building a distinct, credible identity may also be helped at an institutional level by belonging to a professional institution. In Britain, small independent online media outlets have joined a voluntary self-regulator, IMPRESS, with charity support. It offers a logo "TRUST IN JOURNALISM" which they are entitled to display on their websites [35].

The ambition is to offer a "kitemark", which will distinguish them from the rogues. IMPRESS was set up in the wake of the British phone-hacking revelations which forced Rupert Murdoch to shut down the scandal-hit *News of the World*. (Full disclosure: the author is one of the backers of IMPRESS.)

This project was in its infancy in 2018 and hampered by the widespread hostility of the UK's commercial media. They prefer to promote their own industry-financed self-regulator, known as IPSO [36]. IPSO, as was seen in the above case of the *Daily Mail*'s so-called human rights fiasco, does not levy heavy penalties.

Other news groups—notably the *Financial Times, Independent*, and *Guardian*—run their own well-advertised complaints schemes, while the UK's broadcasters such as the BBC are tied to impartiality requirements, supervised by a state regulator, OFCOM. The broadcasting regulatory system does work fairly successfully, despite the misunderstanding by many in the US that the BBC is a "state broadcaster". The BBC has a history of rows about bias, cowardice, attempted political interference, and clumsy corporate internal censorship. But nonetheless, the broadcaster remains so far as an intensely important landmark—a mainstream media organisation whose output is, by and large, believed. This should be the dream of all of us.

HOW TO FIGHT FAKERY
POLICE OTHER JOURNALISTS
CALL OUT LIES
REPORT TRANSPARENTLY
BUILD AN HONEST BRAND

REFERENCES

1. Rais, Guy. 1973. Crash Town Feared Air Shows. *Telegraph*, June 4.
2. Judgment. 2017. Kamil Najim Abdullah Alseran and Ors v Ministry of Defence. [2017] EWHC 3289 (QB). Accessed November 16, 2018. https://www.judiciary.uk/judgments/kamil-najim-abdullah-alseran-and-ors-v-ministry-of-defence/.
3. Cathcart, Brian. 2018. A Day of Shame for Britain's Corporate Press. *Inforrm's Blog*. Accessed November 16, 2018. https://inforrm.org/2018/01/20/a-day-of-shame-for-britains-corporate-press-brian-cathcart/.
4. IPSO. 2018. Khan v. Daily Mail. Decision of the Complaints Committee. Accessed November 16, 2018. https://www.ipso.co.uk/rulings-and-resolution-statements/ruling/?id=20912-17.
5. Greenslade, Roy. 2017. How Blurring of Fact and Comment Kicked Open the Door to Fake News. *Guardian*. Accessed November 16, 2018. https://www.theguardian.com/media/commentisfree/2017/oct/09/how-a-blurring-of-fact-and-comment-kicked-open-the-door-to-fake-news-roy-greenslade.
6. Conway, Kellyanne. 2017. Meet the Press. *NBC News*. Accessed November 16, 2018. https://www.youtube.com/watch?v=VSrEEDQgFc8.
7. Robertson, Geoffrey. 2018. *Rather His Own Man*. London: Biteback.
8. Editorial 2018. Useful Idiots. *Times*, September 15.
9. McIntyre, Ben. 2018. *The Spy and the Traitor*. London: Viking.
10. Frolik, Josef. 1975. *The Frolik Defection*. London: Leo Cooper.
11. Foot, Michael. 1995. My Reply to the KGB Smear. *Observer*, February 26.
12. Erdely, Sabrina. 2014. A Rape on Campus. Internet Archive Wayback Machine. Accessed November 16, 2018. http://web.archive.org/web/20141119200349/http://www.rollingstone.com/culture/features/a-rape-on-campus-20141119.
13. Coronel, Sheila, Steve Coll, and Derek Kravitz. 2015. An Anatomy of a Journalistic Failure. Columbia University Graduate School of Journalism Report. Accessed November 16, 2018. https://www.rollingstone.com/culture/culture-news/rolling-stone-and-uva-the-columbia-university-graduate-school-of-journalism-report-44930/.

14. ABC News. 2017. What Happened to Jackie? 20/20. Accessed November 16, 2018. https://www.youtube.com/watch?v=dfdqBHeXLB0.
15. MacArthur, Brian. 1991. Up in Smoke. *Sunday Times*, June 9.
16. Sagar, Mike. 2016. The Fabulist who Changed Journalism. *Columbia Journalism Review*. Accessed November 16, 2018. https://www.cjr.org/the_feature/the_fabulist_who_changed_journalism.php.
17. Bissinger, Buzz. 2007. Shattered Glass. *Vanity Fair*, September 5.
18. Barry, Dan et al. 2003. Correcting the Record; Reporter Who Resigned Leaves Long Trail of Deception. *New York Times*. Accessed November 16, 2018. https://www.nytimes.com/2003/05/11/us/correcting-the-record-times-reporter-who-resigned-leaves-long-trail-of-deception.html.
19. Morrison, Blake. 2004. Ex USA TODAY Reporter Faked Major Stories. *USA Today*, March 19.
20. BBC News. 1998. Carlton Fined £2m for 'Faked' Documentary. *BBC Online Network*. Accessed November 17, 2018. http://news.bbc.co.uk/1/hi/uk/237715.stm.
21. Vosoughi, Soroush, Deb Roy, and Sinan Aral. 2018. The Spread of True and False News Online. *Science*. Accessed October 28, 2018. http://science.sciencemag.org/content/359/6380/1146.
22. Brauck, Marcus et al. 2016. Lying Press? Germans Lose Faith in the Fourth Estate. *Spiegel Online*. Accessed November 17, 2018. http://www.spiegel.de/international/germany/most-germans-think-the-press-is-lying-to-them-about-refugees-a-1079049.html.
23. Hill, Jenny. 2018. Chemnitz Protests: Far Right on March in East Germany. *BBC News*. Accessed November 17, 2018. https://www.bbc.co.uk/news/world-europe-45328477.
24. Noack, Rick. 2016.The Ugly History of 'Lügenpresse'. *Washington Post*, October 24.
25. Bradner, Eric. 2016. Alt-right Leader: 'Hail Trump! Hail Our People! Hail Victory!'. *CNN*. Accessed November 17, 2018. https://edition.cnn.com/2016/11/21/politics/alt-right-gathering-donald-trump/index.html.
26. Baron, Marty. 2018. When a President Wages War on a Press at Work. *Reuters Institute Memorial Lecture*. Accessed November 17, 2018. https://reutersinstitute.politics.ox.ac.uk/our-research/full-text-when-president-wages-war-press-work.
27. Snyder, Timothy. 2018. *The Road to Unfreedom: Russia, Europe, America*. London: Bodley Head.
28. Davies, Gareth, and Alec Luhn. 2018. Skripal Poisoning Suspects Claim They Were Tourists in 'Wonderful Town of Salisbury' to Visit 'Famous' Cathedral. *Telegraph*. Accessed November 17, 2018. https://www.telegraph.co.uk/news/2018/09/13/skripal-poisoning-suspects-claim-salisbury-visit-historical/.

29. Orwell, George. 1949. *Nineteen Eighty-Four*. London: Penguin Books. 2008 edition.
30. Rusbridger, Alan. 2018. *Breaking News*. London: Canongate.
31. Heren, Louis. 1978. *Growing Up on the Times*. London: Hamish Hamilton.
32. Orwell, George. 1946. Politics and the English Language. *Horizon* 13 (76): 252–265.
33. Hall, Tony. 2018. Satchwell lecture. Society of Editors. Accessed November 17, 2018. https://www.bbc.co.uk/mediacentre/speeches/2018/tony-hall-soe.
34. National Union of Journalists. https://www.nuj.org.uk/about/nuj-code/.
35. IMPRESS. https://www.impress.press/about-us/.
36. Independent Press Standards Organisation. https://www.ipso.co.uk/what-we-do/.

CHAPTER 11

Trafigura: A Classic Investigation

The Trafigura scandal spanned the high seas—from a refinery in Mexico to a port in Texas to Curacao in the Caribbean, and across the north Atlantic to London to France to Switzerland to the Netherlands; then north to Estonia in the Baltic, to Norway and finally a long way south to the polluted shores of West Africa.

This is the inside story of an investigation which pulled together all those threads. It began intermittently in 2006, and efforts went on for several years. Eventually, a handful of reporters working together succeeded in exposing the way thousands of people in a poor country had been lawlessly mistreated by a giant global business—one which used its money and power to create a false narrative.

The story brings together many of the key investigative themes we have studied. These include the global nature of modern business and politics; the key role of journalistic collaboration; the power of simultaneous publication; the need for support from media bosses; the techniques of resistance to legal bullying; the reach of PR falsehoods; the professional value of alignments with lawyers, politicians, and campaigners; and the ability of social media to defeat censorship.

Finally, the Trafigura saga embodies the most fundamental lesson contained in this book—that the problem for investigative reporters is often

© The Author(s) 2019
D. Leigh, *Investigative Journalism*,
https://doi.org/10.1007/978-3-030-16752-3_11

not so much how to find things out: it is how to get them effectively published.

NINE REQUIREMENTS FOR BIG INVESTIGATIONS

1. GLOBAL REACH
2. COLLABORATION
3. SIMULTANEOUS PUBLICATION
4. EDITOR SUPPORT
5. LEGAL PUSHBACK
6. COUNTERING FALSE NARRATIVES
7. ALLIES
8. SOCIAL MEDIA
9. IMPACT

On 2 July 2006, an oil tanker, the Probo Koala, tied up at Amsterdam docks and tried to dispose of 400 tons of stinking slurry. The owners lied about its origins, saying it was routine so-called slops from rinsing out the ship's tanks. This liquid was in fact far from normal. It was toxic chemical waste, the residue of a cheap and dirty refining process called "caustic washing". The experiment had been carried out on board the tanker itself at sea because no-one would any longer allow them to do the process on land.

The owners, Trafigura, were a wealthy firm of London-based oil traders, the third biggest in the world. The group was headed by billionaire Claude Dauphin, a hard-driving son of a French scrap metal dealer. Dauphin had cheaply bought up rights to thousands of tons of so-called coker naptha. Trucked north to the port of Brownsville, Texas, it originated from a Mexican refinery with inadequate equipment, which had found a large amount of this intermediate product left on its hands. Coker naptha was unsaleable as petrol at the pump because it was heavily contaminated with toxic sulphur compounds.

But Dauphin believed it could be cleaned up and sold on for a big profit if some of the sulphur could first be removed by a primitive chemical process. This would involve simply tipping in tons of caustic soda and stirring it around. His traders wrote emails to each other boasting that the

Mexican naptha price was so "bloody cheap" that they could make $7 million this way on each tanker-load.

The fly in the ointment was the resultant toxic residue. As one of them emailed: "Local environment agencies do not allow disposal of the toxic caustic after treatment... This operation is no longer allowed in EU/US and Singapore. Caustic washes are banned in most countries due to the hazardous nature of the waste (mercaptans, phenols, smell)... Under EU law you no longer allowed to transport such waste across EU borders" [1].

Mercaptans had the worst smell of any substance in the world, and could also degrade to release hydrogen sulphide. This not only stank of rotten eggs but in high concentrations could be lethal.

But Dauphin urged his traders to "be creative". One proposed using a ship at sea for the otherwise banned caustic washing process: "I don't know how we dispose of the slops and I don't imply we would dump them but for sure there must be some way to pay someone to take them".

That so-called creative solution was adopted. Trafigura did then try to hire someone in Amsterdam to take their resultant toxic problem away. But the oil traders tried to cheat, and pay too little by misdescribing it as harmless. During unloading, the stench in the harbour led to panicked residents calling the emergency services. The Dutch disposal agency smelled a rat about the purported "routine slops". The firm demanded at least €500,000 to have the waste properly treated. Trafigura refused, and persuaded them to pump it back on to the ship.

Eventually, the following month, the Probo Koala and its foul-smelling waste tanks turned up in an obscure corner of French-speaking West Africa, at the Ivory Coast port of Abidjan. The people there proved less fussy. A man called Salomon Ugborugbo was paid approximately £10,000 to dispose of the material for good. His "contract" for treating the waste was a single scrap of handwritten paper. He agreed "to discharge your chemical slops in a place out of the city" at Akouedo, the local tip [2, p. 46].

When Akouedo refused to accept any more dumping of the noxious sludge, his hired truck drivers tipped the rest around town wherever they could.

The following morning, thousands of people all over the capital of the Ivory Coast woke up retching from an unbearable smell, with stinging eyes, nose-bleeds, and raw throats. More than 3000 of them besieged the hospitals and clinics in panic as the Probo Koala sailed away. The government said that some people miscarried and that 17 died.

Nor was the saga over. Trafigura now hunted for another cheap solution, and eventually found a complaisant firm with a tank farm up a fjord in Norway. They paid them to take the remaining coker consignments and try to treat them. But an onshore tank went up in a huge explosion, thanks to the slurry's unstable chemistry. It doused the residents of the nearby Scandinavian village with more sickening fumes.

As uproar grew back in the Ivory Coast, Trafigura commissioned a report from British technical consultants Minton Traherne & Davies. The traders admitted to their on-board caustic washing attempts, detailing the precise quantities of chemicals used, and they asked how dangerous such waste might actually have been.

Mintons' confidential findings, received on 14 September 2006, were uncompromising: they wrote that exposure to such mercaptans and derivatives "can lead to a cough, headaches, nausea and breathing difficulties… contact with acid will lead to hydrogen sulphide production…contact with skin can lead to permanent ulceration…inhalation of mist may lead to lung damage…dimethyl sulphide…is judged to be very toxic to humans and dangerous to the environment". Hydrogen sulphide gas, if released, would cause eye irritation and, at high levels, "vomiting, breathing difficulties, loss of consciousness and death".

The report concluded that Trafigura's dumped wastes "by their very nature" would have contained very high concentrations of these dangerous substances with noxious smells "and by degradation are likely to release hydrogen sulphide into the atmosphere". The reported "severe human health effects" in Abidjan were, they concluded, precisely those to be expected. The report finished up by noting that such dumping would have been completely illegal in the EU [3].

Minton's conclusions were later backed up by Dutch official analysis of actual samples of the slurry that went on to Africa. This confirmed the presence of noxious and highly toxic compounds in the liquid, including "substances which, when the pH is lowered, decompose into (extremely) toxic mercaptans and hydrogen sulphide". The illegally exported and dumped waste, Dutch authorities found, was "extremely hazardous" [2, p. 70].

THE FALSE NARRATIVE

Faced with this catastrophic situation, Claude Dauphin and Trafigura did not tell the truth. When challenged, they continued to claim that the waste was merely the by-product of routine tank rinsing. They said that the slurry was quite harmless; that they had not gone specially to Abidjan to dump it; and that in any event the dumping was not their fault, but the fault of Salomon Ugborugbo, who they had thought in their innocence to be the head of a reputable disposal company.

Dauphin supplied this false narrative to an aggressive firm of British libel lawyers—Carter-Ruck—and a politically well-connected team of British lobbyists—Bell Pottinger. The duo were paid handsomely to threaten journalists worldwide who wrote hostile articles, whilst simultaneously burnishing the company's image with public relations stunts. It was the classic one-two punch of so-called reputation management.

Ordinary news journalists were easy enough to confuse. Many of the British reports did not even grasp the simple point that Trafigura's secretive activities were directed out of London. They called the company "Dutch" or "Swiss" because its corporate entities were registered in those countries, with shareholdings offshore in Curacao largely no doubt for tax reasons. The company's unadvertised nerve-centre was actually Portman House, over a fashion store in the middle of London's famous Oxford St.

On 19 September 2006, in the immediate wake of the Abidjan medical emergency, Trafigura issued the first of several carefully worded statements. It claimed their tanker had been merely "used for floating storage". Trafigura went on: "Cleaning with caustic soda takes place each time it receives a new load of gasoline blend stock". The waste was simply "the result of washings from gasoline blend stock delivered to the vessel" [4].

The Dutch journalist Jeroen Trommelen was the first to seek to puncture this opaque Trafigura narrative. The environmental activists Greenpeace in Amsterdam and the Dutch authorities were already getting leaks from concerned insiders. As Greenpeace campaigners prepared to travel north to blockade the tanker Probo Koala (by now docked in Estonia), Trommelen wrote in the Netherlands paper *Volkskrant* a piece headlined "Poison ship produced deadly waste at sea". Without being able to publish any documents, he alleged that the ship had really been a "floating refinery" using a primitive caustic wash process which generated "lethal" waste [5].

The next day, Trafigura issued a statement in London denying the allegations:

TRAFIGURA TESTS CONTRADICT MEDIA SPECULATION ...Tests conducted by the company and others show the washings to have little or no toxicity...the composition of the 'chemical slops'; gasoline, spent caustic soda and water, is a normal by-product from the cleaning of gasoline blend-stock cargo ... Trafigura's own analysis and that of a French company, show that hydrogen sulphide level was not detected in the 'chemical slops'. The slops are entirely in line with industry practice and international regulations ... for the disposal of residue washings. [6]

Trommelen's claims in a relatively small Dutch-language paper had only limited resonance. The *New York Times* did pick up the story but reacted uncertainly. They wrote: "Exactly where the waste originated remains unclear. A spokesman for Trafigura, Jan Maat, said the Probo Koala had served in the Mediterranean "as a floating storage tank" and had taken on loads from several different ships, but he declined to give details. Reports in the Dutch press said the Probo Koala had been secretly used as a floating refinery during the summer, when selling gasoline had become unusually profitable. Mr. Maat denied that. 'This is absolutely untrue' he said [7].

Graham Sharp, a British Trafigura director, was deputed to refute the unwelcome US publicity. The *New York Times* agreed to publish his letter a week later. He wrote: "We believe that the vessel slops we discharged in Ivory Coast were not capable of causing the harm that happened there. In particular we are certain that they did not contain hydrogen sulphide" [8].

Trafigura sought to buy their way out of the trouble with the Ivorians. Dauphin flew to Africa to appease the regime there. They promptly locked him up with two fellow-executives until the company paid $198 million for a clean-up and his release. (The company could afford it. Its profits continued to run at more than $400 million a year). The hapless Ugborugbo was arrested. But the Ivory Coast ministers agreed in return for Trafigura's cash, not to proceed against the company itself for the illegal dumping.

The lobbyists Bell Pottinger devised a PR blitz to present Trafigura in a more benign light. The firm offered to help fund a British Lions rugby tour of South Africa. Bell Pottinger were listed as the contact-point for a new charitable "Trafigura Foundation". The foundation was to donate in Britain to a helpline for sufferers from autism, and in the US to an arts centre for hurricane-stricken New Orleans [9].

Another Trafigura public relations effort was to hire a veteran British Conservative politician, the late Peter Fraser QC, Lord Fraser of Carmyllie, to launch a so-called independent inquiry into the dumping. The shine was almost immediately taken off this move when Fraser was arrested for being drunk on a plane. (The drink charges were disputed and later dropped.) [10]

Producing little in the end, Fraser pronounced himself a "frustrated bunny" because of impending litigation. The bitterly fought lawsuit to which he referred was launched in London by a human rights lawyer, Martyn Day, seeking damages for eventually more than **30,000** poverty-stricken Ivorians who were eager to join in.

Day had good links with some of the British press, and this pioneering case as it proceeded, was to throw up facts which found their way to journalists. But, in reporting the initial launch of the action, the *Guardian*'s environment editor, John Vidal, still could not say how the waste really originated. He wrote "Allegations that the waste had high levels of caustic soda, as well as a sulphur compound and hydrogen sulphide, have been strongly denied by Trafigura". He quoted yet another Trafigura statement:

> The slops were the result of normal maritime gasoline trade operations and did not contain active hydrogen sulphide …Hydrogen sulphide would have caused immediate serious illness to the ship's crew and the workers at the petroleum berth where the slops were offloaded. There were no such illnesses. [11]

These references to hydrogen sulphide were a play on words. The traders had by now shifted position to deny only that "active" hydrogen sulphide was present in the waste compounds. The Minton Report had actually identified the danger to health as something different— the likely release of the poisonous gas when activated by further chemical reactions. Such further chemical breakdowns could be expected after exposure of the dumped slurry to the open air and to downpours of African rain. In the absence of key documents, it was easy enough to blind non-specialist journalists with science.

Trafigura also had their lawyers make an unusual move to crush more publicity. They announced they would sue the other side's lawyers personally for libel. They exploited the then-unreformed British libel law under which, among other things, companies could sue as though they were real individuals. Actual financial loss did not need to occur. Trafigura announced, threateningly, that they had:

> issued proceedings for libel against solicitors Leigh Day & Co in respect of a press release and website publication in which Trafigura is wrongly accused

of causing death and injury to the population of Abidjan in the Ivory Coast and widespread environmental damage. [12]

The threat did not altogether close down Martyn Day's vigorous campaigning. The BBC began to take an interest. Their local Africa correspondent went to Abidjan with the lawyer to film interviews with alleged victims. But another Trafigura director, Eric de Turckheim, appeared onscreen in order to discredit the item when it was transmitted in London. He told Newsnight interviewer Jeremy Paxman: "The slops were a mixture of water, gasoline and caustic soda...The discharge of slops is a routine operation which is carried out worldwide...The slops it was carrying were absolutely not dangerous" [13].

In another part of the world, two reporters from Norwegian TV meanwhile began to probe the mysterious explosion in their northern fjord. It had left the inhabitants of the little village of Slovaag retching and choking. The pair worked hard, and discovered that the chemicals in the exploding tank had originated from Trafigura ships. They also found out that the explosion involved waste from the illegal caustic washing processes carried out over a considerable period by the tank farm owners, and they linked the blast to the toxic dumping scandal in Africa.

Trafigura refused to comment or be interviewed. Norwegian TV nevertheless gave them a preview of their documentary, "Dirty Cargo". The reaction was a tirade from lobbyists Bell Pottinger about "inaccurate comments". The lobbyists threatened that Trafigura had already made "legal complaints" against other media organisations worldwide.

It was imperative that the Norwegians transmitted Trafigura's vigorous denials, Bell Pottinger said. Trafigura and its independent experts were going to prove in the English High Court that the waste "simply cannot have caused the deaths and mass injuries alleged". The spin doctors asserted that Trafigura were entitled to assume Ugborugbo's firm was safe and qualified [14].

Pressure from Greenpeace activists now led to a Dutch decision to prosecute Trafigura for exporting the toxic waste and lying to the authorities about its nature. This was eventually to generate a further source of genuine facts. But in the meantime, Trafigura's PR blitz on the media intensified. Even journalists in Estonia and at small Lesotho news agency Afrol said they were threatened and complained about [15].

Bell Pottinger objected to the Associated Press agency about their international news dispatches and then complained to the *Guardian*, which had reproduced an AP story online. "Please note that in view of the gravity of these matters and of the allegations which have been published, I am copying Trafigura's solicitors, Carter-Ruck, into this email" [16].

The PR firm demanded the *Guardian* add a statement saying "The Probo Koala ...left Amsterdam with the full knowledge and clear approval of the Dutch authorities". The statement also asserted that Trafigura had been asked "without any credible justification" for extra fees to process the waste, and that "Ship's slops are commonly produced within the oil industry. To label Trafigura's slops as 'toxic waste' in no way accurately reflects their true composition" [16].

Rather than become embroiled in litigation, *Guardian* editors deleted the whole story.

On 16 September 2008, Trafigura posted a further statement on their website claiming "Trafigura is in no way responsible for the sickness suffered by people in Abidjan ... Independent experts have analysed the slops and concluded that they could not have caused the illnesses alleged ....The discharge of slops from cargo vessels is a routine procedure that is undertaken all over the world... People living near these sites were suffering health problems...long before...This is an environmental tragedy, but it is not one caused by Trafigura" [17].

The statements echoed Trafigura's published annual report for 2007, in which the company once again denied all liability; concealed the fact they had experimented with a floating refinery; and repeated falsely that their waste was only "a mixture of gasoline, water and caustic soda". The Amsterdam port had asked for extra disposal fees, they said, "without any credible justification", and many of those Africans suing had probably been already sick from other diseases.

On 22 September 2008, the *Guardian*'s East Africa correspondent, Xan Rice, asked Trafigura some questions, in view of the then impending trial of Salomon Ugborugbo in the Ivory Coast. The lobbyists Bell Pottinger said it would be "wrong and potentially irresponsible" for the paper to comment and implied that to do so might attract legal action: "These are concerns we would urge you to consider with your own legal advisers...I am copying this email to Carter-Ruck". Bell Pottinger claimed the "legal team" were alarmed by the nature of the reporter's questions.

Xan Rice's article was not published by the *Guardian*.

When Ugborugbo, the toxic waste scapegoat, received a 20-year jail sentence, Dutch Greenpeace activist Marietta Harjono said gloomily: "My strong impression is that some media have simply stopped writing about

Trafigura. I was supposed to do an interview on British radio the day that the court in Abidjan had come to a decision ... I was told that I should in no way mention Trafigura because of possible libel claims" [18].

At the *Guardian*, Xan Rice did ask some more questions after the trial: Bell Pottinger's man repeated the claim that the lawyer Martyn Day was going to be sued for libel. The lobbyist said—meaninglessly—that further Leigh Day allegations "are the subject of a complaint in Malicious Falsehood" and warned "I am copying this correspondence to Carter-Ruck and to the Guardian's legal department". He added: "Any suggestion, even implicit, that Trafigura ... should have stood trial in Ivory Coast would be completely unfounded and libellous ... We insist that you refer in detail to the contents of the attached summary" [16]. A closely typed six-page Trafigura statement was attached.

The waste, this document repeated, was merely "a mixture of gasoline, water and caustic soda ... The slops in question simply cannot have led to the deaths and widespread injuries ... [Ugborugbo] was fully informed as to the nature of the slops ... The company acted at all times in good faith in accordance with applicable regulations...The company certainly welcomes the fact that those involved in the indiscriminate dumping of the material have been brought to justice ... The slops, while having an unpleasant smell, could not have led to the widespread illnesses and injuries alleged ... Independent expert advice on Trafigura's obligations under the respective treaties and independent expert chemical analysis...supports Trafigura's stance...As the evidence from the independent experts forms an important element of Trafigura's ongoing defence...this information clearly cannot be disclosed at the present time ... The strong and unpleasant smell ... prompted local people to seek hospital treatment following the offer of free health care" [16].

Again, *Guardian* editors did not publish. By now, international media coverage had been reduced to little more than a strangled whisper. But this provoked an interesting development. Trafigura's worldwide blizzard of threats to the media was so relentless that it became counter-productive.

Trommelen, the Dutch reporter, tried to publish fresh allegations of attempted witness-nobbling. When he experienced the usual legal pressure, he discovered that Norwegian TV had also been receiving threats, as had the BBC in London. They all started to compare notes. Trommelen accused the lawyers of co-ordinated attempts at suppression. Carter-Ruck did not deny it:

"Trafigura has been obliged to engage my firm to bring complaints against Volkskrant...It is indeed the case that we have on Trafigura's behalf, written to a number of other media outlets around the world in respect of their coverage of this matter." The hired lobbyists Bell Pottinger also admitted they had contacted journalists who "did not accurately reflect Trafigura's position", but added defensively "We completely disagree with your description of Trafigura's involvement in an 'aggressive media campaign'" [19].

In London, BBC Newsnight's Meirion Jones now got the bit between his teeth. He linked up with Trommelen in Amsterdam, and with the two Norwegian TV journalists, Synnove Bakke and Kjersti Knudsen, to attempt a new TV programme.

The final link in this chain came when the *Guardian*'s editor Alan Rusbridger arrived from London to speak at a journalists' conference in Bergen. The explosion at nearby Slovaag was the talk of the journalist delegates. He was buttonholed by the pair of Norwegian reporters. They asked why they were all being pressured by the British lawyers Carter-Ruck. Their complaints stimulated Rusbridger, who had never heard of Trafigura. Once back in London, he consulted the present author, and a full-scale collaborative investigation was decided upon.

This personal backing from the *Guardian*'s then editor was to prove crucial in the warfare that would soon erupt. It is a lesson for investigative reporters everywhere—getting the editor interested makes a big difference. So, of course, does having the right editor in the first place.

THE COLLABORATIVE INVESTIGATION

The four groups of cross-border investigators, along with campaigners from Greenpeace and reporters from Estonia, agreed to pool information; to withstand the threats; and to publish their renewed investigations simultaneously. The company's efforts to pick off its media opponents had backfired. It had driven the journalists in several different countries, both in print and in broadcasting, to start working closely together.

This gave them legal protection: it was harder to gag information published simultaneously in different jurisdictions. Also, the collaboration was painless, without much professional rivalry. Their stories would all naturally emphasise different angles. The Dutch newspaper was focused on illegal waste-handling in Amsterdam. The Norwegian-language state broadcaster was trying to get to the bottom of illegal tank explosions in a

Scandinavian fjord. Neither of them was in direct competition with the Anglophone media, who were mainly concerned with the civil litigation in London. Print outlets wanted words: TV's priority was to have pictures. Furthermore, the journalists' interests in getting information were straightforwardly aligned with those of campaigners from Greenpeace and Amnesty International, who were trying to get the criminal authorities to act; and with the English lawyers who were trying to win damages for their clients.

But it would also be true to say that all the journalists rapidly developed a common state of mind. They felt exasperated at the legal harassment, and they wanted to see wrongdoing exposed.

The group shared hard pieces of evidence contradicting Trafigura's narrative. These documents included a preliminary official analysis of samples taken during the tanker's docking at Amsterdam; and files from the ongoing court cases. The paperwork confirmed that the waste was highly toxic, and that it came from "caustic washing" experiments at sea, not from "routine" tank rinsing. The BBC and the *Guardian* published their first fresh reports simultaneously in May 2009 [20]. The BBC's footage was particularly harrowing—Meirion Jones and Liz Kean had journeyed to the Ivory Coast and filmed victims talking of deaths and miscarriages after the dumping.

Trafigura reached for their lawyers once again. Carter-Ruck announced that libel proceedings had been issued against the BBC for a "wildly inaccurate and libellous", "one-sided", "misleading", "sensationalist and inaccurate" programme. Trafigura had "no choice but to take legal action", they said: "Trafigura has always denied that the slops caused the deaths and serious health consequences presented by the BBC—a position fully supported by independent expert evidence".

The libel lawyers demanded that the *Guardian* delete its parallel articles on the subject, claiming they were "grossly defamatory" and untrue, as well as being "highly sensationalist". The lawyers repeated: "It is untrue that the slops caused or could have caused the numerous deaths and serious injuries...Trafigura cannot be expected to tolerate unbalanced and inaccurate reporting of this nature. Accordingly, Trafigura requires the Guardian to...remove these articles from its website forthwith".

The campaigners met together in Amsterdam for a council of war. The BBC filed a fighting defence to the libel suit, and this time, the *Guardian* was in a stronger position. The paper declined to roll over, saying its articles were all true. The *Guardian*'s lawyer Gill Phillips wrote bluntly, "My client believes that publication of the articles is justified and should not be removed".

Behind the scenes, a harshly fought legal battle for compensation was taking place in the London civil courts. Many millions of pounds were at stake, along with the very survival of Day's own law firm. Trafigura's strategy was to try and keep the history of its criminal behaviour out of court, and purely focus on one test: could Day's team prove to a legal standard that each specific injury to his thousands of clients had been caused by them? Precise proof of such causation was hard. Day, for his part, wanted to swing the focus round to allegations of Trafigura's prior bad faith and dishonesty.

As so often happens, such a contested legal process generated key raw material for investigative journalists. Trafigura were eventually forced to disclose quantities of their emails to the court. Many of their internal discussions about what to do with the waste (which the traders referred to as "crap" and "the shit") proved highly incriminating. Not only did the emails finally prove that "caustic washing" experiments had taken place at sea: they also proved that Trafigura knew perfectly well that export of the subsequent waste was hazardous and illegal.

A final sensational leaked document now also came to light from one of the journalist groups. This was a copy of the long-concealed Minton Report. It told the collaborators that, all along, Trafigura had known that its waste could injure and even kill. The company's three years of threats and protestations seemed to the reporters to have been little better than a pack of lies.

The teams determined to publish all the devastating material simultaneously on 17 September 2009. But they encountered a classic problem. Ethics (and in Britain, the libel law) require that journalists give their targets the chance to respond before attacking them. But as soon as Trafigura were tipped off that their opponents had obtained the Minton Report, the company rushed back to court in Britain.

Thanks to the weak protection for free speech there, Trafigura's lawyers were able to persuade a judge to grant an unprecedented gag. The *Guardian* were banned from publishing any information from the document, on the grounds that it was Trafigura's confidential commercial property. Furthermore the paper was even gagged, in what was termed a "superinjunction", from revealing that Trafigura had gagged them. Nothing at all was allowed to be said.

Defeating the Legal Gag

The way Trafigura's superinjunction was defeated by this small group of reporters is instructive. It demonstrates that journalists too can think creatively. It also demonstrates that in an online age, even the most expensive lawyers and lobbyists will sometimes end up like King Canute, vainly trying to keep back the waves.

What happened with Trafigura is not, of course, an exact template for other journalists blindly to follow. The detailed manoeuvres employed were very specific to the moment and very culture-specific (as of course is all investigative journalism). Investigative reporters need to have a feel for their own particular environments, legal, social, cultural, and political, in order to thread their way through obstacles to the truth.

That is why a textbook such as this does not prescribe detailed playbooks for every circumstance. What is necessary instead is the right problem-solving mindset. (A team at the UK *Daily Telegraph* were to defeat a slightly different legal gag in a parallel way nine years later.) [21]

Thanks to the differing legal jurisdictions involved, the journalists in the Trafigura cross-border team did not all face identical problems. Trafigura triumphantly circulated the Dutch and Norwegians with news of the High Court injunction Carter-Ruck had gained against the *Guardian* in London. But it was all bluff. These injunctions had no legal force outside England.

With resolute lawyers of their own, the Norwegian broadcasters published a copy of the entire report on their website. So did Greenpeace in the Netherlands. A copy was posted up on Wikileaks for all to see around the world. (It was still there at the time of writing.) These online postings were a testament to the value of cross-jurisdiction collaboration. They were legally unstoppable [22].

However, the British journalists were still faced with their own apparently insurmountable barriers. Under the terms of the superinjunction, they were forbidden from revealing that the gagged information could be found elsewhere, or even disclosing that it existed at all. The journalists on whom all this secrecy was imposed were left speechless by reports of the judge's bizarre reasoning: "If the Guardian publish that named claimants have applied for an injunction against them, it is something that could be seen by some members of the public as indicating an attempt by the claimants improperly to muzzle the press" [23].

Yes, indeed!

In legal theory, such interference with the media was temporary and only meant to hold the ring until there could be a proper trial of a claim of "breach of confidence", against which the *Guardian* could argue its own rights of "public interest".

But in the real world, it made no sense whatever for the *Guardian* to try and fight its way out of this legal mire. Months or even years later, they would be arguing in successive courts at a cost of hundreds of thousands of pounds, in the face of an unsympathetic UK legal establishment, about a case that would no longer be relevant. The only winners would be the lawyers and their huge fees. It was a classic case of censorship by legal process.

Was there an alternative? A friendly British MP, Paul Farrelly, discovered what was going on. He was a former journalist on the *Guardian*'s sister-paper, the *Observer*, so the cause of free speech was close to his heart. Later, a Carter-Ruck partner complained bitterly at the way the firm had been outsmarted: "Given that there was a "superinjunction" in place, how on earth did Paul Farrelly MP, find out about it?" [23].

But it was hard to feel sympathy for the fuming solicitors: Trafigura had already sent copies of the injunction to unrestrained journalists abroad, presumably in the hope of browbeating them into silence [24]. And more careful footwork by the supporters of free speech was now to follow. It is a quirk of the British system that the only place safe from legal restraint is the Houses of Parliament. MPs can say what they like, and no lawyer can ever interfere with Parliamentary publications. So Farrelly decided to put down a lengthy and obscure written parliamentary question about the general practice of "superinjunctions" which would in fact also reveal the existence of Trafigura's gag.

His "PQ" read: "To ask the Secretary of State for Justice what assessment he has made of the effectiveness of legislation to protect (a) whistleblowers and (b) press freedom following the injunctions obtained in the High Court by (1) Barclays and Freshfields solicitors on 19 March 2009 on the publication of internal Barclays reports documenting alleged tax avoidance schemes and (2) Trafigura and Carter-Ruck solicitors on 11 September 2009 on the publication of the Minton Report on the alleged dumping of toxic waste in the Ivory Coast, commissioned by Trafigura" [25].

This duly appeared on the Commons order paper.

The real mystery was not how Farrelly, the MP, had first heard of the gag. It was how he was able to get away with tabling that question.

Normally, he would never have been allowed to do it, for despite their freedom of speech, MPs are required by Commons rules to avoid statements about live legal proceedings. This is usually a necessary piece of self-restraint to keep the two branches of government safely apart.

But Carter-Ruck's over-reaching had left a loophole that was almost comic in its effect. Parliamentary officials would routinely check questions that referred to legal events to see if there was any active court proceeding under that name. When they looked up Trafigura injunctions, they found nothing, and waved Farrelly's question through. This was because, as a result of Carter-Ruck's triumph in obtaining a totally secret superinjunction, it was listed only under the deliberately meaningless initials "RJW". The lawyers had been too clever by half, and it had tripped them up.

So the words on the Commons order paper were now printed, privileged, and free for anyone to report. But the comedy continued.

In view of the total gag, how was attention to be directed to the public existence of Farrelly's subversive PQ? The *Guardian* wrote a letter to Carter-Ruck, pointing out that the details had now been published by Parliament, and the *Guardian* must therefore be free to report them. The lawyers fell into the trap. They wrote back telling the *Guardian* it would be contempt of court for the paper to do so. This gave the newspaper a story it *could* publish, and one which was bound to create a furore about free speech.

"Guardian gagged from reporting Parliament" said the headline:

> Today's published Commons order papers contain a question to be answered by a minister later this week. The Guardian is prevented from identifying the MP who has asked the question, what the question is, which minister might answer it, or where the question is to be found. The Guardian is also forbidden from telling its readers why the paper is prevented—for the first time in memory—from reporting parliament. Legal obstacles, which cannot be identified, involve proceedings, which cannot be mentioned, on behalf of a client who must remain secret. The only fact the Guardian can report is that the case involves the London solicitors Carter-Ruck, who specialise in suing the media for clients, who include individuals or global corporations...The editor, Alan Rusbridger, said: 'The media laws in this country increasingly place newspapers in a Kafkaesque world'. [26]

Rusbridger himself, an online enthusiast, thus poured petrol all over the floor. Now he ignited it by tweeting. Linking to the words of his *Guardian* story, Rusbridger summoned up the spirit of John Wilkes, the eighteenth-century free speech campaigner who had gained the right for the public to know what went on in Parliament. His tweet said: "Now Guardian prevented from reporting parliament for unreportable reasons. Did John Wilkes live in vain?"

The wild west world of Twitter users responded enthusiastically to the provocation. The *Guardian* recounted the next day, poker-faced, what it termed a "race among bloggers to reveal all…Just 42 minutes after the Guardian story was published, the internet had revealed what the paper could not…Trafigura was the most used word on micro-blogging site this morning" [27]. The popular actor Stephen Fry was among those retweeting the details of the MP's question to some 830,000 followers he had at the time [28].

The full contents of the Minton Report, freely searchable as it already was online, thus soon also became generally known. And the game was up.

OUTCOMES

In the end, there were several positive outcomes to this long war against Trafigura's falsehoods. The company dropped most of its pointless attempts to suppress reporting [29].

The future use of superinjunctions to suppress free speech was itself curtailed by the courts. In the London civil action, Trafigura was forced to pay £30 million in compensation to the Ivorian citizens whom it had made ill, and another £30 million on account towards the eye-watering legal costs claimed by their pioneering solicitors, Leigh Day. And eventually, in Amsterdam, Dauphin and Trafigura were convicted of what they had repeatedly denied—lying about the toxicity of their waste, and illegally exporting it from Europe. The company were fined €1 million, and Dauphin himself another token ¢67,000 [30].

Of its cut-price dumping in the Ivory Coast, Dutch presiding Judge Frans Bauduin said: "Trafigura—which by that time knew of the exact composition [of the waste]—should never have agreed to its processing at such a price" [31].

The reporters who had joined forces to fight off Trafigura's falsehoods were gratified to be awarded a prize in 2010 by the Washington-based International Consortium of Investigative Journalists, for what the ICIJ termed: "A gutsy, collaborative series by four European news outlets about toxic waste dumping in Africa" [32].

But the news was not all good. The price of the negotiated settlement in the civil damages case was an agreement to seal all the medical reports, and in their place, announce an agreed statement by both sides that "Leigh Day & Co, in the light of the expert evidence, now acknowledge that the slops could at worst have caused a range of short term low level flu-like symptoms and anxiety" [2, p. 162].

This backstairs deal left the BBC journalists exposed in their libel case. They had reported in good faith the far more drastic claims made at the time of death and miscarriages. Under the then-unreformed British libel law, the broadcasters were now left with an uphill struggle to prove the truth of what they had alleged. The BBC decided not to stand by their reporters, but to cut their losses and settle. They paid Carter-Ruck's legal bills, and handed over another relatively modest £25,000 to charity. Viewers were treated to Newsnight's presenter, Emily Maitlis, opening the next evening's programme by saying through gritted teeth:

> In May of this year, we reported on the oil company Trafigura and the disposal of waste in Abidjan on the Ivory Coast. We claimed the waste caused miscarriages, deaths and other serious and long-term injuries. Following the settlement of a personal injury action brought by residents of the Ivory Coast, we have reviewed the evidence and Trafigura's response to our allegations. We accept the independent experts have considered this matter in detail and were unable to establish any link between the waste and these serious consequences. We withdraw those allegations and apologise to Trafigura. [33]

It was a strange experience to see those soon to be convicted as criminals being presented to the public in this way as the innocent victims. And given an apology. But that is the kind of outcome investigative journalists sometimes have to get used to.

References

1. Leigh, David. 2009. Dirty Business: How UK Firm Covered up Toxic Oil Disaster. *Guardian*, September 17.
2. Greenpeace/Amnesty. 2012. The Toxic Truth. *Joint Report.* Accessed November 18, 2018. https://www.greenpeace.org/international/publication/7245/the-toxic-truth/.

3. Minton, Treharne & Davis Ltd. 2006. Re: Caustic Tank Washings, Abidjan, Ivory Coast. Report. Accessed November 18, 2018. https://www.theguardian.com/world/2009/oct/16/carter-ruck-abandon-minton-injunction.
4. Trafigura. 2006. Statement from Trafigura Beheer BV re the Probo Koala. *Clean Abidjan Project.* Accessed November 18, 2018. http://clean-abidjan.blogspot.com/2006/09/statement-from-trafigura-beheer-bv-re.html.
5. Trommelen, Jeroen. 2006. Gifschip produceerde dodelijk afval op zee. *Volkskrant,* September 23.
6. Trafigura. 2006. Trafigura Tests Contradict Media Speculation. Press Release, September 24. Accessed November 18, 2018. https://web.archive.org/web/20061105054741/http://www.trafigura.com:80/press_releases/press_statement_240906.aspx.
7. Polgreen, Lydia, and Marlise Simons. 2006. Global Sludge ends in tragedy for Ivory Coast. *New York Times,* October 2.
8. Sharp, Graham. 2006. Letter. *New York Times,* October 9.
9. Leigh, David. 2009. How Oil Traders Trafigura Tried to Limit the Damage Over Toxic Waste Allegations. *Guardian.* Accessed November 18, 2018. https://www.theguardian.com/environment/2009/may/13/trafigura-pr-campaign-pollution-ivory-coast.
10. Nicolson, Stuart. 2007. Air Rage Case Against Tory Peer Dropped. *Daily Mail,* February 3.
11. Vidal, John. 2007. UK Class Action Starts Over Toxic Waste Dumped in Africa. *Guardian.* Accessed November 18, 2018. https://www.theguardian.com/environment/2007/jan/08/pollution.internationalnews.
12. Trafigura. 2006. Trafigura Issue Libel Proceedings Against Leigh, Day & Co. Press Release, November 13. Accessed November 18, 2018. http://web.archive.org/web/20061122053311/http://www.trafigura.com/trafigura_news/probo_koala_updates/131106.aspx.
13. Turckheim, Eric. 2007. Interview. *BBC Newsnight,* August 16. Accessed November 19, 2018. https://www.youtube.com/watch?v=1o4OmZEaXgA.
14. Bakke, Synnove, and Kjersti Knudsen, 2010. Skup Method Report January 15. Accessed November 18, 2018. https://www.skup.no/sites/default/files/metoderapport/2009-20%2520Trafigura%2520hele%2520bildet%2520%28NRK%2520Brennpunkt%29.pdf.
15. Trommelen, Jeroen. 2009. Geen kwaad woord over hetn gifschip. *Volkskrant,* May 2.
16. Rusbridger, Alan. 2009. Written Evidence to Commons Committee on Culture, Media and Sport; Annex. Accessed November 18, 2018. https://publications.parliament.uk/pa/cm200809/cmselect/cmcumeds/memo/press/m13102.htm. See also: Accessed January 26, 2018. https://publications.parliament.uk/pa/cm200910/cmselect/cmcumeds/362/9071417.htm.

17. Trafigura. 2008. Probo Koala Updates. Press Release, September 16. Accessed November 18, 2018. https://web.archive.org/web/20081223045759/http://www.trafigura.com:80/our_news/probo_koala_updates.aspx.
18. Leigh, David. 2009. How Oil Traders Trafigura Tried To Limit the Damage. *Guardian.* Accessed November 18, 2018. https://www.theguardian.com/environment/2009/may/13/trafigura-pr-campaign-pollution-ivory-coast.
19. Trommelen, Jeroen. 2009. De volledige reacties van de woordvoerders van Trafigura. *Volkskrant,* May 1.
20. Leigh, David. 2009. Papers Prove Trafigura Ship Dumped Toxic Waste. *Guardian,* May 14.
21. A peer, Lord Hain, used parliamentary privilege on October 25 2018 to name businessman Sir Philip Green as the subject of sexual harassment allegations which were covered by so-called Non-Disclosure Agreements. Accessed November 19, 2018. See https://www.telegraph.co.uk/news/2018/10/25/watch-sir-philip-green-named-parliament-businessman-centre-britains/.
22. Bakke, Synnove, and Kjersti Knudsen. 2009. A Spreading of Toxic Gags. *Guardian.* Accessed November 19, 2018. https://www.theguardian.com/commentisfree/2009/oct/26/spreading-toxic-injunctions.
23. Tait, Nigel. 2011. The Trafigura Story: Who Guards the Guardian? *Inforrm legal blog.* Accessed November 19, 2018. https://inforrm.org/2011/10/13/the-trafigura-story-who-guards-the-guardian-nigel-tait/.
24. Bakke, Synnove, and Kjersti Knudsen. 2009. Trafigura and the Monton Report. Accessed November 19, 2018. https://www.nrk.no/dokumentar/trafigura-and-the-minton-report-1.6816347.
25. Leigh, David. 2009. Gag on Guardian Reporting MP's Trafigura Question Lifted. *Guardian.* Accessed November 19, 2018. https://www.theguardian.com/media/2009/oct/13/guardian-gagged-parliamentary-question.
26. ———. 2009. Guardian Gagged From Reporting Parliament. *Guardian.* Accessed November 19, 2018. https://www.theguardian.com/media/2009/oct/12/guardian-gagged-from-reporting-parliament.
27. Booth, Robert. 2009. Trafigura: A Few Tweets and Freedom of Speech is Restored. *Guardian.* Accessed November 19, 2018. https://www.theguardian.com/media/2009/oct/13/trafigura-tweets-freedowm-of-speech.
28. https://twitter.com/stephenfry/status/4831036632.
29. Leigh, David. 2009. Trafigura Abandons Attempts to Keep Scientific Report Secret. Accessed November 19, 2018. https://www.theguardian.com/world/2009/oct/16/carter-ruck-abandon-minton-injunction.
30. Milmo, Cahal. 2010. Trafigura Found Guilty of Toxic Waste Offence. Accessed November 19, 2018. https://www.independent.co.uk/news/world/europe/trafigura-found-guilty-of-toxic-waste-offence-2034313.html.

31. BBC. 2010. Trafigura Found Guilty of Exporting Toxic Waste. *BBC News Africa*. Accessed November 19, 2018. https://www.bbc.co.uk/news/world-africa-10735255.
32. International Consortium of Investigative Journalists. 2010. Daniel Pearl Awards. Accessed November 19, 2018. https://www.icij.org/about/awards/daniel-pearl-awards/.
33. Maitlis, Emily. 2009. BBC Newsnight Apology to Trafigura. *Newsnight*. Accessed November 19, 2018. https://www.youtube.com/watch?v=aMYvFlqLpv8.

CHAPTER 12

Conclusion: A Golden Age for Investigative Journalism?

If you're an investigative reporter, the world around does look gloomy sometimes. There are so many enemies, internal and external, who can seem arrayed against you. But the reality is not all dark. These can actually be marvellous times for journalists who want to stand up to power. The gifted investigative reporter and academic from the Philippines, Sheila Coronel, told her first class of Columbia University students in New York back in 2006 "We are at the dawn of a Golden Age of global muckraking" [1]. I believe she was right.

While it is true that investigative journalism has many enemies, it also has some new friends. They may enable it to survive the current turbulent transition of the mass media from one shape to another. And even prosper.

The International Consortium of Investigative Journalists

Some of the new friends of investigative journalists are philanthropists. Quite a number of rich people out there are nowadays tipping money into successful investigative non-profits. I detailed in earlier chapters the particularly fruitful history of the International Consortium of Investigative Journalists [ICIJ], and its original US parent the Center for Public Integrity [CPI]. They partner with mainstream media outlets to get

© The Author(s) 2019
D. Leigh, *Investigative Journalism*,
https://doi.org/10.1007/978-3-030-16752-3_12

noticed, and their business model is, "We give away our work for free". In 2017, the ICIJ obtained donor pledges of almost $7 million [2].

MAJOR DONORS TO ICIJ 2017–18
ADESSIUM FOUNDATION
AFTENPOSTEN
FORD FOUNDATION
FRANKLIN PHILANTHROPIC FOUNDATION
FUND FOR NONPROFIT NEWS AT THE MIAMI FOUNDATION (NEWSMATCH)
HOLLYWOOD FOREIGN PRESS ASSOCIATION
JOHN AND FLORENCE NEWMAN FOUNDATION
GREEN PARK FOUNDATION
HURD FOUNDATION
JONATHAN LOGAN FAMILY FOUNDATION
LAURA AND JOHN ARNOLD
KCIJ NEWSTAPA
MOSES LUBASH FAMILY FUND
NEO4J
OMIDYAR NETWORK
OPEN SOCIETY FOUNDATIONS
PHALAROPE FOUNDATION
RUTGERS PRESBYTERIAN CHURCH
SWEDISH POSTCODE FOUNDATION
IN-KIND SUPPORT FROM GRAEME WOOD. [3]

Typical of the new kind of philanthropic backer is Adessium. This low-profile family foundation was set up in 2005 by Dutch commodities trader Gerard van Vliet. He told a magazine that he spotted ICIJ's potential for truth-telling early on: "A very important element of a free democratic society is that we are not misled with information" [4].

Van Vliet says he "aspires to a society that encourages people to live in harmony with each other and with their environments". He and his family distributed a total of ₡19 million in various directions in 2017. They realise that investigative journalism is short of money. Hence Adessium puts cash not only into ICIJ, but also into "Reporters Without Borders"; the Bureau of Investigative Journalism, European Investigative Collaborations; the Global Investigative Journalism Network; journalismfund.eu (which provides grants for collaborative investigations), and British "open source" investigator Bellingcat—as well as helping fund some of the NGOs which assist journalists, such as the Committee to Protect Journalists; Media Legal Defence Initiative; Transparency International, Global Witness; Greenpeace Netherlands; Human Rights Watch; and the Tax Justice Network.

Adessium's rationale for what they do for journalism is "We promote the search for truth, the availability of quality information, and public discourse in a digital environment. This way, we contribute to an ethical, democratic, and effective Europe"

Another significant ICIJ donor is a different type of person—the American billionaire entrepreneur Pierre Omidyar, founder of the online marketplace Ebay. His starting-point is that "People are basically good" [5]. Omidyar's Democracy Fund was distributing around $12m a year in 2017 to various causes, including "investigative journalism". He also backed the US "fearless adversarial journalism" website The Intercept, run by activist lawyer Glenn Greenwald, which promoted many of the Edward Snowden 2013 NSA surveillance revelations.

Omidyar's further contribution to the iconography of investigative journalism was to co-finance Spotlight, a 2015 movie chronicling the feats of the *Boston Globe* and its then editor Marty Baron, in exposing sex-abusing Catholic priests. The $20m production was well received: it was also estimated to have actually made a profit [6].

The full range of donors to ICIJ includes the billionaire financier George Soros' Open Society Institute, which has been vigorous in promoting democracy in Eastern Europe; the rather smaller Rutgers Presbyterian Church on Manhattan's upper west side; and a non-profit foundation in Stockholm which distributes Swedish lottery funds. In 2018, this body financed development of an ICIJ digital platform. Its reasoning was again quite idealistic: that human societies throughout the entire world were threatened by "polluting industries, international crime, false news, and corruption" [7].

THE BUREAU OF INVESTIGATIVE JOURNALISM

The existence of teams like ICIJ does not directly help aspiring young investigative journalists to get started in their careers. Apart from a few young staffers, they tend to recruit into their network only those who have already established a reputation.

One direct route into working for donor-funded reporting in Britain comes through websites like the small London-based Bureau of Investigative Journalism. They hire some young reporters. It was launched in 2010 largely through the effort of an old hand from the *Sunday Times* Insight team, Elaine Potter, together with her husband David Potter. He made his money through development of the early Psion home computer. Elaine Potter says: "We want to be a force for good… pursuing the truth and disentangling lies from reality" [8].

While some other attempts at investigative websites have crashed and burned, TBIJ overcame its early misadventures over sex abuse (see Chap. 8). Under its subsequent editor, Rachel Oldroyd, the Bureau flourished. Working to reliable professional standards, its revenue rose from £490,000 in 2014 to over £1 million in 2017. Its income comes from the Potters and a group of further donors whose identities overlap to a considerable extent with those of the ICIJ.

The Bureau's basic model, like that of the ICIJ, is to give away its work, partnering with mainstream outlets who provide publicity and credibility. The mainstream "co-publishers" also—crucially—provide legal defence in depth. This is essential in a British—and to an extent also a US—legal landscape, where one big lawsuit can otherwise crush the finances of a small non-profit. Organisations like TBIJ find things out which are not being investigated elsewhere—such as, for example, their painstaking bodycount of those killed by drone strikes. TBIJ's charitable sister organisation, the Centre for Investigative Journalism, provides training, particularly in data journalism, and an annual summer school which showcases current work by reporters.

MAJOR DONORS TO TBIJ 2017–18
ADESSIUM FOUNDATION
AGORA JOURNALISM CENTER
BERTHA FOUNDATION

CHANGING MARKETS
THE EVAN CORNISH FOUNDATION
SIR DONALD AND ELIZABETH CRUICKSHANK
EUROPEAN JOURNALISM CENTRE
FREEDOM OF THE PRESS FOUNDATION
THEGUARDIAN.ORG
GREEN PARK FOUNDATION
GOOGLE DIGITAL NEWS INITIATIVE
JOSEPH ROWNTREE CHARITABLE TRUST
OPEN SOCIETY FOUNDATIONS
OXFAM
PEARS FOUNDATION
DAVID AND ELAINE POTTER
THE REMOTE CONTROL PROJECT
REVA AND DAVID LOGAN FOUNDATION
RUDOLF AUGSTEIN STIFTUNG
STAMP OUT POVERTY

Propublica and Center for Investigative Reporting

In the US, these non-profit sites have been going for long enough now to have become a venerable part of the investigative landscape. They too collect funds from a range of civic-minded donors, many of them US billionaire families, and they push out their radio, TV, and online material via mainstream partners. The CIR is based in the San Francisco area and collected some $13 million in donations and grants in 2017. The distinguished TV journalist Lowell Bergman (see Chap. 4) was one of its original co-founders in 1977.

On the East coast, New York-based Propublica was founded in 2007 and defines its productions as "investigative journalism with moral force". It was headed from the outset by Paul Steiger, who had been managing editor of the Wall Street Journal. In 2017, a bumper year following the election of Donald Trump, it brought in $43 million in pledges from donors.

Propublica had an explicitly hostile stance towards the powerful. It started out proposing an adversarial "journalism that shines a light on exploitation of the weak by the strong", although by 2018, they were offering a slightly more centrist mission statement: "To expose abuses of power and betrayals of the public trust by government, business, and other institutions ... to spur reform through the sustained spotlighting of wrongdoing" [9].

OCCRP, BIRN, EIC, GIJN, IRE, SKUP

A variety of other investigative networks that publish news have sprung up in the decades since the collapse of the old Soviet Union. Some in Europe offer strength through numbers to the fragile democracies or near-democracies of the former communist empire. OCCRP, set up in 2006 and substantially funded from US government sources, originally focused on corruption and crime in eastern Europe, but has since expanded internationally [10]. BIRN, the Balkan Investigative Reporting Network, was also launched in 2006 and performs a training and publishing role in former Yugoslavia, Greece, and Albania. It is backed by EU and US government money as well as support from private foundations [11]. EIC, the European Investigative Collaborations, is a different model of a more commercial kind, led by the German magazine Der Spiegel with a group of minor European partners. It was set up after 2015 as a rival to the US-based ICIJ [12].

The Global Investigative Journalists Network, GIJN, sees investigative reporters in distinctly warlike terms, as the "special forces" of the regular journalistic world. Under the energetic leadership of US-based journalist David Kaplan, GIJN is not a publisher, but more of a federation of national journalist organisations: the services they offer include valuable access to training and regular large international conferences. GIJN has been a seed-bed of collaborative journalistic enterprise since its first worldwide conference in Copenhagen in 2003 [13]. In the domestic US, a comparable role is performed by Investigative Reporters and Editors, which has been in operation since 1975 (see Chap. 8).

One of GIJN's member organisations in Scandinavia, SKUP, has been particularly prominent in promoting investigative reporting. This Norwegian group, otherwise known as the Association for Critical and Investigative Press, was founded in 1990, and holds regular conferences with international speakers. They were one of the first journalist organisations to spot the significance of the work of Wikileaks and Julian Assange: they invited him to speak in Norway in March 2010.

A more chilling testimony to SKUP's investigative worth came the following year. The far-right terrorist Anders Breivik made plans to kill every journalist attending their 2011 conference. Only when his timing got delayed did he decide instead to slaughter 69 youngsters on the island of Utoya [14].

Greenpeace, Open Democracy, and Advocacy Organisations

The line between advocacy organisations and professional journalists is blurring as a result of this non-profit ferment. Organisations such as Greenpeace [15], Global Witness, and Open Democracy [16] are now hiring professional journalists to run investigative sections. They produce reports which can be marketed to mainstream partners, or published on their own sites. And mainstream papers like the *Guardian* in London are beginning to take money directly from philanthropists. *Guardian Australia*, for example, was set up with start-up finance from entrepreneur Graeme Wood [17]. The *Guardian* itself runs on an unusual hybrid business model: owned by a trust, it operates on commercial lines but is not required to make a profit for shareholders. Under those happy circumstances, it can focus, among other things, on turning out "public interest" investigative journalism.

Donor-Driven Journalism and Its Problems

Of course, it doesn't do to be too optimistic about journalism's future. Donor-driven journalism has its own problems. One is that the editors of small non-profits can find themselves spending all their time chasing money, rather than doing the journalism itself. Foundations will tend to fund only for one, two, or three years, resulting in endless exhausting rounds of fundraising simply in order to make sure the staff get paid.

Another headache is that the journalists can become prisoners of donor caprice. In the early days of ICIJ, it was always easy to get funds in order to investigate Big Tobacco. But it was hard to get funding for the unglamorous task of regular international conferences to build the organisation. The donor who pays the piper, understandably often wants to call the tune.

Another potential trouble-zone is always conflict of interest. Even the most high-minded donors can be a source of awkwardness. In 2015, journalists working on the leak of HSBC Swiss bank files were dismayed to discover that members of the philanthropic Potter family were keeping the equivalent of up to £70 million in previously unadvertised Swiss accounts.

The Potter's three sons had quite legitimately inherited "non-domicile" status from their father, whose origins were South African. Some held British passports and had houses in London. They were entitled to keep their money abroad and not pay British tax on it. They had done nothing illegal, but the British tax concession was controversial.

I experienced personal embarrassment about this. The *Guardian*, where I was employed, had been busy for months investigating such holders of Swiss bank accounts. At the time, I was on the board of the Potter-funded Centre for Investigative Journalism in London, but sworn to secrecy by my *Guardian* obligations. I had to quietly resign from the CIJ board to avoid a potential clash of interests. It was just as well: eventually, the *Guardian* decided to publish all the details of the Potters' holdings, in the interests of transparency. One of the problems of a life in investigative journalism is that you can't have friends [18].

A similar headache cropped up at the headquarters of the Washington-based International Consortium of Investigative Journalists. They discovered the equivalent of £12m had been passed through the Swiss bank in the name of Sigrid Rausing. The Swedish Tetrapak heiress, who lived in London, had purchased control of the literary magazine *Granta* and was also a benefactor of many good causes, to which she distributed some £20 million a year. These included donations to the ICIJ itself, which had received a total of £220,000. The ICIJ's partners went ahead and published details of her use of a Swiss bank, and of Rausing's hereditary "non-dom" tax-privileged UK status. Although it was all perfectly legal in Britain, Rausing was not happy at some of the Swedish publicity she received as a result. She is no longer listed as an ICIJ donor [19].

THE RISE OF THE INVESTIGATIONS EDITOR

Dependence on donors is caused by revenue collapse. This has eviscerated conventional mass media, particularly print newspapers, since advertising migrated online. At the same time, people, particularly young people, have stopped reading print to get their news, and the Internet has become awash with free news-related "content".

These well-known economic calamities have also however, had one, unexpected, positive effect on investigative journalism. It has become one of the relatively few ways in which mainstream media outlets can brand themselves. Precisely because serious investigations are expensive, time-consuming, and require sophisticated professional judgement, they have become a mark of distinctiveness in a crowded and chaotic market.

As a result, twenty-first century editors became investigation enthusiasts. British mid-market papers hurried to set up "investigation units" with "investigations editors", modelling themselves on their once-lonely highbrow predecessors. It is cheering to see investigative journalism become fashionable in this way, even as its financial underpinning remains precarious.

Universities too are now starting to teach investigative journalism as a specific subject. The present author was funded by the family of distinguished British writer, the late Anthony Sampson, to launch the first postgraduate course in investigative reporting at City University, part of the University of London. It began in 2006 with further funding from the Sainsbury supermarket family's Gatsby Foundation, and is now being imitated by others. Over its 12-year course, the programme steadily seeded would-be investigative journalists—and their exposure stories—into the British mainstream.

A more ambitious set of synergies were built up in California, where Lowell Bergman, hero of "The Insider" tobacco exposures, held the Reva and David Logan Distinguished Chair in Investigative Journalism, at Berkeley, University of California. He spent 20 years there, promoting the work of his graduate students into the mainstream, and working closely with PBS "Frontline" to produce a series of heavyweight TV documentaries [20].

Conclusion

Investigative journalists have managed in all these ways to become genuinely esteemed over the last half-century. It is certainly good for the soul to feel useful and even glamorous, rather than just a hack in a grubby raincoat. And it has also been very heartening to see a new phenomenon emerging over the years—the camaraderie of the international foot-soldiers of investigative journalism. Many have discovered that their common ideals (and obsessions) transcend the narrow interests of their employers, and produce better results than the egotism of old-fashioned diva reporters.

But we should never forget that underpinning this sense of social validation has been an information revolution. It's all about the technology. There is a cornucopia of information riches now available to the present generation of investigative journalists. This is utterly transformative and makes the pre-Internet journalistic era look medieval.

We used to have to attempt research by riffling through paper scraps cut out of newspapers by librarians with scissors, then laboriously indexed, stuffed into cardboard folders, and stacked on shelves. But now we have huge, free search engines, backed up (for the price of a Nexis subscription) with even more gigantic instantaneous worldwide keyword-searchable news databases.

Great masses of other data are found online: land registry files, company records, word for word parliamentary debates and reports, registers of politicians' financial interests, registers of political donations, copies of birth certificates, registers of doctors and lawyers, and biographies posted on LinkedIn, Wikipedia, Facebook, and so on. Unusual is the corporation that doesn't have some sort of website. Every fellow-journalist, academic, or expert on the entire planet is just a mouse-click away.

Access to some of this treasure-trove has indeed been a struggle. Property ownership files and court records, for example, were sealed in the UK until relatively recently, and many battles remain to be fought. But the information explosion has already brought us Freedom of Information rights, satellite images, and citizen video. Every day, we can find out so much more.

So even though the environment in which investigative reporters work is never going to be easy, they should be optimistic about what is possible. In the twenty-first century, journalists are successfully illuminating many unexpected dark worlds of wrongdoing—rendition and torture by intelligence agencies; undercover police fathering children on environmental activists; politicians wrongfully deporting elderly citizens; organised sexual harassment by businessmen [21, 22, 23, 24, 25].

These are just a handful of examples of the ways in which otherwise powerless people are being defended by determined reporters. If investigative journalists do learn how to survive and effectively publish truths about the world, they may find Sheila Coronel was justified in those cheerful predictions she made to her students at Columbia journalism school. As she said, the coming years could well become our trade's golden age.

REFERENCES

1. Coronel, Sheila. 2016. A Golden Age of Global Muckraking at Hand. *Global Investigative Journalism Network*. Accessed November 19, 2018. https://gijn.org/2016/06/20/a-golden-age-of-global-muckraking/.
2. ICIJ. 2017. Annual Report. Accessed November 19, 2018. https://www.icij.org/about/corporate/.

3. Donors. 2017. Our Supporters. *ICIJ website*. Accessed November 19, 2018. https://www.icij.org/about/our-supporters/.
4. Keidan, Charles. 2017. Interview: Adessium Foundation. Alliance for Philanthropy and Social Investment Worldwide. Accessed November 19, 2018. https://www.alliancemagazine.org/interview/interview-adessium-foundation/.
5. Accessed November 19, 2018. https://www.omidyar.com/people/pierre-omidyar.
6. ———, 2018. https://www.hollywoodreporter.com/news/oscar-profitability-goes-martian-872507/.
7. ———, 2018. https://postkodstiftelsen.se/en/blog/projekt/framjande-av-internationellt-samarbete-mellan-journalister/.
8. ———, 2018. https://www.thebureauinvestigates.com/.
9. ———, 2018. https://www.propublica.org/about/.
10. Organised Crime and Corruption Reporting Project. Accessed November 20, 2018. https://www.occrp.org/en.
11. Balkan Investigative Reporting Network. Accessed November 20, 2018. http://birn.eu.com/about-birn/donors/pages/4/.
12. European Investigative Collaborations. Accessed November 20, 2018. https://eic.network/.
13. Global Investigative Journalists Network. Accessed November 20, 2018. https://gijn.org/.
14. Kromke, Kathrine, and Anette Stensholt. 2014. SKUP-konferansen i Tønsberg var et mål for Anders Behring Breivik i 2011. *NRK News*. Accessed November 22, 2018. https://www.nrk.no/vestfold/500-journalister-samles-i-tonsberg-1.11646698.
15. Jackson, Jasper. 2015. Greenpeace Hires Team of Investigative Journalists. *Guardian*. Accessed November 22, 2018. https://www.theguardian.com/media/2015/sep/09/greenpeace-hires-investigative-journalists-meiron-jones.
16. Accessed November 22, 2018. https://www.opendemocracy.net/uk/about.
17. Meade, Amanda. 2018. Guardian Australia Reports Its First Profit. *Guardian*. Accessed November 22, 2018. https://www.theguardian.com/media/2018/jul/31/guardian-australia-reports-first-profit-2018-annual-results.
18. HSBC Files. 2015. HSBC Files Reveal How UK's Non-dom Concession is Being Exploited. *Guardian*. Accessed November 20, 2018. https://www.theguardian.com/business/2015/feb/11/hsbc-files-reveal-how-uks-non-dom-tax-concession-is-being-exploited.
19. Eriksson, Niklas. 2015. Rausing undviker skatt pa miljoner. *Aftonbladet*. Accessed November 19, 2018. https://www.aftonbladet.se/nyheter/a/G16dWV/rausing-undviker-skatt-pa-miljoner.

20. Accessed November 22, 2018. https://journalism.berkeley.edu/person/bergman/.
21. Grey, Stephen. 2006. *Ghost Plane: The Untold Story of the CIA's Secret Rendition Programme*. London: C. Hurst.
22. Cobain, Ian. 2013. *Cruel Britannia: A Secret History of Torture*. London: Portobello Books.
23. Lewis, Paul, and Rob Evans. 2013. *Undercover: The True Story of Britain's Secret Police*. London: Guardian Faber.
24. Rawlinson, Kevin. 2018. Guardian's Amelia Gentleman Wins Prize for Windrush Reporting. *Guardian*. Accessed November 22, 2018. https://www.theguardian.com/culture/2018/jun/19/the-guardian-amelia-gentleman-paul-foot-award-windrush-generation-reporting.
25. Marriage, Madison. 2018. Men Only: Inside the Charity Fundraiser Where Hostesses are Put on Show. *Financial Times*. Accessed November 22, 2018. https://www.ft.com/content/075d679e-0033-11e8-9650-9c0ad2d7c5b5.

Appendix: Basic Public Sources

Basic UK Public Sources

1. *Companies House*

- Names, addresses, dates of birth, nationalities, shareholdings and commercial connections of individual directors, and basic accounting info
- Online subscriptions give more detail and dissolved firms. Basic data is currently free

2. *192.com*

Uses electoral rolls to search for individuals, addresses, phone numbers, directorships, history of movements, occupants of same addresses [spouses, children, flatmates, neighbours]. Online subscriptions or buy credits.

3. *Land Registry*

Postcode-based. Ownership of property, mortgages, and, frequently, last price paid. *Limitation*: shy owners can hide behind offshore companies Can buy proprietorship register and other documents online. Also possible to access previous owners.

© The Author(s) 2019
D. Leigh, *Investigative Journalism*,
https://doi.org/10.1007/978-3-030-16752-3

4. *Google, Bing and other search engines*

Should need no introduction.

5. *Newspaper/media sites*

Archives are generally searchable (mainstream newspapers have own pool arrangements) + Lexis/Nexis + limited online archive searching of free sites (e.g. *Guardian*)

SECONDARY PUBLIC SOURCES

1. *General register office (GRO)*

Birth and marriage certificates show names and addresses and occupations of parents, children.
Buy online

2. *Westminster Library archives centre*

Contains GRO hard indexes for inexact dates of birth and so on.
Visit in person

3. *Parliament & local councils*

Online registers of MPs' and councillors' financial interests, peers' interests, researchers' interests, commercial/political sponsors of all-party interest groups.
Searchable archives of speeches, motions, questions, council planning applications.

4. *Electoral Commission*

Online registers of donations to central political parties, and individual constituencies, referenda, and individual party leadership campaigns

5. *Who's Who*

Always useful starting-point. NB: entries are written by prominent individuals themselves. Good part—by definition, they are reliable. Bad part—they leave stuff out
Free hard copy in UK reference libraries

6. *Charity Commission*

Financial accounts of UK charities
Free online

7. *Court files, civil cases*

Access as of right to High Court files in London of civil cases. Not online
Access as of right <u>during hearings</u> to skeleton arguments of counsel on each side, and to witness statements.

NB: these are recently won rights, subject to endless obstructiveness

Personal application. Sizeable copying fees for court files. Some parts of file not accessible—only the "pleadings", not the correspondence or exhibits.

8. *Court judgments*

Major judgments available free online via BAILLI or HM Courts Service

9. *US civil court files*

Available online via PACER on payment of smallish fee

10. *US company information*

Stock exchange information (SEC) on quoted companies available free online via EDGAR

11. *Foreign company registers*

Many available online on pay-per-item, for example, Netherlands, Belgium
Minimal online information also available on offshore tax haven companies, for example, Jersey, Isle of Man, Curacao, BVI
Good lists of international company registries at http://www.rba.co.uk/sources/registers.htm

12. *Social network sites*

For instance, Twitter, Facebook. LinkedIn often have biographical info

13. *Google Earth, Google images, Bing maps*

Aerial pictures, maps, street views, pictures of people

NB: Ordnance survey maps show public rights of way—can be useful for picture access

14. *Whois*

Owners of domain names. Sometimes gives useful contact names and addresses

15. *Wayback Machine*

Internet archive. Collects deleted pages. Can be useful when earlier information has been removed

16. *UK National Archives*

Free online searchable catalogues of past government files held at archive centre, Kew, near London

17. *Postcodes*

Free online postcode finder and phone directory inquiries [not mobile numbers]

18. Links to further technically useful UK and US sites

Paul Myers Research Clinic. http://researchclinic.net
Global Investigative Journalism Network (GIJN) Online Research Tools.
    https://gijn.org/online-research-tools/
Margot Williams. Investigative Research Links. https://drive.google.
    com/file/d/1pLjKuNjFyHGDiOAW7sLmX7L9o2j5kdbF/view
The UK Centre for Investigative Journalism (CIJ) based at Goldsmiths
    College, University of London, runs practical classes and conferences
    on data journalism. https://tcij.org/

19. Freedom of Information (UK)

FOIA Without the Lawyer (Logan Handbooks) is a good place to start for
    advice https://tcij.org/handbooks/foia-without-the-lawyer/. See also
    the Campaign for Freedom of Information. https://www.cfoi.org.uk/

NB WHAT YOU <u>CAN'T</u> GET FROM PUBLIC SOURCES

1. Reverse phone numbers in UK. Illegal in UK
2. Reliable information off Wikipedia (unless it's verified !!)

Index

© The Author(s) 2019
D. Leigh, *Investigative Journalism*,
https://doi.org/10.1007/978-3-030-16752-3

CPSIA information can be obtained
at www.ICGtesting.com
Printed in the USA
LVHW020459041120
670660LV00010B/294